Life After Death

Born in London in 1941, Ian Wilson graduated in history from Magdalen College, Oxford in 1963. His first book, *The Turin Shroud*, published in 1978 by Doubleday became a bestseller, translated into ten languages, and accompanied a BAFTA-award-winning television documentary which he co-scripted.

He became a full-time author in 1979, immediately choosing to write on reincarnation, or claims of 'past lives', for his first investigative topic, published as *Mind Out Of Time?* in 1981. *Jesus: The Evidence*, published in 1984, became another international bestseller, linked to a controversial Channel 4 television series of the same name. In 1987 he returned to the life-after-death theme with *The After Death Experience* in which he exposed the Spiritualist medium Doris Stokes as a fraud.

Ian has subsequently explored the serious evidence for ghosts in his *In Search of Ghosts*, published in 1995, and has lectured widely on life after death topics. After some twenty-five years residency in and around Bristol, England, he and his wife Judith currently live near Brisbane, Australia.

Also by Ian Wilson

The Turin Shroud
Mind Out of Time
Jesus: The Evidence
The Exodus Enigma
The Evidence of the Shroud
Worlds Beyond
Undiscovered
The After Death Experience
The Bleeding Mind
Superself
Holy Faces, Secret Places
The Columbus Myth
Shakespeare: The Evidence
In Search of Ghosts

Ian Wilson

Life After

Death?

THE EVIDENCE

Near-Death Experiences
Visions of the Dying
Ghosts

From all around the world,
the serious evidence that something
of us survives physical death . . .

PAN BOOKS

First published 1997 by Sidgwick & Jackson

This edition published 1998 by Pan
an imprint of Macmillan Publishers Ltd
25 Eccleston Place, London SW1W 9NF
and Basingstoke

Associated companies throughout the world

ISBN 0 330 35394 2

9 8 7 6 5 4 3 2 1

A CIP catalogue record for this book is available from
the British Library.

Typeset by SetSystems Ltd, Saffron Walden, Essex
Printed and bound in Great Britain by
Mackays of Chatham plc, Chatham, Kent

Contents

List of Plates   ix
Author's Preface and Acknowledgements   xi
Note on Style and Quotations   xvii

Chapter One
Back from the Dead?   1

Chapter Two
The Oldest Belief   11

Chapter Three
Sifting the Wheat from the Chaff   27

Chapter Four
'Something Everyone on Earth Has to Know About'   56

Chapter Five
But Can You Really Leave Your Body?   78

Chapter Six
And Can You Really Reach a Realm of the Dead?   108

Chapter Seven
A Question of Judgment   136

Chapter Eight
On Time, Space and 'Reality'   162

Chapter Nine
A Transforming Experience 182

Chapter Ten
On Not Leaving God Out 201

Chapter Eleven
Conceiving the Inconceivable 228

Notes & References 255
Bibliography 276

To all those who even at the risk of public scorn or humiliation have been willing openly to share experiences that they believe to be evidence for life after death – without whom this book would not have been possible

List of Illustrations

The soul departing the body, and floating over it after death. From an engraving of the English artist-poet and visionary William Blake (1757–1827).

German cancer specialist Dr Josef Issels. One of his patients described herself floating outside her body, and down the hospital ward, just moments before her physical death (*courtesy Gordon and Edith Thomas*).

The Swedish engineer and visionary Emanuel Swedenborg (1688–1772) from a contemporary engraving.

Swedenborg's fellow-engineer Christopher Polhem, also from a contemporary engraving.

Abercrombie House, near Bathurst, Australia, scene of the author's encounter with an apparent 'ghost' in January 1994 (*author's collection*).

Retired engineer Eddie Burks of Lincoln, England, who appears to have a special ability to sense ghosts (*author's collection*).

Thomas Howard, Fourth Duke of Norfolk, whose 'ghost', haunting the head office of Coutts' Bank, was perceived and laid to rest by Eddie Burks (*private collection*).

Lord Jenkins of Hillhead, 'visited' in a dream by fellow-MP Anthony Crosland moments before his death (© *Popperfoto*).

Anthony Crosland, who died in February 1977 (© *Popperfoto*).

Dr George Ritchie, who as a young army private 'died' in 1942, thereupon to have a quite extraordinary near-death experience during which an out-of-body element of him visited Vicksburg, Mississippi (*courtesy Dr George Ritchie*).

American Vicki Umipeg, who despite being born blind, 'saw' during an after-death experience (*courtesy Vicki Umipeg*).

American former art professor Howard Storm, who had a life-transforming near-death experience in Paris in 1985 (*courtesy Revd Howard Storm*).

The English philosopher A. J. Ayer, who although staunchly atheist, had an experience strikingly resembling one of the near-death variety (© *Popperfoto*).

Australians Edwin and Laurel Lloyd-Jones, who together had extraordinary experiences associated with Laurel's near-death experience in 1980, totally transforming their lives (*author's collection*).

The rock formation near Goobarragandra above which Laurel described herself out-of-bodiedly flying (*courtesy Laurel and Edwin Lloyd-Jones*).

Matilda Everingham, the deceased great-grandmother whom Laurel described appearing to her (*courtesy Laurel and Edwin Lloyd-Jones*).

Author's Preface and Acknowledgements

What if you really *knew*, beyond any possible shadow of a doubt, that you will live on after you die? Also, that not only everything of your life's behaviour, but even all your innermost thoughts, will stay preserved on some near-unimaginable kind of permanent record? Would you continue conducting your life much as you do now? Or would you do at least some things differently? These are the issues we are about to confront in the light of the evidence to be explored in the course of this book.

Let me make clear immediately that this is not my first essay into the evidence for life after death. In *The After Death Experience*, published in 1987, I looked across the whole spectrum of claimed evidence of this kind, from the activities of show-biz spiritualist mediums such as the late Doris Stokes, to the purported 'past life' memories retrieved via hypnotic 'regressions'. Although I found much of this material either unfounded or downright spurious, one facet of the subject deeply impressed me and enabled me to come to a positive conclusion. This was the phenomenon of near-death experiences, that is, the testimonies of those ordinary individuals who, in a variety of circumstances, have clinically died, have been resuscitated, and have then returned to tell remarkable stories of viewing themselves from outside their bodies, meeting up with other-worldly beings, and much more. Those experients whom I met personally, together with the innumerable testimonies of others as published by specialist researchers, so impressed me that I determined that if there was indeed some form of life after death, then this must be the evidence for it.

For this reason, with the active encouragement of my publishers, I have devoted the present book to concentrating very specifically on this serious evidence, deliberately omitting all other material that I have already weeded out as spurious, though including, for their possible relevance, some of the more reliable reportings of ghosts, visions of the dying, and the like. As a further aid to focus, I have also forgone any exhaustive assembly of my own collection of near-death experience cases, since this has already been done so many times by other researchers, in an attempt to make real sense of those published cases already in the public domain worldwide. For the issues are startlingly clear: these cases are either the most seemingly 'real' of hallucinations, that have cruelly deceived some highly intelligent and self-critical individuals from all walks of life, or they are evidence for something way beyond our present-day scientific ken.

Which to choose? This is the task that I have set myself, not without much the same misgivings as expressed more than fifteen centuries ago by St Augustine:

> If anyone can track down and definitely understand the causes and mechanisms of these visions . . . I would rather listen to him than be expected to hold forth on the subject myself. I make no secret of my views. But I hope the learned will not regard me as dogmatizing, nor the unlearned as teaching them. Rather that both will look on me as somebody discussing and exploring rather than knowing already.

Accordingly this book is particularly indebted to *all* those individuals, from all over the world, who have had near-death experiences, who have returned from these (to use St Augustine's terminology) 'definitely understanding' that there is life after death, and who have had the courage – particularly in the face of likely ridicule – openly and without hope of reward to tell the stories of those experiences to whoever may be prepared to listen. Without those individuals – far too many for me to have been able to interview them all personally – this book would have been much the poorer, and this is why it is unhesitatingly dedicated to them, and to those who have been similarly open concerning experiences possibly related to life after death.

Additionally, of course, I am deeply indebted to those particular near-death experients who, and not necessarily for the present book, have personally shared their experiences with me, and allowed their true names to be used. Here I have particularly in mind, from the UK David Ayre of Bristol, Gillian McKenzie of Eastbourne, and Captain Edmund Wilbourne of Chippenham; from the USA Dr George Ritchie, who kindly checked my chapter about him, and the Rev. Howard Storm, who did the same and most kindly made available to me a tape-recording of one of his lectures; and from Australia Pat Venn of Brisbane, Dr Cherie Sutherland of Sydney, and Laurel Lloyd-Jones. Laurel and her husband Edwin made me particularly welcome during a memorable overnight stay at their home near Tumut, in the foothills of Australia's Snowy Mountains, and again carefully checked my chapter about them.

Additionally, and particularly in view of the very nature of this book as an overview, I am unusually indebted to those now internationally recognized and respected leaders among near-death experience researchers from whose published cases I have quoted very liberally. I refer in particular to Dr Raymond Moody, author of the pioneering *Life after Life*, and currently of Alabama, to Dr Kenneth Ring of Connecticut who gave a most memorable lecture in my present 'home' city of Brisbane and was most helpful and gracious in subsequent correspondence, and to Dr Michael Sabom of Florida. Also to Dr and Mrs Peter Fenwick of London, whose book *The Truth in the Light* proved most timely, and to Dr Cherie Sutherland of Sydney, who as a direct result of being a near-death experient herself went on to research the subject as the theme of her Ph.D., and on my coming to Australia very kindly agreed to be interviewed even while she was on vacation.

My personal thanks for a variety of favours are also due to: Eleanor O'Keeffe of London's Society for Psychical Research, whose efficiency and helpfulness were as ever boundless; Dr Michael Hough of the Australian Institute of Parapsychological Research and the Department of Behavioural Sciences, University of Sydney; David Lorimer of the UK's Scientific and Medical Network; the Rev. Thomas Barnett of Missouri, who led me to the Rev. Howard Storm; Deacon Anthony Lawrence; Peter Brookesmith for most helpful information concerning the case of Durdana Khan; Egyptologist Professor Naguib Kanawati of Macquarie University, Sydney, who while introducing me to Egyptian hieroglyphs on a memorable 'crash' course at the University of Queensland, helped me better understand Egyptian attitudes to life after death; the Stepping Stone Centre, Brisbane; also the ever-helpful staffs of the University of Queensland Library, the Brisbane Central Library and the Indooroopilly Library.

Finally, my thanks are due to former Macmillan editor Carey Smith for inviting me to write this book as a follow-up to *The After Death Experience*, which she most efficiently edited; to publisher William Armstrong for supporting this commission; to present editor Catherine Hurley and Yvette Taylor for steering this book to publication, and above and beyond all else, to my wife Judith, who single-handedly typed transcriptions of the several tape-recorded interviews and lectures used for this book, who carefully checked every chapter, and who shared much of the research, not least, our encounter with the Abercrombie House ghost!

With a subject like life after death there are no half-truths. It is impossible to sit on the fence. Whether you decide 'Yes, there is life after death' or 'No, there isn't', you can only either be wholly right, or wholly wrong, and I can offer no guarantees either way. All I can promise, in words that used to be my late parents' encouragement to me in whatever I ventured to do, is that I have 'done my best'. And one day we shall all know (or not know), whether I was right or wrong . . .

Bellbowrie, Queensland, Australia
August 1996

Note on Style
and Quotations

As a matter of style, it has long been my policy to avoid the jargon and initializing that psychical researchers so frequently adopt in communication with each other, and which then make their writings so unintelligible to others. For instance, to save much typing it would have been very tempting here to use the now widely recognized initials NDE instead of the undeniably cumbersome 'near-death experience'. However, even this seemed one initialization too many.

It is also my normal policy to leave quotations exactly as in the original. However, in this instance, with so many quotes themselves transcribed from tape-recordings that bear the quirks of each transcriber, I have sometimes opted for editing and repunctuating these to maintain my own book's overall continuity, while at the same time always acknowledging their source.

Finally, there are instances in this book in which I have used initial capital letters where a near-death experient has felt himself or herself to be in the presence of some 'divine' Being. Such capitalizations are intended simply as expressions of the experients' perceptions of this Being, rather than indications of any loss of descriptive objectivity.

Chapter One

Back from the Dead?

*I'm not telling you everything, doctor. Just enough so that
you won't get too uptight with me.*

American near-death experient

We are familiar enough with the scene from television
hospital dramas. The patient is undergoing surgery on
the operating table, wired up to every conceivable support
system and monitoring device. Although he has been
anaesthetized into deep unconsciousness, dials and gauges
show that he is breathing, that his heart is pumping, and
that his brain is active. Then an ominous warning buzzer
sounds. Above their surgical masks the operating team's eyes
register alarm as they look towards a monitor that had
previously been showing a steadily fluctuating line. That line
is now flat. Instrument-wise, the patient is 'dead'.

Frantic activity breaks out. External heart massage is tried,
following by a direct injection into the heart. The monitor
line still registers flat. A surgeon goes to the wall telephone
and puts out a coded message over the hospital's Tannoy.
Duly alerted, a 'crash' team rush their high-tech trolley
through crowded hospital corridors. Moments later they
burst into the operating theatre, connect their equipment to

1

the theatre's electricity supply, and position it alongside the operating table. Commanding, 'Stand back!', the senior technician claps two hand-sized applicators to the patient's chest, jolting this with x-hundred amps of electricity that momentarily cause the 'corpse' to rise from the operating table. Everyone looks anxiously at the monitor, but the line remains flat. An increased amperage level is called for, and the procedure repeated, again with everyone looking to the monitor. This time the line that had previously stayed so inert flickers into a feeble blip that then begins to strengthen and steady. Relief shows in the eyes above the surgical masks. The patient who was 'dead' has come back to life . . .

Such scenes, now relatively commonplace in hospitals across the world, reflect the huge advances in resuscitation procedures that medical technologists have developed during the last twenty to thirty years. Thanks to them there are now literally thousands of people who would previously have been left for dead, and who indeed were 'dead', but have been enabled to return to a full and active life. Particularly fascinating for us is that among those thousands of people there are about one in three who claim surprisingly vivid memories of the time that their life-signs monitors registered zero. Many speak of their having seen their body from a vantage-point as if they were hovering about it, watching all the attempts to resuscitate them. Some even describe themselves as having gone to an indescribable 'other world', and having met and talked with 'dead' relatives and friends and encountered radiant beings before being told that they had to 'go back'. Almost invariably the experience has so moved them that even if they were completely atheistic previously, they return with an altered, markedly more 'religious' attitude towards the future conduct of their lives. And almost to a man – or a woman – they have lost all fear of death.

All this confronts us with the paradox and the mystery

that form the focus of this book. The paradox is that at the very time when medical science has developed such high-tech methods of preventing and indeed reversing 'death', there should be people on the receiving end of that technology who return with talk of floating out of their bodies and going on to some 'other-worldly' dimension. For, given our sophisticated microscopes capable of probing everything down to its tiniest atom, one wonders where within us any 'soul' or 'spirit' that could leave our physical bodies in such a manner might conceivably reside. And with our radio-telescopes capable of looking out many billions of miles to our universe's outermost reaches and detect spectra otherwise invisible and undetectable to us, where might anyone find any 'heaven', or 'hell', or any other conceivable abode of the dead? Surely, as we approach the twenty-first century, such strange experiences reported by those who have been brought back from 'death' must be dismissible as mere hallucinations? Mustn't they?

Herein lies the mystery confronting us. For in the very face of all the scientific orthodoxy that there can be no life after death, some very well-qualified and seemingly equally well-balanced researchers worldwide, mostly from scientific disciplines such as psychology, psychiatry and cardiac surgery, have listened very carefully to those returned-from-the-dead individuals who have described 'out-of-the-body' and 'other-worldly' experiences, and have opted to treat these seriously and sympathetically – as if they might indeed hold clues to an afterlife existence that we have yet to encompass within our understanding of the universe.

Particularly well-known of these researchers is the American psychiatrist Dr Raymond Moody, who came upon his first experient who had returned from 'death' while studying philosophy at the University of Virginia in 1965. This led to his subsequently collecting some 150 further examples, based on which, twelve years later, he wrote *Reflections on Life after Life*, the world best-seller which introduced the term 'near-death experience' into the English language, and inspired many other researchers to take an interest in the phenomenon.

In Moody's wake, among the earliest to develop such an interest was Dr Kenneth Ring, a University of Connecticut social psychologist who patiently and methodically began assembling his own collection of more than a hundred cases, from the evaluation of which he published *Life at Death* in 1980. Although Ring's book lacks Moody's more popular touch, it introduced a valuable measured and statistical approach to the subject.

Similarly early to enter the field was Dr Michael Sabom, then a young cardiologist at the University of Florida. Although he first expressed outright disbelief because no patient of his had ever mentioned a Moody-type experience, he rapidly changed his mind when he began making specific enquiries with people whom he and others had resuscitated from cardiac arrest. This resulted in the assemblage of his own substantial dossier of cases published in 1982 as *Recollections of Death*.

Moody, Sabom and Ring had all largely ignored near-death experiences in children, but in the mid-1980s this deficiency was rectified by paediatrician Dr Melvin Morse of the Children's Orthopedic Hospital, Seattle, who discovered that a greater proportion of children who had clinically 'died' reported such experiences, compared to adults, despite the fact that they were much less likely to have had some prior knowledge of the phenomenon.

Outside America the distinguished British neuropsy-chiatrist Dr Peter Fenwick likewise took up a strong interest in such experiences, seeing in them a potentially important link to his specialization in the mind/brain interface and the mysteries of human consciousness. Aided by his journalist wife Elizabeth, Fenwick collected more than 300 examples of near-death experients from around the United Kingdom. The Fenwicks published their findings from these as recently as 1995 under the title *The Truth in the Light*.

In Australia, even as early as 1971, and therefore before the publication of Moody's book, housewife Cherie Sutherland had had her interest sparked by a near-death experience she suffered while giving birth to her first son, Eden. This prompted her not only to study for and gain a doctorate in sociology, but painstakingly to interview and correspond with more than 400 fellow-experients from around the Australian continent. Like the Fenwicks, Dr Sutherland has only comparatively recently released her findings, published under popular titles such as *Transformed by the Light* (1992), and *Within the Light* (1993).

The attitude of all these researchers to the near-death experients whom they have studied and interviewed may be best summarized as mostly clinical and sympathetic, usually erring on the side of caution in preserving their professional reputations, and simply relaying what experients tell them rather than trying to put it all into some overall cosmological context. Although they feel that if there is indeed life after death, then theirs must be among the best available evidence for it, they are acutely aware that some aspects of near-death experients' stories put a considerable strain on the credulity of those who have never been through the direct experience. They are also very conscious that the tide of current scientific orthodoxy remains very firmly set against them.

For certainly in this latter respect the overwhelming consensus of contemporary science would be that that which is 'contained' within our physical bodies and brains is all there is to us, and that there is not a shred of truly 'hard' evidence to suggest that there might be anything that could detach at death in the manner that near-death experients

describe. For example, the behaviourist school that has dom-
inated psychology since the 1920s resolutely maintains that
the part of ourselves which we fondly call our 'I', or our
'consciousness', or our 'mind', is but an illusion created by
our physical brains, a mere 'epiphenomenon', or useless
evolutionary by-product. It has no real existence and will die
completely and utterly when our brains die.

Likewise, even when they are presented with the most
convincing examples of near-death experiences, the propo-
nents of scientific orthodoxy will unhesitatingly dismiss
these as evidentially worthless. Particularly vocal in this
respect is British psychologist Dr Susan Blackmore of the
University of the West of England, Bristol, a frequent participant in popular radio and television chat-shows on the
subject. In her string of publications on this theme, including
most recently her book *Dying to Live*, published in 1993, Dr
Blackmore confidently and authoritatively explains away
near-death experiences as due to experients' dying brains
being starved of oxygen, or to the brain manufacturing its
own opiates to take it through into death. She maintains that
whatever the precise chemical process, ultimately it is all just
a hallucination. Because we are no more than our physical
bodies, death really is death. After death each and every one
of us goes back to Absolute Nothing.

But is this truly the last word on the matter? Of course, if
we want to please all the trendier gurus and scientific jour-
nalists, the safe option is to accept all that Dr Blackmore and
her orthodox colleagues insist upon. Choose anything else,
and the media pundits will automatically lump us in with
the New Agers and UFOlogists, however uncomfortable we
may feel with these bedfellows.

If we are concerned with real truth, however, can anyone
be *that* confident that modern science knows so much of
everything that there is to be known that we should just

close our minds to anything and everything that might challenge its current wisdom? Indeed, could it be that what near-death experiences relate, rather than being an embarrassment to anyone's intelligence, might actually further our understanding of the truly big questions of life – and death – if only we could find the right way of interpreting it all correctly and then relating it to the otherwise solid world with which we are so familiar?

In this regard it has long seemed to this author that if near-death experiences do indeed constitute valid evidence for some form of life after death, then they cannot exist in a vacuum, as they have mostly been treated hitherto. They must be linked in some as yet undetermined way to other of the better-authenticated phenomena similarly purported to be evidence that something of us survives physical death. Ghosts, for instance, have been reported for thousands of years, sometimes by very reliable witnesses, and it may be no coincidence that near-death experients report as part of their experience seeing living people exhibit the apparent substancelessness associated with ghosts. As we will discover, near-death experients also seem to become significantly more prone to perceiving ghosts than they may have been before their experience.

Many perfectly down-to-earth people have also been puzzled by some of the strange phenomena associated with the deaths of friends and relatives which they have witnessed, such as premonitions and visions. A surprising number of similarly down-to-earth people have also reported a relative or friend appearing to them at the time of the latter's death, even though that death may have occurred thousands of miles away. If there is validity to any or all of these, surely they must be linked to whatever may happen in a near-death experience, better understanding of both thereby offering some potentially truly fresh light on the whole life-after-death mystery?

If there is any value in such thinking, then clearly what is needed is more than yet another researcher going around collecting yet more examples of near-death experiences. From even the first books of the previously mentioned researchers we have already more than a thousand published or semi-published cases in the public domain. So who could possibly want to collect more? Either they are all just useless and misleading fantasies – or they already hold the key to unlocking the mystery of life after death, if only we could gain some better grasp or comprehension of what lies behind the lock.

Instead, therefore, what is far more crucial for any true advance in our understanding of the subject is an intelligent overview of all evidence that others have already so painstakingly assembled. Particularly important, for instance, is an assessment of just how consistent and repetitive may be the various elements of near-death experiences as they are found among experients living in widely different cultural circumstances and widely separated parts of the world. Equally important is to determine how those elements, if indeed convincingly consistent, might relate to other of the potentially reliable evidence for life after death that we have mentioned. And not least, all needs to be weighed against the arguments of determined sceptics such as Dr Susan Blackmore.

Accordingly, although I have conducted some of my own interviews with near-death experients – English, American and Australian – this book will mostly be devoted to cross-evaluating the near-death experiences already published by the researchers named earlier, in combination with potentially relevant material from other facets of purported evidence of life after death. The method is not without its difficulties, not least because of the different researchers' often quite varied styles and approaches. The Americans Raymond Moody and Kenneth Ring, for instance, rarely if ever provide a name, pseudonymous or otherwise, for their informants, let alone anything of their personal background. Only slightly improving on this, Dr Michael Sabom usually provides an age and occupation, but gives no name. To their credit, Peter and Elizabeth Fenwick invariably cite all their informants' real names, but relatively little about their background. Perhaps the most ideal approach is that of Dr Cherie Sutherland, who while identifying every informant by a pseudonymous Christian name, more than compensates for this by providing far fuller details than anyone else of each person's background, and exploring the possibly more 'way-out' aspects of their experience in greater depth.

Our concern, however, is not to try to judge any one researcher against another, as any differences are incidental, and fall away when their work is studied in parallel. Far more important instead, are the testimonies of the informants. For it cannot be stressed enough that it is the experients themselves, and in particular those willing to share their experiences with others, who hold the key to whatever the truth may be regarding life after death: they are this book's real heroes. In today's materialist world which tries to brush death and everything associated with it under the carpet, it takes real courage to talk about coming out of your physical body and looking down upon it, or of floating towards a bright light and meeting up with dead relatives, or of seeing everything you ever did replayed before you from the perspective of those whom you may once have hurt, or humiliated, or cheated, or lied to.

In this regard, as noted by every researcher, among near-death experients' commonest hang-ups is a fear of being thought 'mad'. As an English housewife told Peter and Elizabeth Fenwick: 'Ten years ago I could not tell anybody about my experience, even my husband, because I thought people would think I was crazy.'[1]

And an Australian high school student told Dr Cherie Sutherland: 'I was quite embarrassed about it and thought I must have been losing my mind . . . I couldn't talk about it with anyone.'[2]

Even those willing to talk may feel constrained to hold back on certain details for fear that these might be too over the top, as for instance a middle-aged night watchman from Florida who told Dr Michael Sabom, regarding what he experienced following a cardiac arrest: 'I'm not telling you everything, doctor. Just enough so that you won't get too uptight with me. Maybe later, when I know you better and know how serious you really are.'[3]

Well, for the benefit not only of that night watchman, but of every other near-death experient, we are indeed serious. In reality there can be no one, atheist or religious, erudite or illiterate, hedonist or reclusive, for whom the post-mortem fate of the 'I' part of them is not of some serious concern or interest. However much anyone may have decided in his or her own mind that after death there is just oblivion, even that decision cannot but have put a stamp on the way they conduct their life. As that most inspiring of UN Secretary-Generals, Dag Hammarskjöld, put it in a remarkable series of jottings found after his own untimely death: 'No choice is uninfluenced by the way in which the personality regards its destiny, and the body its death. In the last analysis, it is our conception of death which decides our answers to all the questions that life puts to us.'[4]

So this is our quest, and our task will therefore be to try very hard to listen to and evaluate near-death experients' testimony without getting uptight (to use the night watchman's phrase), and mentally shutting them off as candidates for the nearest asylum for the insane.

But first we need to gain some thorough perspective on the whole historical background to belief in life after death. And as we are about to discover, people from all around the world have been seriously 'mad' about it for a very long time indeed . . .

Chapter Two

The Oldest Belief

> *To the Zulu . . . the existence and presence of the shades [i.e.*
> *the spirits of the dead] is not doubted. They are a reality*
> *which is so strongly interwoven into kinship relations that a*
> *world without them is not possible.*[1]
>
> Axel-Ivar Berglund

For us of the near-twenty-first century little is likely to arouse a greater sense of our own 'civilized' superiority than viewing what ancient peoples buried with their dead, or being told what present-day tribal peoples believe concerning the spirits of the dead. I vividly remember from my schooldays a visit to London's British Museum during which, with dozens of others, I gaped at the naturally mummified corpse of a 5000-year-old ancient Egyptian displayed in a shallow grave surrounded by clay pots that once contained the food and drink that relatives had provided for him to enjoy in his afterlife. Affectionately known as 'Ginger', this particular Egyptian is still there, still a favourite with visiting parties of schoolchildren, for many of whom he is their first encounter with a real-life dead body.

But it is the sight of those food and drink pots that really brings out our sense of superiority. Imagine: the ancient Egyptians provided food and drink for *dead* bodies, as if they were still alive! Just how quaintly primitive – how 'mad', even – can you get?

The real difficulty, in today's scientific-minded society, is for any of us to try to comprehend the sheer scale of that 'madness'. 'Ginger' himself was of course just one of the many millions of ancient Egyptians who were too ordinary and lived too early to have left us with any record even of their names. And if you visit the Cairo Museum's display of Tutankhamun's funerary provisions, you will usually be shown just the visually spectacular items, such as the gold coffins, the exquisite face mask, the ornate thrones, the tasteful chairs, beds and stools, the chariots, and the musical instruments. Because such items are seriously costly and inanimate, our modern minds too often interpret them just as over-elaborate furnishings for the coffining of a *dead* body.

Yet as we should be reminded by inscriptions from the Pyramids, ancient Egyptian monarchs went to their deaths with the firm assurance: 'No, not as a dead king did you depart; as a *living* king did you depart.' In Tutankhamun's tomb, rousing much less interest than the furnishings and goldwork, were found no fewer than forty-eight boxed joints of meat and poultry; hundreds of baskets of vegetables, fruits, spices and condiments; dozens of different kinds of bread and cakes; jars of honey; and over thirty jars of vintage wine.[2] All these were for Tutankhamun's living spirit, or *ka*, to enjoy within the confines of his earthly 'house of eternity', while another aspect of him, his bird-like *ba*, which only came into being at his death, soared freely between this world and the next.

For Tutankhamun, as for all his more ordinary subjects, such consumable funerary provisions were provided along with the imperishables precisely because all Egyptians expected that on death their *ka*s and *ba*s did not just lie immobile inside the mummy cases, but went on *living* in a very real way in the spaceless, boundless world for which the *ka*-house or tomb was merely a point of earthly contact. This is why in life everyone who had the necessary means to do so made preparations for the building of his or her personal tomb or family tomb with much the same care and forethought that modern-day business executives devote to their pension plans. Most of these tombs were provided with an on-the-surface chapel for living relatives to deposit their offerings of food and drink (perceived as we would flowers for the hospital patient, rather than as the deceased's only means of sustenance), and a false door for the *ka* to come and go to partake of these. Everything about the design and decoration of every tomb, such as the painted scenes of eating and drinking, music and dancing, hunting and fornicating, reflected the confident expectation that the deceased would continue to enjoy such pleasures after he or she died. And in a manner highly reminiscent of modern-day near-death experiences, the funerary artists commonly depicted the deceased's *ba*-bird/soul hovering over its parent *het* – in ancient Egyptian literally the 'thing' or shell of its physical body – or even perching in a tree and detachedly but interestedly watching its own funeral.

Again, it needs to be stressed that none of this was peculiar to the ancient Egyptians. Because of the world fame of their Pyramids, their Valley of the Kings and their elaborate mummification practices, the Egyptians are often thought of as a people somehow peculiarly obsessed with life after death. Yet this is a totally false impression that has come about solely because of the unusual survival of so much of their culture due to Egypt's dry climate. The plain fact is that whoever and wherever we look to among ancient cultures, the peoples exhibit a similarly quite overwhelming conviction of the *fact* of life after death, to the extent that the amount of gross national product they put into providing for this can only seem totally mad by our modern standards.

For instance, if we look to the Sumerians in what is today Iraq, we know from Sir Leonard Woolley's famous discoveries at Ur how a richly caparisoned palace household of more than seventy persons could all seemingly peacefully and voluntarily commit suicide in order to go on serving their dead king or queen in an afterlife in which they clearly assumed they would all share. Even Sumer's most ordinary citizens were granted a victuals allocation of seven jars of beer and 420 loaves of bread, together with two measures of grain, to take with them into death.[3]

Among the ancient Chinese and Japanese there were similar customs of real flesh-and-blood servants and horses being killed outright to join the deceased royal, until gradually, as in ancient Egypt, token figurines became acceptable as substitutes (though in Japan the burial of *living* servants and horses with a dead prince persisted until well into the Christian era.)[4] When the tomb of the Lady Dai, a short, arthritic Chinese lady married to a high official of the Western Han Dynasty, was excavated by Chinese archaeologists in the early 1970s, she was found surrounded by 162 token figurines of servants and entertainers, together with hampers packed with beef, venison, pork, rabbit, dog, chicken, fish, eggs, pickled vegetables, fruit and rice. The discovery in the same tomb of a T-shaped banner depicting the deceased already in other-worldly realms shows that, just like the ancient Egyptians, the Chinese believed that the dead person could both inhabit these realms and at the same time partake of any delicacies left at or in the tomb. The practice of bringing offerings of food and drink to the tombs of the dead has indeed continued among traditional Chinese to this very day.

If we look to the graves of the ancient Greeks we find

these to have been fitted with feeding tubes that seem to indicate that it was once customary for broths and soups to be poured down them into the jaws of the corpse lying below. An ancient Greek painted *krater* in New York's Metropolitan Museum features a mourning boy stuffing food into the mouth of a dead relative.[5] The earliest inhabitants of Scotland's Orkney islands are known to have taken choice cuts of meat to the bones of their ancestors in a special 'house of the dead' at what is now Isbister on South Ronaldsay.[6] The Etruscans built whole villages for their dead, decorating each tomb's walls with frescoes of feasting and entertainments, as in Egypt. As for the Romans, however pragmatic their culture may have seemed, between 13 and 21 February each year they held a special feast of the dead, the Parentalia, during which, according to Susan Walker, Assistant Keeper of the British Museum's Department of Greek and Roman Antiquities, they: 'specially opened [tombs] for the purpose of sharing meals with the dead. . . . Food and drink were offered to them through the necks of *amphorae*, pottery storage jars used for burial of the poor.'[7]

Nor has this custom of treating the dead as if they were still living been confined to the Old World. When the Spanish conquistadors arrived in Inca Peru, whose inhabitants had theoretically had no contact with the Old World for many thousands of years, they found a culture in which the dead were again being fed with tubes leading down from the surface into each subterranean burial chamber, while the mummified bodies of the Inca kings were cared for by special attendants who gave them food and drink, kept the flies off them, and even helped them to 'urinate'. Nor have such practices entirely died out even today. Just a few hundred miles north of where I am typing this chapter, the Toraja people on the Indonesian island of Sulawesi can leave a dead chieftain embalmed but unburied for perhaps several years while they rustle up sufficient sacrificial buffalo to give him the right send-off. Toraja funerary protocol dictates that during this time his widow must never leave his side. She will attend his corpse day and night, just as if he were still alive, while visitors come regularly to bring him betel nuts and palm wine, and, if he was a smoker, tobacco.[8]

What cannot be emphasized enough is that all this has to have its base in something rather more than just 'fear and superstition', the clichéd phrase that modern-day sceptics use far too unthinkingly of such practices. For peoples throughout such a long period of time, and in such widely separated parts of the world, to have honoured their dead with offerings of funerary items of foodstuffs and material goods that represented huge inroads into their available resources, is evidence of some universally understood and seriously powerful impetus for their doing so.

But what was that impetus? If we look among today's less developed peoples, we find the clues plainly enough. Common to virtually all tribal peoples' attitudes towards their own dead, and indeed to those of everyone throughout the world, is the prevailing idea, amounting to a certainty, that the dead are still alive and close to them, and can actually be *felt* at certain times, particularly at night, in the vicinity of their graves, and in special ceremonies.

For instance, A. M. Duncan-Kemp, an Australian woman who grew up among one of the continent's communities of traditional aboriginals, noticed that no matter how hard these people worked during the day, at night they seemed to acquire a new energy that came from their renewing contact with their deceased ancestors. On her expressing her curiosity about this to one aboriginal whom she knew well but could never persuade to open up properly on the subject, he told her simply: 'It is our life, miss. We live again at night, and our spirit folk come to us after sunset and leave before sunrise.'[9]

In Mexico, whole family groups of Nahuatl-speaking Indians, who have descended from the Aztecs, band together each 2 November to take specially baked breads, baskets of fruit, *jalapeño* peppers, wine, beer and flowers to their local cemeteries. Exactly as in the case of the Roman Parentalia, they bring these for the delectation of their dead ancestors and other kin. They speak of the latter without the slightest dread or cynicism as their 'little dead ones', and are absolutely insistent that they can feel them around them.[10]

Of the Zulus of South Africa the Scandinavian anthropologist Axel-Ivar Berglund has written: 'To the Zulu . . . the existence and presence of the shades [i.e. the spirits of their deceased ancestors] is not doubted. They are a reality which is so strongly interwoven into kinship relations that a world without them is not possible.'[11]

Of the Makgabeng tribe, also of South Africa, the anthropologist Adrian Boshier, who most unusually became honoured with initiation as one of their witch-doctors, has similarly reported:

> From both the tribal and the witch-doctor schools my tutors' instructions continually emphasized the remarkably close ties the living have with their departed relatives. Virtually all their waking life they contend with the whims and fancies of these very real entities. More likely than not their sleep will be influenced by them, for dreams are considered direct communications from the spirits. Their discussions about these ever-present beings are absolutely matter-of-fact and completely free of embarrassment . . . On very rare occasions they even indulge in humorous songs like bemoaning the vain nature of a long-deceased great-aunt whose continual demands for ornate bangles and colourful beadwork leave no money for food.[12]

Repeatedly we come across examples of what could be, and in modern eyes would be, 'wasted' upon the dead. For instance, among the pre-Islamic Arabs there could have been few more prized possessions than a camel, yet as the missionary M. S. Seale has written of those who inhabited Syria and the Lebanon:

> In Arab society, friends and relatives kept in touch with the deceased, lingered at the burial place, and even pitched a tent at the graveside; they could not tear themselves away. Coming upon the grave of an acquaintance, they would call his name and greet him: the deceased was believed to return the greeting . . . Besides food [the pagan Arab] would also provide the deceased with a riding camel which was tethered at the graveside and left there to die without food or water.[13]

We can be confident, therefore, that the reason why peoples of the ancient world expended so many precious resources on their dead, and why less developed peoples continue to do so even today, is that they could actually sense the closeness of these around them, in a way that our developed society has lost. This could seemingly extend even to perceiving the presumed spirit of the dead person hovering in the vicinity of his body in the immediate aftermath of death, looking upon his grieving family in the exact manner of the near-death experience. The modern Chinese writer Jung Chang, who carefully recorded her mother's memories of living in pre-Revolutionary China, has written of what the Manchurian Chinese understood in this regard:

> On each of the last seven nights before his interment the dead man was supposed to ascend a high mountain in the other world and look down on his whole family; he would

only be happy if he saw every member of his family was present and taken care of. Otherwise, it was believed, he would never find rest.[14]

Likewise the great nineteenth-century anthropologist J. G. Frazer wrote of the central Melanesians:

They imagine that as soon as the soul quits the body at death, it melts into a tree where there is a bird's-nest fern, and sitting there among the ferns it laughs and mocks the people who are crying and making great lamentations over the deserted tabernacle. There he sits, wondering at them and ridiculing them: 'What are they crying for . . . whom are they sorry for? Here am I.'[15]

Similarly among the traditional aboriginals of south-eastern Australia, a man's corpse would initially be strapped to a frame and left to decompose and dry during the first phase of his funerary rites, and during this time his spirit was believed to be so close that it was thought most inadvisable to mention his name, lest if he heard this he whisked the utterer off to join him and his ghostly companions.[16]

But upon just what perceptions were/are these beliefs based? Certainly one very widely recognized method for the dead making their post-mortem survival known to the living was via dreams. As long ago as 1850 BC the Egyptian widower Merertifi wrote the following supplication to his dead wife Nebeyotef:

I am your beloved upon earth. Fight on my behalf and intercede on behalf of my name . . . Remove the infirmity of my body. Please become a spirit before my eyes, so that I may see you fighting for me in a dream. Then I will deposit offerings for you when the sun has risen.[17]

Life After **Death**

In ancient China, as in other cultures, it was believed that in dreams a living person's spirit could leave his body and travel into the realms of the dead, just as a dead person might sometimes disturb a living person's dreams to plead for some special favour. A Chinese governor called Wen Yung, for instance, reportedly dreamed of a man in wet clothes who pleaded that his grave had been dug too near a river, as at high tide it filled with water. Shown the grave-site in his dream, on waking Yung visited it, found its conditions just as described, and had the body transferred to a more congenial location.[18] Earlier we noted from Adrian Boshier's insights how South Africa's Makgabeng tribe believed their dead relatives to communicate with them via dreams. The same idea is shared by today's Nahuatl Indian descendants of the original Aztecs of Mexico, as exemplified by what one Nahuatl told American anthropologist Amanda Parsons of his dream of his dead mother: 'I now live in Mexico City and did not return to Chilac to honour my mother's grave. Then, I dreamed of her. She called sadly to me. Every year since, I have returned.'[19]

Likewise among the Maoris of New Zealand the 'Atua', or god-like ancestors, are purported to communicate their wishes to the living via dreams.[20]

Another purported method for the dead making their presence known to the living was via waking manifestations which today we call ghosts and spirits. Again common to virtually all cultures around the world from the earliest times, is that ordinary non-psychic people, whatever their particular beliefs on life after death, on occasion see, hear, or otherwise sense ghosts of the dead, the universally understood distinctive feature of these being that however solid these ghosts might look, they can pass through walls as if these did not exist. In the words of a Babylonian exorcism, written some 3000 years ago:

20

> *. . . the thickest walls, like a flood they pass*
> *From house to house they break through.*
> *No door can shut them out . . .*
> *Through the door like a snake they glide,*
> *Through the hinge like the wind they blow.*[21]

Likewise in Homer's *Iliad*, the ghost of the dead hero Patroclus is described as passing through Achilles' hands 'like a wisp of smoke' when the latter tried to clasp him.[22]

From both the ancient literary sources and more recent folkloric studies, at least two fundamentally different types of ghost seem to have been distinguished. The first, or non-haunting type, usually took the form of a recently deceased friend or relative who might appear anywhere in the world to a person to whom they wanted to impart some message (generally, by their very appearance, that they have died), after which they were never seen again. The Greek Patroclus was essentially one of these, the message in his case being that he needed a decent burial – once this had been attended to there was no question of him disturbing Achilles, or anyone else, ever again.

As for the second, more traditional haunting-type ghost, this might be construed as representing what might have happened with Patroclus had Achilles not performed the appropriate funeral rites. For this type of ghost seems perennially unhappy and able to appear only in one particular place, literally its 'haunt', but over a long period of time, making his or her presence known to anyone who might wander into this. He or she also always seems to need some form of placation in order for the hauntings to cease. The ancient Babylonians certainly knew of and feared this second type, as did the Chinese, who reported such ghosts from as long ago as 500 BC, interpreting them then, as some still do today, as the spirits of individuals who have died unprovided with offerings. As reported by the Chinese folklorist Arthur P. Wolf, who interviewed many modern-day Chinese still adhering to their traditional religion: 'When pressed to explain their conception of ghosts, most of my informants compared them to bullies or beggars. Why do you have to make offerings to ghosts? "So that they will go away and leave you alone."'[23]

The Romans certainly experienced such ghosts. The historian Suetonius, for instance, reported serious manifestations following the murder of the unbalanced first-century emperor Gaius Caligula.[24] Among the world's less developed peoples there is also widespread experience of, and recognition of, the *fact* of ghosts, the sheer power of this being particularly well conveyed by an example from a community living in the jungles of the Malabar country of south-western India, reported by the anthropologist W. Y. Evans-Wentz:

A European planter . . . having died in the jungles . . . was buried there by the people. Some years after, a friend of the planter found the grave carefully fenced in and covered with empty beer and whisky bottles. At a loss to understand such an unusual sight, he asked for an explanation, and was told that the dead *sahib*'s ghost had caused much trouble and that no way had been discovered to lay the ghost until an old witch-doctor declared that the ghost craved whisky and beer, to which it had long been habituated when in the flesh and which were the real cause for its separation from the fleshly body. The people, although religiously opposed to intoxicants, began purchasing bottled whisky and beer of the same brands which the *sahib* was known to have used, and with a regular ritual for the dead, began sacrificing them to the ghost by pouring them out upon the grave. Finding that this kept the ghost quiet, they kept up the practice in self-defence.[25]

Especially notable here, underlining our point about what we regard as ancient and undeveloped peoples' quite irrational profligacy bestowing expensive commodities upon the dead, is that these Indians of Malabar, in purchasing whisky and beer to appease the ghostly planter, actually went against their own traditional aversion to intoxicants in order to procure them, besides inevitably spending money that they could ill afford.

But also particularly to be noted about this story is that while the planter's ghost reportedly disturbed, and was therefore experienced by, a generality of the people, it was one man, in this instance described as a witch-doctor, who seemed to have perceived the ghost more fully than the rest, and was able to discern that what he craved was whisky and beer, and that it was in the people's best interests to provide these for him.

This leads us to what seems yet another powerful contributing factor to the deep-seatedness of beliefs in life after death around the world, that throughout antiquity (and almost certainly way back into the mists of prehistory), almost every tribe and culture seems to have had, and in many instances still has, certain individuals variously termed 'seers', 'shamans', 'witch-doctors', 'witches', *wus*, 'mediums', *wirinun*, etc., accredited with quite exceptional powers of making contact with the realm of the dead.

Biblically we find one such in the Book of Samuel in the person of the famous Witch of Endor, whom King David's predecessor Saul (generally thought to have flourished c.1030–1010 BC) secretly sought out at dead of night because (in conformity with the law of Moses) he had personally outlawed anyone trying to communicate with the dead. In this instance King Saul felt impelled to go against his own laws because, finding himself very reluctantly at war with the Philistines, and believing along with everyone else of his time that the dead could see into the future, he desperately wanted someone to put him in touch with his dead spiritual mentor Samuel, so that he could find out what fate had in store for him. What followed is fascinating for the insights it affords into spiritualist medium-type practices 3000 years ago, with the witch, in conjuring Samuel's spirit, describing the occasion in sufficient detail for Saul to feel that this was indeed he, and conveying to Saul predictions that the latter definitely did not want to hear.[26]

The Chinese had their equivalents of Saul's witch in male or female seers called *wu*s, who could similarly perceive spirits of the desired dead when others present could not, could tap into their supposed knowledge of distant and future events, and even on occasion affect being possessed by them. As an example, when during the Western Han Dynasty the then emperor's succession was disputed by his brother Hsü, a female *wu* pronounced on the matter: 'The Emperor Hsiao Wu [a revered earlier emperor] descends in me. It is my strict order that Hsü shall become the Son of Heaven [i.e. Emperor].'[27] Hsü's succession duly became recognized. In the late tenth century AD a *wu* prophesied to Chau Tsu, the ancestor of China's House of Kin, the birth of four children, accurately describing their various characteristics. Of a *wu*'s perceptions of the realm of the dead, one of the ninth century AD interestingly made almost exactly the same distinction in varieties of ghosts that we earlier noted. In her words:

> There are two kinds of spirits, those which enjoy happiness and blessing, and others which are poor and mean; the former have a vital spirit which is so vigorous and healthy that it enables them to speak with men from time to time, while the latter have a breath which is so weak and a *shên* [soul] which is so exhausted that they are obliged to employ me as their mouthpiece.[28]

Again among tribal peoples of the present day there can be found all over the world near-exact equivalents of Saul's witch and China's *wu*. Among Australian aboriginals these are known as *wirinun*, or magicians. According to Cyril Havecker, a blood-brother of the Warramunga tribe, the *wirinun* makes:

> regular journeys to the *Dowie* or subtle world, [where] he is said to contact ancestral beings who have passed on from their physical bodies. He does this in order to obtain past and future information beneficial to the livelihood of the tribe.[29]

For more about the *Dowie*, see Chapter 11.

Anthropologist C. A. Valentine has reported native magicians of the Lakalai people in New Britain, part of the Papua New Guinea islands, professing both to go on flights 'to the dwelling places of ghosts and ancestors' and to be able directly to summon ghosts Witch of Endor-style.[30] Oxford lecturer Dr Audrey Butt, who has made a special study of the Amazonian Indians of South America, has reported how the Akawaio tribe's shamans affect to fly bird-like out of their physical bodies and reach the world of spirits of the dead,[31] inevitably recalling the ancient Egyptian conception of the *ba*. Again, these are all accredited with learning about the future on such trips. But these are just incidental examples of equivalents to be found among undeveloped peoples from all over the world.

If, then, we try to summarize all that we have learnt concerning the broad concepts of life after death held by peoples of ancient civilizations and of less developed cultures than our own time, we find they believed the following:

1 something of us separates from the physical body at death, and continues some form of independent existence;

2 this can remain in touch with living friends and relatives, and in certain circumstances manifest itself to them, either during dreams, or as a non-haunting ghost;

3 this appears to have access to certain fields of knowledge, such as of the future, that were not available to the individual when he or she was alive;

4 there are, however, certain circumstances in which dead persons do not 'transform' in this way, but become a traditional 'haunting' ghost;

5 there are certain individuals who are far more readily able to perceive dead persons' 'spirits' than the rest of us.

Almost all this is of course based on how matters of life after death were and are understood on the part of ancient and undeveloped peoples, among whom there has mostly been unquestioned acceptance that there is life after death, and that something of a dead person remains perceptible to the living.

But what happens when we look to those experiences of ghosts and the like claimed to be still occurring in our altogether more sceptical-minded age of science – experiences which we can arguably use our own scientific-minded methodology to check out? Are we going to find that all these turn out to be no more than make-believe and charlatanry, thereby devaluing those experiences that we have been unable to check? Or are we going to find that some at least simply cannot be lightly dismissed, impelling us to treat the whole subject of life after death that bit more seriously . . .?

Chapter Three

Sifting the Wheat from the Chaff

> GLENDOWER: *I can call spirits from the vasty deep.*
> HOTSPUR: Why, so can I, or so can any man;
>   *But will they come when you do call for them?*
>   Shakespeare: *Henry IV Part I*, 3:1, 53–5

Quite apparent from as early as antiquity is that there were people who deceived the gullible with their claims of being able to 'tune in' to the realm of the dead. As long ago as the fifth century BC the Greek playwright Euripides put into the mouth of the Messenger in his play *Helen* remarks concerning the seers or *manteis* who were the Greeks' equivalent of shamans and mediums:

> I perceived how seers' craft is rotten and full of falsehoods
> . . . Why . . . do we have seers at all? We should ask good
> things directly from the gods with sacrifices and leave seers
> alone. For this invention was a snare and a delusion.[1]

With the emergence in the last century or so of spiritualist mediums claiming to be the heirs of the old seers and shamans, there has certainly been no shortage of modern-day frauds in this field. One such in the late nineteenth century was the young and attractive Florence Cook, who while seated inside a curtained cabinet in the near total darkness of her séance room, produced 'materializations' of white-clad 'spirits' that convinced even the eminent physicist Sir William Crookes. Florence's wiles were exposed – almost literally – by Sir George Sitwell, father of the famous Edith, Osbert and Sacheverell, who during one sitting, contravening all the séance room rules, grabbed the spirit of the moment, purportedly one 'Marie', and found her impressively solid and resistant to his clutches. On Sir George's calling for the lights to be turned on, 'Marie' was revealed as none other than a very angry and embarrassed Florence herself, clad only in her Victorian underwear. Florence ended her days as a prostitute in Battersea.

During the 1930s and 1940s another medium, Helen Duncan, in the darkness of the séance room, made an impression when there manifested from her mouth copious quantities of a supposed other-worldly substance called ectoplasm. Upon investigation this was found to be no more than lengths of cheesecloth and surgical gauze that she had ingested, and in 1944 she was put on trial at the Old Bailey and gaoled for nine months specifically for 'conspiracy to pretend that she was in touch with spirits'.[2] In the early 1950s the male medium William Roy likewise duped many bereaved who came to him by affecting to produce 'spirit voices' of their dead loves ones, until it was revealed that he had an accomplice who, while the sitters were with Roy in the séance room, searched whatever belongings they had left outside, then whispered any usable information – together with louder, appropriate-sounding voices – into a tiny radio receiver hidden in Roy's ear.

In the same tradition was one of the most famous mediums of recent years, the late Doris Stokes, who during her demonstrations at mass auditoria such as the London Palladium and the Sydney Opera House convinced many by producing personal, detailed and apparently random messages that individual audience members would tearfully identify as from their dead loved ones. When I attended just such a show at the London Palladium on 16 November 1986, accompanied by two television researchers, Beth Miller and Siobhan Hockton, I was personally able to discover how Doris rigged such messages.

As we had planned, during the show's interval Beth and Siobhan approached each individual for whom Doris had so far produced messages, ostensibly simply collecting their names and addresses so that I could interview them afterwards at greater leisure. Far more quickly than we had anticipated, however, it emerged that each individual had had some significant, and on their part quite innocent, contact with Doris some time before the show. The repeated pattern was that either they or a friend had written to Doris a few weeks previously, had told her of their recent loss of a loved one, and had asked her for her help to put them in touch. Doris had then personally phoned them, offered them complimentary tickets to her show, and of course chatted seemingly casually about this loss. Flattered and grateful, when in the course of the show each invitee heard Doris impart 'spirit' messages with names and family circumstances unmistakably belonging to them, they would publicly claim these with palpably genuine emotion, completely failing to recognize them as based on details that they themselves had given Doris in the course of their conversations with her.

Nor was the London Palladium night that I attended just some isolated aberration. Journalist Joanna Moorhead told me how two years previously, while working as a reporter for the *Halifax Courier*, she had happened to cover a show that Doris Stokes staged at the Halifax Civic Theatre. Joanna was particularly impressed by the detail that Doris produced for one woman in the audience, and said so on meeting up with the woman afterwards. Deflatingly, the woman told her that she had come to the show by special invitation through her daughter having written to Doris on her behalf. Doris had then telephoned her twice beforehand for a chat. While it is impossible to be sure that Doris cheated throughout her career, there can be absolutely no doubt about her rigging of such stage demonstrations, and of her telling blatant untruths in her published books.

Sadly, many of the same tabloid newspapers and magazines that so uncritically brought Doris Stokes her unde served fame and credence have also continued to popularize other unworthy claims of 'proof' of life after death, such as purported reincarnation memories, psychic dreams and modern-day stories of ghosts. Time and again, some hypnotist or other will make headlines with claims of having 'regressed' some housewife or media celebrity back into remembering having lived before, perhaps in Victorian England, or even as long ago as ancient Egypt. Elsewhere I have explored such 'past life' claims far more thoroughly than would be relevant here,[3] but suffice it to say that on proper investigation even the best turn out to derive from a historical novel or some such that the hypnotized person read perhaps decades before, and then completely forgot so far as his or her conscious awareness was concerned. Somehow hypnosis seems to reactivate such long-forgotten memories. And just as, for stage-show purposes, a hypnotized person can very abandonedly and realistically mimic a farmyard animal, so the command to 'go back to times before you were born' can activate them to a sometimes very convincing impersonation of someone from the historical past, without the slightest conscious intention on their part to deceive, or awareness of having done so.

Interpretation of dreams has also fallen victim to every form of media misinformation, the unscrupulous cheerfully passing themselves off as 'experts' in the subject, when in reality dreams remain as mysterious as so many other aspects of the mind. The same is true of the phenomenon of ghosts, which has generated a whole genre of books of the most anecdotal material, thrown together without checking of sources or serious thought to what might constitute a true ghost. Exacerbating this is television's increasing tendency to celebrate the feast of Hallowe'en with wacky people dressed up as House of Horror ghosts, with the result that the idea that there just might be real dead relatives living on in some form of afterlife could not be further from anyone's mind.

Inevitably, against such a background, extreme wariness is needed as we now turn to those examples of evidence of life after death which I regard as potentially more valid, and which may also tie in with the insights from ancient and tribal peoples. Our first consideration concerns whatever serious evidence may be available for whether there might genuinely be something of us that can and does separate from the physical body, either when close to death, or in other exceptional circumstances.

Evidence of this kind most usually derives from the dying, a classic example being one that was told to the eminent pioneer psychical researcher Frederic Myers (1843–1901) by the sisters Alice and Mary Ellis, towards the end of the last century. According to the Ellises, just one day before their father's death in Kensington, London, he told them he was out-of-bodily seeing their brother Robert, then 11,000 miles away in Normanton, Queensland, close to Australia's Gulf of Carpentaria. In Alice Ellis's words:

On Wednesday, 29 December 1869, my father, who was dangerously ill at the time, awoke from a sleep, and raising himself up in the bed pointed and looked most intently to one corner of the room and said to us (my sister Mary and me), 'Look! Don't you see? It is my poor boy Bob's head!' Then turning to me he said, 'Normanton. Don't forget. Gulf of Carpentaria.' He then sank back exhausted. This happened about three p.m. . . . My father died on Thursday, 30 December 1869.[4]

Interestingly, and in corroboration of the Ellis sisters' insistence that their father was 'not in the least delirious', their brother Robert, for his part, seems reciprocally to have seen his father across all those miles. As Alice Ellis went on:

When my brother returned from Australia a few years after, he told us that one night, while camping out, he had gone to rest and had slept, and he awoke seeing my father's head distinctly in one part of his tent. It made such an impression on him that he went to his mate in the adjoining tent and said, 'I have seen my father, you must come and stay with me.' By the next mail he received my letter telling him of my father's death. My brother said it must have been about three a.m. when he saw my father. Would not that correspond with our three p.m.? I always think they must have seen each other at the same time.

If we look to more recent examples, there can be few better than one described in the biography of the highly clinical and down-to-earth Dr Josef Issels, founder of Bavaria's Ringberg Cancer Clinic, concerning a woman patient of his who was dying:

I was doing my morning round on Ward One, the ward reserved for the acutely ill. I went into the room of an elderly patient close to death. She looked at me and said: 'Doctor, do you know that I can leave my body? . . . I will give you proof, here and now.' There was a moment's silence, then she spoke again: 'Doctor, if you go to Room 12, you will find a woman writing a letter to her husband. She has just completed the first page. I've just seen her do it.' She went on to describe in minute detail what she had just 'seen'. I hurried to Room 12, at the end of the ward. The scene was exactly the same as the woman had described it, even down to the contents of the letter. I went back to the elderly woman to seek an explanation. In the time I had gone she had died . . .[5]

Note here that just as something of Mr Ellis had seemed to travel the 11,000 miles to 'see' his son in northern Queensland, so something of Issels' patient seems to have been able to float down the hospital ward and observe things impossible from the vantage-point of her physical body – but only when she was on the very brink of death. Note also that Issels insisted that he was able to verify that what she told him she had out-of-bodily 'seen' was in fact correct, strongly suggesting that it was no mere hallucination.

Our second consideration concerns the surprisingly common instances of those close to death reporting seeing, and seemingly conversing with, one or more relatives who have already died. Although today such experiences are all too often interpreted as no more than delusions due to strong pain-killing drugs and the like, there remain many examples that cannot be explained away so easily, such as where no drugs were involved, or where the details reported have too much corroborative validity.

To cite just one classic example: the evangelist Billy Graham reported of his dying grandmother how she suddenly sat up in bed – even though she had been too weak to do so earlier – and said, 'There is Ben, and he has both of his eyes and both of his legs!' Ben was her husband, Billy

Graham's grandfather, who had lost a leg and an eye during the American Civil War.[6]

In another example, the American paediatrician Dr Melvin Morse recorded the experience of a woman patient of his who in 1979 suffered the death of her ten-year-old son Tom from leukaemia, swiftly followed by her mother being diagnosed as having incurable cancer. This patient described one of her daily visits to her dying mother:

> One day when we entered the room, she was talking to someone. She was looking at them as though they were standing right next to her, but we could see no one.
>
> 'Who are you talking to?' I asked.
>
> 'I am talking to Tom,' she said.
>
> Over the course of the next two weeks my mother had long conversations with Tom as well as with her dead mother and sister. In the hours before she died she was received by all three of them.[7]

Particularly convincing was a similar case told to me personally by a very down-to-earth Bristol housewife called Janet whose first child, a daughter, tragically died of pneumonia after just two days, in 1968. Before the baby's death Janet and her husband had named her Jane after Janet's long-widowed grandmother Jane Charles, a ninety-six-year-old who at that very time lay dying 100 miles away in a tiny village near Abergele in North Wales. Janet's father, Geoffrey Charles, a newspaper reporter, was attending his mother's bedside at this time, and when told the news of Janet's baby's death decided it best not to pass this on to her, in order not to upset her during what were obviously going to be her last hours.

Accordingly Geoffrey was quite unprepared for the shock when, with every indication of being totally lucid, his mother began telling him of being able to see around her, in the classic 'Billy Graham's grandmother' manner, people whom he could not see. First she talked of a woman who seemed to bother her, then she became 'calm and happy', announcing that she 'knew what it was all about now.' Very contentedly, she told Geoffrey that she was seeing his father John, her husband who had died back in 1942.

But then, with a very puzzled expression, she remarked that the only thing she couldn't understand was that John *had a baby with him*. Then she said very emphatically, as if the knowledge of who this baby was had suddenly come to her: 'It is one of our family! It's Janet's baby! Poor Janet. Never mind, she will get over it.' A few moments later she was dead.

Highly important to note is that, in full accord with the ancient and tribal concepts of life after death discussed in the previous chapter, the dying Jane Charles shifted from what may be considered a normal understanding to suddenly exhibiting knowledge of events relating to family members many miles removed from her, and of some 'other-worldly' realm. She also accurately foresaw the future for her relatives, for in accordance with her prophecy Janet, after her initial devastation, did indeed get over her loss and went on to give birth to another daughter and son, both now in adulthood. Later in this book we will come across similar prophetic insights reported by near-death experients. It should also be stressed that all this happened in a family with absolutely no special religious or psychic inclinations: Janet was completely unaware of other examples of this genre until I brought them to her attention.

It is perhaps helpful now to turn from these instances of dying persons' experiences of meeting up with their some-times long-dead relatives and friends to examples of living persons experiencing manifestations of relatives and friends who have just died. Such manifestations mostly occur before the person has been told of their relative's or friend's death, and when they may be separated by some considerable physical distance. It should be noted that during these the living experient's state of awareness can vary from the dreamlike to seemingly full waking consciousness.

One particularly remarkable example of the dreamlike state has been reported by the altogether level-headed and non-psychic-inclined former British Cabinet Minister Roy Jenkins, now Lord Jenkins of Hillhead and Chancellor of Oxford University. From his university days, and continuing into his political career, one of the Jenkins's closest friends was a fellow-Labour MP, the charismatic Anthony Crosland. In February 1977 Crosland was ill in Oxford at a time when Jenkins had to go to Rome on political business, but nothing prepared Jenkins for the shock one morning on his awakening in a Rome hotel. As he recorded in his political diary for 19 February:

> I awoke about 6.30 a.m., having had a vivid dream about Tony [Anthony Crosland] being present, and his saying in an absolutely unmistakable, clear, rather calm voice, 'No, I'm perfectly all right. I'm going to die, but I'm perfectly all right.' Then at about 8 o'clock we had a telephone call from the BBC saying that he [Crosland] had died that morning, curiously enough at almost exactly the same moment that I awoke from my dream about him.[8]

The clear inference of this story, deriving from an individual without the slightest predisposition towards matters paranormal, is that seemingly in Anthony Crosland's dying moments something of him reached out from Oxford to be received some 1100 miles away in the mind of his friend Roy Jenkins in Rome.

More recently still, the previously mentioned American

paediatrician Dr Melvin Morse of Seattle has quoted a strikingly similar instance, in which the vehicle was again a dream, the dying/dead person being his own father. In Dr Morse's own words:

> One night in January [1988] I came home late from the hospital. It had been a very difficult day and I was only interested in sleep. I turned off my beeper and my telephone and told my wife that I didn't want to be disturbed for any reason. Then I went to bed. As I fell asleep in the darkened room, my father appeared to me in a dream. He just stood there facing me. He spoke very clearly. 'Melvin, call your answering service. I have something to tell you.' I awoke with a start and charged into the living room. 'My dad just told me to call my answering service,' I said to my wife. I made the call and was told that my mother had been trying to reach me with an urgent message. It was to tell me that my father had died. Since that very personal event I have had little doubt that the human brain has the capacity to communicate telepathically.[9]

Importantly, from the hypothetical perspective of any dead person, Dr Morse's father making contact with his son via a dream was very necessary in this instance, partly because that son was asleep, but more importantly because he had unusually switched off the normal telephone means of communication at this very critical time.

The two foregoing examples are of dream-based manifestations of the newly dead. Surprisingly common are very similar manifestations received by the living in waking consciousness. Indeed, the whole genre dubbed 'crisis apparitions', in the jargon of psychical researchers, is arguably deserving in its own right of just as much serious attention as has been given to near-death experiences.

37

Among the most classic, and extremely reliably reported, of these apparitions is a manifestation, again involving father to son, experienced by Prince Victor Duleep Singh in October 1893 when he was staying in Berlin with the then youthful English aristocrat George Herbert, Lord Carnarvon (later to become better known as financier of the search for the pharaoh Tutankhamun's tomb). Prince Victor's father was the Maharajah Duleep Singh, then some 3500 miles away at the family home in India. According to the Prince's own account:

On Saturday [21] October, 1893, I was in Berlin with Lord Carnarvon. We went to a theatre together, and returned before midnight. I went to bed, leaving, as I always do, a bright light in the room (electric light). As I lay on the bed I found myself looking at an oleograph which hung on the wall opposite my bed. I saw distinctly the face of my father ... looking at me, as it were out of this picture; not like a portrait of him, but his real head. The head about filled the picture frame. I continued looking and still saw my father looking at me with an intent expression. Though not in the least alarmed, I was so puzzled that I got out of bed to see what the picture really was. It was an oleograph common-place picture of a girl holding a rose and leaning out of a balcony, an arch forming a background. The girl's face was quite small, whereas my father's face was the size of life and filled the frame. I had no special anxiety about my father at the time and had for some years known him to be seriously out of health; but there had been no news to alarm me about him. Next morning (Sunday) I told the incident to Lord Carnarvon. That evening, late on returning home, Lord Carnarvon brought two telegrams into my room and handed them to me. I said at once, 'My father is dead.' That was the fact. He had had an apoplectic seizure on the

Saturday evening at about nine o'clock, from which he never recovered, but continued unconscious and died on the Sunday, early in the afternoon. My father had often said that if I was not with him when he died he would try to come to me.[10]

Because Prince Victor's experience occurred at a time when Britain's Society for Psychical Research was still newly formed and enthusiastic, the Society's investigators diligently sought Lord Carnarvon's independent corroboration of the Prince's account. Lord Carnarvon responded with characteristic politeness:

I can [indeed] confirm Prince V. Duleep Singh's account. I heard the incident from him on the Sunday morning. The same evening, at about 12 p.m. he received a telegram notifying him of his father's sudden illness and death. We had no knowledge of his father's illness. He has never told me of any similar occurrence.

In 1986 I learned through my personal contacts of an experience remarkably similar to Prince Victor's, as told to me by London health visitor Krystyna Kolodziej. In Krystyna's case the dying person was, like Prince Victor's, her father, Polish-born Kazimir Kolodziej, and again considerable distance was involved, because Kazimir had emigrated twelve years previously to Australia, and Krystyna had not seen him since. Furthermore, in this particular instance the daughter–father relationship had never been close, particularly because of Kazimir's chronic alcoholism, so when in 1981, as Krystyna was just about to take her B.Sc. final examinations, he contacted her to say that he was dying and urgently wanted her to come to him to Australia, she actually declined to do so, as this would have meant her missing the vital examinations for which she had been studying for three years.

Then, as Krystyna sat one evening with a friend in her flat in Hackney, East London, her father appeared to her in a strikingly similar manner to the way Maharajah Duleep Singh had appeared to his son. In Krystyna's own words:

> My friend had been with me a few hours and . . . she and I were sitting on my sofa talking at about 11 p.m., and she was describing to me some clothes she had bought recently . . . Suddenly, and while still attending to her, my father's face appeared high on the wall to my left, just next to a large mounted picture. Indeed part of it occluded the picture. I saw it out of the corner of my eye, because my face was actually turned toward my friend, and the face imprinted itself onto my awareness in a way so real that I shook my head and looked away, as if trying to shake off the vision in disbelief. This time, I looked directly at the place and saw the face again, after which it disappeared almost instantly. The entire episode lasted only about ten seconds and my friend, absorbed in what she was saying, noticed nothing in my expression. I told her of it the next morning. My father did die within hours of my seeing him, and I woke spontaneously just before the phone rang to tell me . . . What I remember most was the expression on my father's face – there was no expression . . . If I had to describe the feeling the apparition imparted to me, it was as if seeing me, and perhaps being seen, was a duty my father had to perform.[11]

In fact, such 'announcing' manifestations of the newly dead to close living relatives and friends are surprisingly common. Among other examples Harold Owen, brother of the First World War soldier-poet Wilfred Owen, has described how shortly after the latter's tragic death in France one week before the end of the war (and while he, Harold, was still unaware of this), Wilfred manifested to him in his cabin on the ship on which he was serving, stationed off the Cameroons, West Africa. In this instance the manifestation was completely life-like. In Harold's own words:

> I had gone down to my cabin thinking to write some letters . . . drew aside the door curtain and stepped inside and to my amazement . . . saw Wilfred sitting in my chair. I felt shock run through me with appalling force . . . I did not rush towards him but walked jerkily into the cabin – all my limbs stiff and slow to respond. I did not sit down but looking at him I spoke quietly: 'Wilfred, how did you get here?' He did not rise and I saw that he was involuntarily immobile, but his eyes which had never left mine were alive with the familiar look of trying to make me understand; when I spoke his whole face broke into his sweetest and most endearing dark smile. I felt no fear . . . But still he did not speak but only smiled his most gentle smile . . . He was in uniform and I remember thinking how out of place the khaki looked amongst the cabin furnishings. With this thought I must have turned my eyes away from him; when I looked back my cabin chair was empty . . . Suddenly I felt terribly tired and moving to my bunk I lay down; instantly I went into a deep, oblivious sleep. When I woke up I knew with absolute certainty that Wilfred was dead.[12]

Similarly, at the end of the Second World War one of the very last British soldiers to be killed in action on mainland Europe was a Lance Corporal Woodley, who very shortly before his death had married the love of his life, Dorothy. During the VE Day Celebrations of 1995, and having long remarried, the now Mrs Dorothy Williams told BBC journalist Bill Hamilton how at what could only have been the time of Woodley's death a picture fell off the wall at their home in England, followed by Woodley's appearance to her, wearing a blood-stained uniform and extremely life-like. He told her of his death and specifically instructed her that because she was still so young she should remarry rather than grieve for him all her life.[13]

It does not always seem necessary for such manifestations to occur only at the point of death. Certainly this seems to be the case where geographical distance or some hiatus to normal communications seems to be involved, but the apparent purpose of the manifestation may also be one of explanation, for which immediate communication may not be necessary. For instance, when in early September 1977 the German-born economist E. F. Schumacher, author of *Small Is Beautiful*, died of a heart attack while travelling alone by train during a lecture tour to Switzerland, his widow Vreni, back at their home in Surrey, England, learned of her loss swiftly enough because the Swiss police identified her husband quickly from the passport and other documents they found on his body. For Vreni the aching gap lay in not knowing quite how her husband had died. However, a few days later Schumacher himself seems to have filled that by appearing to Vreni in a dream. According to Schumacher's biography by his daughter Barbara:

> A few days later Vreni had a vivid dream. She was sitting in the drawing-room at Holcombe [the family home] in front of the open fire when she suddenly because aware that Fritz was in the room with her. She looked up and saw him sitting in his chair. 'I just wanted to tell you what happened,' he said. 'On the train I suddenly felt ill and thought it was indigestion. I went to the toilets but it got worse. As I came

out I saw a food vendor coming towards me. I asked her for help. Then I died.[14]

Now, an important feature of all these extremely well-attested manifestations of dead persons to their families and friends is that the English-language word that comes most readily to mind to describe them is 'ghost', and although particularly in cases such as Wilfred Owen and Lance Corporal Woodley they died sudden, tragic deaths, they all best correspond to the non-haunting type ghosts held by ancient and tribal peoples to stay in close touch with their families and friends.

Notably, for instance, they have seemed free to make their presence known even thousands of miles from where their own physical body met its death. They have appeared only to those family members and friends whom they chose. They have appeared happy, given the circumstances, and mostly made their appearance on just the one occasion. In other words, in no way could they be considered traditional haunting-type ghosts, associated as these latter are with being unhappy, bound to just one location, and appearing indiscriminately to whoever might wander into that location.

This is not to say, however, that there is not also good evidence for the latter-type ghosts, once the considerable clutter of insubstantial and anecdotal stories concerning these is set aside. As with reincarnation claims, this is a subject that I have explored in greater depth elsewhere, but for me the particularly convincing cases are those in which ordinary families have found themselves so disturbed by what seemed to be a haunting-type ghostly intruder that they have gone to great lengths, not to collect evidence of this, but to get rid of him or her.

Among these a highly important example is the ghost of

a young man who committed suicide early in this century, as experienced by Barbara and Duncan McKenzie and their three daughters. In 1968 the McKenzies moved into a spacious and almost brand-new four-bedroomed house in the pleasant village of Hook, Hampshire, England. This house was so modern and unspooky that when Barbara McKenzie first heard some strange footstep-like noises, she assumed that they must be coming from the central heating system. Although when the noises persisted the thought of something ghostly crossed her mind, she decided to say nothing. Then at Christmas-time, her eldest daughter, just returned from boarding-school and regarded as 'down to earth, practical and unimaginative', came to her in considerable puzzlement, as recalled by Barbara: 'She came to me in the kitchen with a dead-white face, saying, "Mummy, something funny is going on here. I was just about to go upstairs when I heard someone coming down, so I stepped back and waited, but no one came." '[15]

Barbara was just trying to think how to respond to this, when her daughter went on: 'But, Mummy, the footsteps coming downstairs – they weren't coming down where the stairs are, but behind me!'

As Barbara continued:

This really puzzled me for until then I had never actually thought about where the noises were coming from, but had simply accepted that they were associated with the existing stairs – if not the heating system! The next time I heard the footsteps I ran to the foot of the stairs and listened closely as they approached. Yes, my daughter had been right, the footsteps came from a place and position where there were no stairs; in fact they seemed to come from the doorway leading into the lounge.

As Barbara was already aware, the house had been built on the site of a farmhouse formerly owned by the Hayden family, and she discovered from some of Hook's older residents that this had had its staircase precisely where the footsteps were heard. Then, just after Christmas, the footsteps intensified both in frequency and loudness, so that guests also reported hearing them, 'not only coming downstairs, but also pacing to and fro upstairs'. Barbara's mother-in-law, who was visiting them, also reported seeing a young man 'in Teddy-boy's clothes' [i.e. in an Edwardian-style suit] standing in the kitchen. The sound of shots also sometimes seemed to accompany the phenomena, which now continued so obstrusively that they were difficult to ignore.

In the course of inquiries of the villagers Barbara learned that a young son of the Hayden family had committed suicide earlier in the century, and on researching this in contemporary newspapers and coroner's archives, she discovered him to have been Robin Hayden, the eighteen-year-old son of farmer Fred Hayden. Apparently Robin had fallen in love with the local innkeeper's daughter, a match that he knew would meet with intense disapproval from both his almost fanatically puritanical parents and their like-minded employers the Burberrys. During Christmas-time 1913 he had therefore walked out of his room in the old farmhouse and down the stairs, picked up a revolver and went out to a nearby field where he shot himself through the head. Because of the Church of England's strictures against suicides at the time, he had subsequently never been accorded the full burial rites.

Convinced that it was Robin's still unhappy spirit that was responsible for the footsteps and other phenomena, Barbara McKenzie called upon a local clergyman, the Revd Ben Hutchinson, to conduct a simple ceremony of laying him to rest. Thereupon, in Barbara's words, 'Believe it or not, we have had no noises, no walking downstairs sounds, no gunshots, no stampings from that day to this.'

The highly important feature here is not so much the attestation of a ghostly phenomenon, fascinating though this is with elements such as the hauntings intensifying around the anniversary of Robin's death, as the fact that once the ceremony of laying him to rest had been conducted, a very definite result was achieved. In other words, instead of the ghostly phenomenon being just an empty recording-tape of Robin's one-time distress, the strong inference was that something of the dead Robin Hayden's continuing presence had been reached, so that whatever had been causing him to disturb the living was duly quieted.

Importantly, this is not an isolated example. On the files of Canon Dominic Walker, vicar of Brighton Parish Church and head of the Church of England's service for conducting such laying-to-rest ceremonies, is the case of the ghost experienced by a young family of four, whom we will call the Parkers. Around 1979 the Parkers moved into a house in Carshalton, Surrey, and had not been there long before Mrs Parker began seeing the solid-looking apparition of a middle-aged woman with one leg, who would simply vanish into thin air. Because Mrs Parker only experienced the apparitions when she was upstairs and on her own, she initially said nothing to anyone, concerned for her own sanity.

Then one of her daughters came rushing downstairs claiming 'Mummy! Mummy! There's a woman upstairs with only one leg.' Satisfied now that she was not going mad after all, the artistically-inclined Mrs Parker made a sketch of the ghostly woman, and took this round to some of her longer-established neighbours. They immediately identified the likeness as of Anne Allen, who some thirty years before had been a tenant in the upstairs part of the house at a time it had been divided into flats. Anne had suffered the trauma of having her leg amputated in hospital, followed by receiving an eviction notice from her landlord on her return. In despair, she had hanged herself in what was now the Parkers' main bedroom.

Now quite sure that their house was haunted, the Parkers duly called upon the Church of England's 'laying-to-rest' service, and it was Canon Dominic Walker who arrived to conduct this. He chose to do so in the Parkers' bedroom, using their dressing-table as an altar, and not long after commencing was profoundly startled to see an ordinary-looking woman with one leg – clearly Anne Allen – standing next to him. Undaunted, he continued and concluded the ceremony, whereupon she smiled and vanished, and, as in the case of Robin Hayden, never disturbed the Parkers again.

Difficult to believe though such cases may seem, not only do they derive from individuals whom I have directly questioned and completely trust, I have independent reasons for accepting them thanks to a related ghostly experience of my own – shared with my wife Judith – during our first-ever visit to Australia. On 29 January 1994 Judith and I happened to stay overnight at the historic forty-roomed Abercrombie House, near Bathurst, New South Wales, at the invitation of the owners, Rex and Mary Morgan. I had known Rex for some years through a common interest in the Turin Shroud. It was not until after our arrival that our hosts mentioned in all apparent seriousness, that the house had something of a reputation for being haunted. But even so, as Judith and I settled down that night in our allotted bedroom, we assumed that as we were the house's only guests, we were hardly likely to have been given a room the Morgans knew to be thus affected.

It was accordingly with considerable disbelief that little more than two minutes after our turning off the light, I found myself hearing the quite unmistakable and seemingly attention-seeking breathing of someone immediately to my left (Judith was lying to my right). In the pitch darkness I could see no one, and as the breathing relentlessly continued I whispered to Judith, 'Can you hear what I can hear?' To my great relief she replied, 'Yes!' Since I am night-blind, and was therefore unsure whether she could perhaps see something I could not, I then added, 'Can you see anything?' to which she answered, 'No!'

Then, as Judith switched on the light, the weirdest thing happened. As I looked directly at where the breathing sounds had been coming from, immediately to my left, and just a little above my head, they simply seemed to dissolve in the air as I watched. Judith, as the night-sighted partner, got out of bed, explored the gloom of the passageway outside our room, and even went down a flight of steps to the kitchen below us, to see if one of the Morgans' dogs might be sleeping there, and the sound somehow travelling upwards. But she returned baffled. Getting back into bed, she switched off the light, whereupon the breathing almost immediately recommenced, sounding every bit as close, clear and 'real' as before. We listened to it for several minutes, establishing that we were both hearing the inhalations and exhalations at exactly the same time. Then, as Judith turned the light back on, it once again ceased. When she turned the light off once again, it returned again, always just whisper-distance from my ear.

Tired as we both were (for it was now around 12.30 a.m.), and even though neither of us felt frightened, we were now in little doubt of the impossibility of getting to sleep in such close proximity to our invisible but audibly very intrusive visitant. In the circumstances – at that stage I knew nothing of the Robin Hayden and Anne Allen cases – all I could think of was a case I had once read of in which the distinguished

Cambridge classics scholar J. C. Lawson and his wife had been repeatedly disturbed by a nun-like ghostly visitant, whom only Mr Lawson could hear, though both could see. One day when Mrs Lawson was ill, this ghostly figure again appeared at the foot of her bed, whereupon, more in exasperation than piety, she said out loud: 'In the name of the Holy Trinity, poor soul, rest in peace.' As she herself subsequently described it, the apparition almost immediately 'went away to the curtain and I have never seen or heard it since'.[16]

Musing on whether some such formula might achieve the peace that certainly we – if not our visitant – craved, I decided to try a similar prayer. Since my own night-time prayers are said silently before going to sleep, I chose likewise with this one, simply inaudibly pronouncing in my mind: 'Lord Jesus Christ, Son of God: to whoever is with us in this room please grant eternal rest. In the name of the Father, the Son and the Holy Ghost, Amen.' To my utter astonishment, immediately upon my saying the Amen the breathing sound stopped, never to recommence. After I told Judith what I had done, evoking a heartfelt 'Thank God for that!', we both almost instantly went off to sleep, not waking until breakfast-time.

The only logical deduction from the last three cases quoted is that these were all traditional-type haunting ghosts, unhappy, seemingly chained to locations associated with their lifetimes, and manifesting even to complete strangers chancing into those locations – distinctively different, therefore, from the Anthony Crosland and Wilfred Owen-type non-haunting apparitions, but arguably no less valid. It must also be noted that while Billy Graham's grandmother saw her dead yet clearly 'at rest' husband Ben with his lost leg restored, both the Parker family and Dominic Walker saw the unrested Anne Allen as still an amputee. Just as we noted from the ancient and tribal examples quoted in the previous chapter, not everyone's afterlife seems to be the same. While some can manifest anywhere in the world where their loved one might be, others seemingly have no loved ones, and linger unhappily haunting in one spot, until some fortuitous release.

This leaves for consideration one final element that we came across among the ancient and tribal cases: that there seemed to be certain people far more able than others to perceive dead person's spirits, and even to communicate with them and release them on occasion. In the Robin Hayden case, for instance, we observed that Barbara McKenzie's mother-in-law seemed to see Robin's ghost, whereas others only heard his footsteps. But some people seem to be even more sensitive, raising the question of who among those claiming such sensitivities might be genuine in today's world. As we have seen from cases such as those of Florence Cook and Doris Stokes, charlatans undoubtedly abound, but arguably there are also certain individuals with genuine insights.

An interesting example from 200 years ago may have been Swedish engineer Emanuel Swedenborg – a man who, from the scientific point of view, exhibited every form of hard-headedness and could justifiably be regarded as very much of the modern scientific age. For instance, he founded Sweden's Scientific Society. He corresponded with the astronomer Sir Edmund Halley. He advised on decimal coinage. He designed equipment for mines and canals. He founded the science of crystallography. He even invented a successfully marketed hot-air stove.

But Swedenborg's other side, which only emerged following a mysterious Damascus Road-type experience in 1743, was that after this he professed, with completely disarming candour, to be able to see 'into the spiritual world and . . . to converse with spirits and angels'.[17] When, for instance, his one-time teacher, the distinguished Swedish engineer Christopher Polhem, with whom he shared royal patronage, died, he noted matter-of-factly in his diary:

> Polhem died on Monday. He spoke with me on Thursday and when I was invited to his funeral he saw his coffin, and those who were there, and the whole procession, and also when his body was laid in the grave; and in the meantime he spoke with me, asking why he was buried when he was still alive: and he heard also when the priest said that he would be resuscitated at the Last Judgment, and yet he had been resuscitated for some time . . .[18]

When in July 1759 a huge fire broke out in Swedenborg's home city of Stockholm at a time when he was 300 miles away in Gothenburg, he astonished those with whom he was staying by 'seeing' the progress of the fire, only beginning to relax when he perceived that it had been checked before it reached his house. When the hard news of the fire reached Gothenburg by fast messenger two days later, everything he had described proved correct.

In another well-attested incident, Swedenborg even shook the very down-to-earth Queen Louisa Ulrica of Sweden, sister of Frederick the Great of Prussia. As reported at the time by the courtier Count von Höpken:

> Swedenborg was one day at a Court reception. Her Majesty [i.e. Queen Ulrica] asked him about different things in the other life, and lastly whether he had seen or had talked with her brother, the Prince Royal of Russia [with whom, prior to his death, she had been secretly corresponding while Sweden and Prussia were at war.] He [Swedenborg] answered No. Her Majesty then requested him to ask for him and to give him her greeting, which Swedenborg

promised to do. I doubt whether the Queen meant anything serious by it. At the next reception, Swedenborg again appeared at Court . . . and approached her Majesty, who no longer remembered the commission she had given him a week before. Swedenborg not only greeted her from her brother, but also gave her his apologies for not answering her last letter; he also wished to do so now through Swedenborg. The Queen was greatly overcome, and said, 'No one except God knows this secret.'[19]

Now, even assuming that Swedenborg genuinely perceived the dead – in his case a little difficult to establish after more than 200 years – no less difficulty pertains to determining which of his present-day counterparts are genuine, given the fraudulence we noted earlier in this chapter. Nevertheless, one man whom I would unhesitatingly cast in this mould is Englishman Eddie Burks of Lincoln. Today a modest and unassuming septuagenarian, Eddie's early career was not unlike Swedenborg's in that he was an engineer, specializing in airfields and roads, eventually becoming a Civil Service-employed Principal Scientific Officer. And again like Swedenborg, it was only when Eddie was in his early fifties that he discovered in himself an unsought sensitivity towards perceiving spirits of the dead.

Initially this came about following Eddie's loss of his wife at the tragically early age of forty-eight. To his joy, and without any attempt on his part to try to reach her by mediumistic means, he perceived her in his kitchen only one day after her death with all the ease and naturalness that Swedenborg described in connection with his encounter with Christopher Polhem. Subsequently, she even appeared to him in the passenger seat of his car.

It was in 1983 that Eddie's senses heightened to perceiving and communicating with spirits with whom he had no family or friendship connection. Finding himself called upon in instances where families had suffered ghostly disturbances of the Robin Hayden/Anne Allen kind described earlier, he discovered that he could not only easily perceive and communicate with the deceased person, but also help them to be released from whatever it was that kept them tied to their earthly 'haunt'. A classic example was one of the first cases of this kind that Eddie tackled, at a house in Leicester. In his own words:

A local vicar called me, because a young couple in his parish thought their house was haunted. Soon after moving in, they heard footsteps on the landing, a woman crying, and their two-year-old daughter started talking to someone they couldn't see. When the vicar and I went to the house, the daughter was asleep downstairs, in the spare bedroom, and her uncle was baby-sitting. We knew that the previous occupant of the house was an elderly lady who had died from a fall down the stairs. As soon as we went into the child's bedroom I sensed a woman, who was crying. 'What's happened to my house?' she moaned. 'What are these people doing here? I can't use my own bedroom now.' I said to the vicar that I thought she hadn't realised she was dead. 'Ask her about the fall down stairs,' he said to me. Then I turned back to the ghost. Her reply was 'That was a narrow squeak, wasn't it?' I continued with her, until she understood that she was in the next life. It was difficult to persuade her until two people came towards her, and she recognised them as having passed on. The little girl was asleep while we were there, but when she woke up the following morning, she told her mother that she had said goodbye to the lady. She must have seen the old lady in her dreams. It happens quite often with children, because they are much more aware than adults.[20]

Note here how Eddie pereceived the old lady to have been met by 'two people' in the already observed manner of the dying reporting being met by deceased relatives. He also communicated by thought-power, as I had done in respect of the Abercrombie House ghost. And it was via a dream that the old lady seems to have said her goodbyes to the two-year-old.

Inevitably, however, the greatest enigma concerns Eddie himself. Could this man really be genuine? To his considerable credit, he quite deliberately makes absolutely no charge for his services. He has also performed some very convincing 'layings to rest'. For instance, in August 1992, in the case for which he has become best known, he was called upon by Coutts Bank in London's Strand to help them with a ghostly figure in Elizabethan costume that had been disturbing their reception staff. This figure, whom Eddie sensed virtually as soon as he entered Coutts's premises, was identified as almost certainly Thomas Howard, 4th Duke of Norfolk, beheaded, on the order of Queen Elizabeth I, in 1572. After forty-five minutes of mind-to-mind exchange with him, Eddie perceived a woman whom he took to be the Duke's daughter come to receive him and escort him 'towards the Light', whereupon Coutts Bank's disturbances promptly ceased.[21]

In January 1995 I personally took Eddie to an ultra-modern but seriously haunted house on the outskirts of Bristol. Even before getting out of my car, he seemed to make contact with the woman ghost concerned, and less than an hour later he helped her to be received by her other-worldly family, at one and the same time terminating the disturbances that the house's owners had suffered for some five years.[22]

Although it has to be a matter of individual judgment, what I have learnt of Eddie Burks from my own and others' dealings with him leave me with absolutely no doubts concerning his basic integrity – an enormous contrast, therefore, to my attitude towards Doris Stokes and her ilk. Of course, this is not the same as being convinced that his sensitivities represent genuine evidence for life after death, but at this stage this may be the wrong question to be exploring. An arguably far more readily answerable question is why a seemingly ordinary, level-headed and scientific-minded individual like Eddie should have acquired such sensitivities in the first place. The answer seems to lie in the fact that at the age of five he suffered a near-death experience as a result of a tonsillectomy operation going seriously wrong. So was this just a coincidence, or did it somehow trigger Eddie's whole subsequent greater perceptivity to ghosts, even though this took several decades to manifest properly? And if, as I suspect, it was the latter, this indicates that there must be some as yet undetermined link between near-death experiences and ghosts, a link which potentially might shed the most crucial new light on the whole issue of life after death.

Certainly my hunch is that there is indeed such a link. Indeed, we will see later that several other near-death experients besides Eddie Burks had their perceptivity to ghosts significantly heightened in the wake of their experience. Accordingly, it is with this in mind, set against the background of all that we have so far explored, that we will now properly concentrate our attention on the phenomenon of near-death experiences. In particular we will explore both whatever significant links they share with the phenomena we have already touched on, and whatever patterns they share with each other, as manifesting in different people all around the world.

But first, just to give us a real flavour of what near-death experiences are, we will examine a particularly historic, seminal, yet neglected case in its entirety . . .

Chapter Four

'Something Everyone on Earth Has to Know About'

*What if, in some impossible, unimaginable way, I lost . . .
my hardness? My ability to grasp things, to make contact
with the world? Even to be seen?*

Near-death experient George G. Ritchie

The case that follows is historic because it occurred more
than fifty years ago, more than a quarter of a century
before Dr Raymond Moody coined the term 'near-death experience'. It is seminal because it was Raymond Moody's learning
of it, while a philosophy undergraduate, that specifically
sparked off his writing of *Life after Life*, leading in turn to the
present-day scientific acknowledgement of near-death experiences (however these may be interpreted). The case is also a
curiously neglected one, because although Dr Moody actually
dedicated his book to the man to whom it happened, psychiatrist Dr George Ritchie, and has spoken of it as 'one of the
three or four most . . . well-documented "dying" experiences
known to me',[1] Moody and other near-death experience
researchers have mostly shied away from recounting it in any
entirety. Thankfully Dr Ritchie himself has rectified this both
in his first, still all too little-known book *Return from Tomorrow*, published in 1978,[2] and in his recent autobiography *My
Life after Dying*, to which this chapter is heavily indebted.[3]

It was back in September 1943, with the Second World War at its height, and its outcome still far from certain, that the then twenty-year-old George G. Ritchie broke off from his preliminary medical studies at the University of Virginia and joined the US Army, specifically to feel some solidarity with his father, an army major serving with the US forces in Europe. He was sent out with tens of thousands of other raw recruits to the vast, dust-ridden Camp Barkeley, near Abilene, Texas, where that December the temperatures plummeted to only five degrees above zero centigrade, so that when a lieutenant ordered his entire company to sit at attention on icy ground because two soldiers had been talking, Ritchie and several others developed respiratory infections serious enough to require treatment in the camp hospital.

For Ritchie this hospitalization was particularly unwelcome, because as a result of a sudden acute shortage of medical personnel occasioned by the war he had just been specially invited to go back to the Medical College at Richmond, Virginia, to recommence his training as a doctor. For this he needed to be fit enough to make the long journey east within a week.

However, what neither he nor his medical carers realized was that the infection would develop into double pneumonia. In the early hours of the morning of 20 December Ritchie's condition suddenly deteriorated drastically, and he found himself coughing up blood. At the very time when he should have been on a jeep to catch the last available train for his appointment in Virginia, he found himself being rushed by ambulance to the Barkeley Station Hospital's X-ray department. As he tried his best to stand upright at the X-ray machine, his legs buckled beneath him, and his last memory before he lost consciousness was of an army captain shouting out, 'Grab him!'

His next memory was of finding himself sitting up in a

tiny and very dimly lit room that he knew he had never been in before. On the bed next to him there seemed to be a covered mound, but he had no time to investigate this. The thought uppermost in his mind was still the urgency to catch that last train back to Virginia. Unable to find his uniform, he wandered from the tiny room out into the hall and the corridor of the adjoining ward, to see coming towards him a ward assistant carrying a covered tray. Alarmed that the man was going to crash into him, he called out a warning, but to his astonishment not only did the man show no sign of either seeing or hearing him, it was as if he walked right through him . . .

Thoroughly confused, but still too intent on getting to Richmond to rationalize what was happening to him, Ritchie went through an outside door (by what means he really did not know), only with yet more astonishment suddenly to find himself some 500 feet above the ground, and travelling at a phenomenal speed through the night-time darkness. Below him he could see desert and little hills with mesquite trees, gradually giving way to more wooded terrain. From the position of the North Star he gauged that he must be travelling east. Puzzlingly, although the terrain below him looked icy, he had absolutely no feeling of cold.

Soon he found himself crossing a very broad river, noting an impressive bridge spanning it, and a large town on its far side. This prompted the thought that he really ought to slow down at least to check if he was travelling in the right direction for Richmond, whereupon, according to his own recollections:

[As] I came down closer to the ground . . . I noticed the bright blue colour coming from a Pabst Blue Ribbon Beer neon sign in [one of the] front windows of a white café. It was on the corner of the street ahead of me. I saw a tall, thin man, bundled in a dark overcoat, coming up the sidewalk, heading towards the door of this café. I lit down about twelve feet in front of him to ask directions. I had no idea where I was or how far I had travelled.

'What is the name of this city?' Do you know where Richmond, Virginia, is and in what direction I should go to get there?'

For the second time that night, here was another man who acted as though he could neither see nor hear me. In fact, he also walked right through me. This was too much.[4]

Pausing reflectively against the guy-wire of a telephone pole, Ritchie found that this tool appeared to have no substance. He seemed simply to pass straight through it. He then found himself conducting what he freely acknowledged to be 'the strangest, most difficult thinking' that he had ever done in his whole life. In his own words:

The man in the café, this telephone pole . . . suppose they were perfectly normal? Suppose I was the one who was – changed somewhat? What if, in some impossible, unimaginable way, I lost . . . my hardness? My ability to grasp things, to make contact with the world? Even to be seen?[5]

Such concerns immediately raised doubts in him whether there could be any real purpose in this helter-skelter dash for the Richmond Medical College. As he began asking himself:

Will the commandant or any of the professors or students be able to know I am there? What is the use of going on if they cannot? . . . What was that covered mound I left in the bed after I stood up back in the room in Texas? Could that have been a body? I don't like this line of thought: A human isn't separated from their body unless they are dead! If I am, then what is this thing that I am in now? It can go through doors without opening them. It can fly. It does not feel cold. As remarkable as these qualities are, they are no good if I cannot be seen. I have to go back to that hospital in Camp Barkeley and get my other body![6]

No sooner had Ritchie still all too bewilderedly entertained such thoughts than he found himself up in the air again, apparently now going back in the direction from which he had come. As if in no time at all, he found himself back standing in front of the Barkeley Station Hospital.

But now he had a fresh problem: exactly where had he left his body? Again in his own words:

When I left the hospital, I was in such a great rush that I had not taken the trouble to look and see which ward I had left. What had happened with the human beings before was still true. These people, the doctors and nurses now, also could not see or hear me and there was no way I could ask them for information about where my room was located. This was a much larger hospital than I had anticipated since I had been in only two wards and the movie theatre. Now I found myself wandering from ward to ward, room to room, trying to find that little room that I had been in before I left.[7]

Of further alarm to him was the possibility that even if he found his body, he might not be able to recognize it as himself. Several of the soldiers lying in their beds bore some resemblance to him, and sometimes the only way he could be sure that they were not he was when he could see that their left hands lacked the very distinctive Phi Gamma Delta ring with an oval black onyx stone that he knew he had been wearing. So he began to focus his search particularly for anyone wearing such a ring, and not long afterwards came across a tiny, poorly lit room which seemed quite possibly the one he was looking for. Looking inside, he saw on the bed a body with the sheets drawn right up over its head, with only its left arm and hand uncovered.

But this was enough. To his horror he saw that there was a Phi Gamma Delta ring on the hand's ring finger. And it was undoubtedly his own. There was even a chip on the onyx where he had damaged it while going through an obstacle course. A particular cause for his horror was that the hand had precisely the appearance that he recalled of his grandfather's hand just after the latter had died three years before . . .

Although Ritchie desperately wanted to pull away the sheet covering what he felt sure must be his face, there was no way in which he could do so in the form he was in. As he now realized, he had to be dead. Yet despite his having been raised, in typical American 'Bible belt' fashion, as a devout Southern Baptist, nothing seemed to make sense of what his Church's ministers had led him to expect of death. In his own words: 'I . . . carried the concept that when one died, he/she slept until Judgment Day when he/she would be judged and then sent to heaven or hell. The experience I was having now had never been mentioned.'[8]

At last, overcome by the most intense emotions of aloneness, despair and fear that he had ever known, Ritchie mentally cried out: 'Oh God, where are you when I am so lost and discouraged?'

The very next moment, the absolutely impossible happened. The light at the end of his bed began to grow brighter and brighter. At first he thought it was the tiny night-light that was the room's only illumination. But then he saw that it was coming from beside the white bedside table at the head of the bed. Furthermore, it continued to increase so dramatically in intensity that had it been any ordinary light he knew he would have been instantly blinded. The next moment there flooded into his mind the words 'Stand up! You are in the presence of the Son of God', whereupon out of the light stepped what he could only describe as 'the most magnificent Being I have ever known'.

With 'a kind of knowing, immediate and complete' Ritchie recognized that this Being had to be Jesus, but not the Jesus of his Southern Sunday School books. Instead, in his perception, this Jesus was 'power itself, older than time and yet more modern than anyone I had ever met'. More even than anything else, he was also, in Ritchie's own words:

> unconditional love. An astonishing love. A love beyond my wildest imagining. This love knew every unlovable thing about me – the quarrels with my stepmother, my explosive temper, the sex thoughts I could never control, every mean, selfish thought and action since the day I was born – and accepted and loved me just the same.[9]

Nor was it by any mere guesswork that Ritchie knew that this loving Man knew so much about him. It was because, as the two of them watched in that tiny room, to his utter amazement every single episode of his entire life replayed itself before them. Although Ritchie felt sure that they remained in the room, it was as if its walls offered not the slightest barrier and every single moment of his life was recurring before him at one and the same instant as part of some enormous, three-dimensional 'sight and sound' mural.

Among so much that was odd and astonishing, Ritchie found himself now seeing every tiny detail of his life as if from a perspective that was not his. For instance, his mother had died very shortly after giving birth to him by Caesarean section, and for the first time he saw her in her dying moments, along with himself at just two-and-half pounds panting for breath in a nearby incubator. He also saw himself growing up: standing at the blackboard at school, running the fastest mile in a race, and wheeling his grandfather on to the verandah at his grandparents' home.

But there was a further dimension to this observation of himself from the perspective of others: the dimension of his emotions, particularly the more unlovely ones. Although he regarded himself then (and indeed continues to do so now), as having developed into 'a pretty normal teenager',[10] he saw with no little pain his early and persistent distancing of himself from Mary, the tall young woman whom his father brought home to become his stepmother. With like pain he saw his deep resentment when Mary gave birth to his stepbrother Henry, feeling the heat of his own fury on the occasion when the still infant Henry had smashed his model aeroplane. He perceived also the undue pride with which he received his Eagle badge in front of his Scout troop; and the smugness with which he punctiliously attended church every Sunday, counting himself as superior to those children who did not. Even his surely commendable urge to be a doctor, he recognized, cloaked a darker ambition to buy a Cadillac and his own private aeroplane with the wealth that he expected to earn from such an occupation.

Behind every scene there seemed to lie the Man of Light's burning question: 'What have you done with your life to show Me?' And as he watched himself, he always seemed to have all too little to offer in response. Even the seemingly reasonable excuse, 'But I'm only twenty. I haven't properly started yet,' brought the never less than loving response: 'No one is too young to die.'

With Ritchie still trying to formulate more excuses in his mind – 'Why didn't someone tell me that this was what life was all about?' – he suddenly found himself on the move again, rising straight up through the hospital roof and then across the surface of the Earth at an immense speed, his only advice from the Man being, 'Keep your eyes on Me'. Moments later he found himself approaching a large American-looking industrial city beside a large expanse of water.

Here he at once noted something very odd about the streets and offices and factories. They were all impossibly crowded. In one street he watched two men walking down a pavement. One simply passed through the other, as if he wasn't there. In an office he saw a man dictating a purchase order, seemingly oblivious to another, older man standing behind him desperately telling him to change his mind: 'No! If you order a hundred gross they'll charge more. Take a thousand gross at a time. Pierce would have given you a better deal.' In a factory he saw a group of assembly-line workers having their coffee break, with behind them a woman pleading for a cigarette 'as though she wanted it more than anything in the world'. When one of the workers, clearly blind and deaf to the woman behind him, actually took out a cigarette from a packet and began to smoke it, the woman behind repeatedly snatched at it, but as if she was clawing at thin air . . .

Ritchie expressed his reactions to all this:

I thought of that guy-wire on the telephone pole. The sheet on the hospital bed. I remembered myself yelling at a man who never turned to look at me. And then I recalled the people here in this town trying in vain to attract attention, walking along a sidewalk without occupying space. Clearly these individuals were in the same substance-less predicament I myself was in. Like me, in fact, they were dead.[11]

There then sprang into Ritchie's mind 'like an electric shock' the words of Jesus that he remembered from Sunday School: 'Lay not up for yourselves treasures on earth.' As he now saw these people, they must somehow be like ghosts. Even though dead, they remained chained to the material world by all the things they had deemed most important about it in their lifetime – their jobs, their cigarette smoking, their material possessions – just as in Chapter 2 we heard of the Makgabeng deceased great-aunt's spirit being chained to her love of 'ornate bangles and colourful beadwork', and the Malabar planter's ghost being chained to his cravings for whisky and beer. As for Ritchie, in the predicament he found himself in, his thoughts inevitably turned to his own failings. What about his pride in his Eagle Scout badge, his desperation to get back to Virginia, and his urge to own a Cadillac? Were these going to be his chains?

But the Man was moving him on, taking him 'as fast as thought' on a journey from city to city, always with everywhere seeming over-populated, because of all the beings who could only be dead mingling with the still living ones unable to perceive them. And Ritchie now became aware of a new group of such 'ghosts'. As he recollected:

In one house a younger man followed an older one from room to room. 'I'm sorry, Pa!' he kept saying. 'I didn't know what it would do to Mama! I didn't understand.' . . . The old man was carrying a tray into a room where an elderly woman sat in bed. 'I'm sorry, Pa,' the young man said again. 'I'm sorry, Mama.' Endlessly, over and over, to ears that could not hear . . . Several times we paused before similar scenes. A boy trailing a teenaged girl through the corridors of a school. 'I'm sorry, Nancy!' A middle-aged woman begging a grey-haired man to forgive her. 'What are they so sorry for, Jesus?' I pleaded. 'Why do they keep talking to people who can't hear them?' Then from the Light beside me came the thought: They are suicides, chained to every consequence of their act.[12]

Here we may well feel reminded of the ghost of Robin Hayden, haunting his parents' home, also of Anne Allen's ghost, haunting the house of her evicting landlord, in the previous chapter. But Ritchie found himself moved onward again to what seemed to be a US Navy base, and being zoomed into a dingy bar, another impossibly crowded place, where he watched ghost alcoholics mingling with living drunks, like in a scene from a horror movie. He observed with particular fascination how whenever a drunk lapsed into unconsciousness a desperately thirsty ghost seemed to spring inside him, so that they became one. As he began to recognize, the living people could be distinguished from the ghosts by a faint cocoon of light around their bodies, but whenever anyone lapsed into an alcoholic stupor this light cocoon faded, enabling one of the hovering ghosts to take over, or literally 'possess' him or her.

So horrific was the scene that the world 'hell' began to float into Ritchie's thoughts, and as it did so he began to wonder why all these dingy dead people, so desperately clutching at the real-life beer glasses they could not hold, could not see the so obviously amazingly brilliant Man beside him. Was it because he, George Ritchie, confirmed as a Christian at age eleven, had been specially privileged to have his eyes opened? Or was it because they, with their hearts so set on alcohol or whatever else, had simply blinded themselves to Him? Indeed was this why he had been so firmly told 'Keep your eyes on Me'?

His odyssey was by no means finished, however. Once more he found himself on the move, and whereas everything that he had seen so far comprised dead people existing seemingly invisibly and inaudibly alongside the living, now he found himself on what appeared to be a vast plain, seething with yet more beings, among whom the lack of light cocoon indicated that they were all dead. From Ritchie's description of these, he might have been looking at a painting by Hieronymous Bosch:

> At first I thought we were looking at some great battlefield: everywhere people were locked in what looked like fights to the death, writhing, punching, gouging. Although they appeared to be literally on top of each other, it was as though each man was boxing the air; at last I realized that of course, having no substance, they could not actually touch one another . . . These creatures seemed locked into habits of mind and emotion, into hatred, lust, destructive thought-patterns. Whatever anyone thought, however fleetingly or unwillingly, was instantly apparent to all around him, more completely than words could have expressed it, faster than sound waves could have carried it. And the thought most frequently communicated had to do with the superior knowledge or abilities, or background of the thinker: 'I told you so!' 'I always knew!' 'Didn't I warn you!' were shrieked into the echoing air over and over. With a feeling of sick familiarity I recognized here my own thinking. This was me – my very tone of voice – the righteous one, the award-winner, the churchgoer. At age twenty I hadn't yet developed any truly chaining habits, not like the beings I'd seen scrabbling to get close to that bar. But in these yelps of envy and wounded self-importance I heard myself all too well.[13]

Ritchie noted that from the Man beside him there came absolutely no feeling of condemnation of these unfortunates, only compassion. As part of his 'knowing' he sensed that it was their will, not his, that was keeping them where they were. And as he pondered why it was that they all stayed together and didn't try to get away from each other, the answer came to him loud and clear. There was nowhere for them to get away to. This wall-less realm of thoughts had no private corners, no separate spaces. Everything and everyone was ever-present everywhere at once.

And literally everything and everyone. For as Ritchie suddenly became aware 'with a shock that left me stunned', hovering over this very same plain, and over each and every individual on it, there were beings of the very same immense light as the Man Jesus who had taken him on this extraordinary journey. Indeed, as he also realized, these Beings had always been right there all along beside all the 'ghost' figures he had seen in the offices and bars and factories. It was simply that he had not previously registered them, or been conscious of their presence. So were they angels? Or were they somehow innumerable clones of the self-same Man Jesus who had made his presence known to him?

Before being able to obtain any answers, however, Ritchie next found himself wafted to a world seemingly way out of time with his own war-torn 1943. He came to a sunny park with enormous buildings that seemed to comprise partly a study centre, but also a place in which people sat before elaborate consoles whose purpose, even though Ritchie had had a scientific education, was way beyond him. In a studio music was being composed and performed to complicated rhythms and unfamiliar scales. There was a library 'the size of the whole University of Richmond', with rooms lined floor to ceiling with every conceivable document on every conceivable writing material. One building was a huge sphere with a tank inside containing what appeared to be ordinary water. Others seemed to be laboratories, yet another may have been a space observatory. Although Ritchie again asked in his mind what he was being shown, he received no answer. Equally enigmatic was a journey that seemed to be into the vastness of outer space in which, immensely far off, he seemed to glimpse a city of bright buildings and bright beings, only tantalizingly to find himself moving away from it as fast as he had been moving towards it . . .

Then, as if he had been a whole lifetime away, he suddenly found the walls of the cell-like room in the Camp Barkeley hospital solid and confining again. He saw that his sheet-shrouded body was still beside him, and the Man told him that he now had to rejoin this. As it dawned upon him that this meant unbearable separation from this wonderful individual whom he had only just got to know, suddenly he felt real physical pain once again. His throat was burning, his chest was aching as if crushed by a steam-roller, and his breathing was impeded by something covering his face. As he tried to move his arms to push this away, they felt like lead bars and refused to move. Once again he lost consciousness.

When eventually he regained a properly sustained consciousness, the nurse who greeted him told him that it was Christmas Eve. He had been 'out' for four days. Although, amidst painful coughing, he desperately tried to tell the medical staff of his experience as 'something everyone on earth has to know about', they were all too busy with what had become a full-blown epidemic of influenza and pneumonia, so severe that it had necessitated the cancelling of their Christmas leave.

However, as Ritchie became stronger, he gradually learned what had happened to at least the physical part of him while the 'something else' of him had seemingly been on its travels. Apparently, shortly after his collapsing unconscious in front of the X-ray machine, he had been taken to the little isolation room where his condition had steadily worsened until twenty-four hours later the young ward attendant, on doing his rounds, found him with no pulse, no respiration, and no blood pressure. The attendant had duly summoned the duty medical officer who, on running the same tests, confirmed that he was indeed dead. The medical officer had then straightened his arms, pulled the sheet over his face, and given instructions for the attendant to prepare the body for the morgue after he had finished the rest of his rounds. As remarked by Ritchie: 'That must have been the point at which I, in my desperate disembodied search, arrived back at that little room and saw a figure covered with a sheet.'[14]

Nine minutes later the attendant had apparently returned to the little room to carry out his instructions, only to hesitate on seeing what he thought was a movement in Ritchie's chest. He called for the duty medical officer, who once again checked Ritchie's vital signs, all of which still registered zero. The medical officer once again pronounced him dead. Astonishingly, however, not least because he was questioning the judgment of a very busy senior officer, the attendant refused to accept his diagnosis. 'Maybe,' he suggested, 'you could give him a shot of adrenalin directly into the heart muscle?'

Now, as Ritchie subsequently learned, at that time such an injection was not even considered medically appropriate, being used only occasionally in sudden trauma cases such as cardiac arrest, but not when death occurred from a progressive illness such a pneumonia. Nor was it regarded as medically advisable when the patient's brain had been starved of oxygen for as long as Ritchie's seemed to have been. Yet remarkably, the medical officer acceded to his junior's recommendation, tried the procedure, and as the two watched incredulously, first Ritchie's pulse returned, then he began breathing, then his blood pressure rose back to a sustainable level.

During the ensuing days Ritchie slowly but steadily went on to make a full recovery. To his delight he found that his place at the Richmond Medical College had been kept open for him, and exactly a month after his collapse he was pronounced fit enough to make that so eagerly anticipated train journey east. As his train drew in to Richmond station, his stepmother was waiting on the platform, and on her greeting him she immediately sensed that something had changed him, something so profound that late that evening she felt bound to ask him what it was. Having never been able up to this point to tell his story properly to the Camp Barkeley's medical staff, Ritchie suddenly found himself pouring it all out to the one person whom he had steadfastly resisted communicating with throughout his whole life.

As his stepmother listened to him attentively and sympathetically, he suddenly realized that his whole perception of her had changed. She was no longer just an outsider who had become his stepmother, but Mary Skeen Ritchie, a thoroughly caring woman who while still young had most courageously taken on himself and his sister, in full knowledge that their father would mostly be away from home except at weekends. He also now appreciated something about her that his father had once told him but he had put to the back of his mind, that she had quite deliberately opted not to become pregnant during the first three years of their marriage, specifically so that she could have time to get to know him and his sister. When he finished telling her his story she sat with him in silence for some while, then said simply, 'George, God has entrusted you with enormous truths.'

Indeed they are enormous truths, the most enormous possible, the crucial question for us being, can we really believe them to be genuine? If they are, then they are most certainly something that everyone on earth needs to know about. They need to be shouted from the rooftops. If they are genuine, then there really is life after death; there really are ghosts and spirits all around us, just as the ancients and

71

the tribal peoples have always said; Jesus truly was someone special, and what he taught is something that we really do need to shape our lives around.

But inevitably a first, important question is whether even George Ritchie himself could be sure he did not hallucinate the whole experience. With regard to this he is emphatic that he received his own subsequent proofs. One of the most important of these occurred only ten months later. Because of the time he lost recuperating he failed his first-year medical exams. As a result, and because the war was still on, he was summoned back to the dreaded Camp Barkeley. Three medical students in the same predicament and intending to drive to the Camp offered him a seat in their car for the long journey, in the course of which they stayed the night of Tuesday, 2 October in Vicksburg, Mississippi, a town Ritchie was quite sure he had never visited before. As he recalled:

> While driving down the street the next morning, I could look over to the right and see the Mississippi River. Then I thought, 'Something looks very familiar to me.' I looked over to the left and there stood the white all-night café with the Pabst Blue Ribbon neon sign in the front window. I looked down the river and there was the big bridge crossing the Mississippi, the one I had seen that night I was trying to get back to Richmond. Now I had tangible proof I was not hallucinating.[15]

Because of the medical experience Ritchie had already gained, on his getting to Camp Barkeley the army trained him as a medical and surgical technician, and in this role he was shipped to Europe in the closing stages of the Second World War. There he confronted scenes of human suffering that taught him that he must no longer keep looking for the Man in the other-worldly form that he had been privileged to see, but instead in the injured and troubled people he encountered in his work each day.

He also learned to listen to a voice deep inside him that on at least one occasion directly saved his life. One morning, having boarded an army personnel carrier for a coveted excursion to visit the Cathedral of Rheims, he inwardly but unmistakably 'heard' the stern instruction, 'Get off, and go write Marguerite [his intended wife back in the USA] a letter.' Although it seemed absurd, for he had only just written to Marguerite and was genuinely looking forward to the excursion, he reluctantly complied and gave his place to another soldier. Minutes later the carrier with twelve of Ritchie's companions on board, having travelled no more than eight miles, hit a landmine. The soldier who had taken Ritchie's place was killed instantly, and almost all the rest received horrific injuries requiring long hospitalization in England and the USA.

At the end of the war Ritchie married Marguerite, was allowed to resume his still-coveted full medical training, qualified successfully, and spent thirteen years as a general practitioner at Richmond, Virginia's Memorial Hospital, during which he was elected President of the Richmond Academy of General Practice. Then in 1963, feeling that general practice did not allow him enough time to get to know his patients as people, he decided to specialize in psychiatry, uprooting his wife and two children to Charlottesville, where as resident psychiatrist attached to the University of Virginia School of Medicine he became popular among students and patients alike for his invariable warmth, kindliness and good humour.

His extraordinary experience always remained uppermost in his mind, and whenever he found a receptive ear he would enthusiastically tell his story, sometimes being invited to lecture on it at university gatherings. It was on just one such occasion, at the University of Virginia in 1965, that the audience included philosophy undergraduate Raymond Moody, then much the same age as Ritchie had been when he underwent his experience. Impressed, Moody filed the lecture away in his mind, and when a few years later, on giving a lecture of his own at East Carolina University, he learned of other cases like Ritchie's, he began the research that led to the writing of *Life after Life*, the coining of the term 'near-death experience', and the whole explosion of interest in the phenomenon.

Here the curiosity is that although Moody actually dedicated *Life after Life* to 'George Ritchie, MD' adding cryptically 'and, through him, to the One whom he suggested', Ritchie's story went unchronicled throughout the book itself, being referred to only most glancingly,[16] with Ritchie not even named. Now it is possible that this was because Moody did not want to subvert Ritchie's plans to tell his story in his own words, for Ritchie's own *Return from Tomorrow* was published three years later, though with nothing like the worldwide sensation which Moody's book had created.

But there may well have been another reason, indeed quite possibly the same one which accounts for why Ritchie's book did not enjoy Moody's success, why Ritchie's story, when told in its entirety as here, is quite literally too difficult to believe. Even in his most passing references to it Moody twice uses the word 'fantastic', and we ourselves may well feel this to be by no means an unfair description. Moody managed to make near-death experiences credible because when dealing with the 150 or so that he collected for his first book he carefully broke them down into individual elements, so that he could compare them element by element. Following standard practice for medical case histories, he also deliberately omitted the names of any of the experients, and gave few if any other details by which they might be identified. In so depersonalizing each case he managed to sanitize it and maximize its credibility, and avoid the sort of material that might have got his book laughed out of court. And such is the lore of its own that has grown up around the subject of near-death experiences, that with only the partial exception of Australia's Dr Cherie Sutherland, essentially, every subsequent serious researcher has followed Moody's lead.

The question for us, however is: hang the idea of any sanitization – when a case such as George Ritchie's is looked at *in toto*, as we have tried to do, is it true? If we accept the evidentiality of near-death experiences in general, as researchers such as Moody, Ring, Sabom, Fenwick and Sutherland all have, then there can be no denying that Ritchie's is in the same mould, simply being far fuller – with the exception of any meeting with deceased relatives – than most other first-hand accounts so far published.

Nor can Ritchie himself easily be written off as just some hallucinating religious freak. He has insisted upon the experience as 'the most entirely real thing that's ever happened to me'.[17] We have seen his credentials as a sane, qualified, longstanding practising physician. And as an even more long-standing psychiatrist he has commented: 'I've had a chance to study . . . hallucinations. I've had patients who were hallucinating. There's just no resemblance.'[18]

As for whether he might simply have concocted the story, even the thought is unworthy, and may be discounted out of hand. Although, because of the lapse of time, the subsequent whereabouts of the medical officer and the ward attendant are not known, both the doctor in overall charge of the Camp Barkeley hospital ward, and the nurse who cared for Ritchie after his 'coming back to life' have been traced and identified. The former, Dr Donald G. Francy, made the following notarized statement: 'Speaking for myself [I] feel sure that his [Ritchie] virtual call from death and return to vigorous health has to be explained in terms of other than natural means.'[19]

As for the nurse who treated him, the then 1st Lieutenant Rhetta Irvine, she attested on being traced in 1957:

> Although fourteen years have elapsed and some of the details are not quite clear, I remember that this patient was pronounced dead at two different times by the Medical Officer who was on duty, yet after he was given an injection into the heart muscle the patient revived and in due time regained his health. During his convalescence Private Ritchie asked me how near dead he had been. When I told him what had happened he said that he thought he had been dead. Although he did not go into detail he told me that he had an experience that would probably change his life. Even though this experience was most unusual, I did not doubt this man's sincerity either then or now.[20]

If Ritchie were a sensationalist who wanted to make money out of his story, he could have easily beaten Moody to publication, but he showed no inclination to do so. And in terms of his ambitions for a medical career, the knowledge, which he never tried to suppress, that he had had such an experience was always more of a burden than an asset. When he applied for his psychiatric post with the University of Virginia (notably long before the publication of Moody's book), he was directly asked during the very first interview whether it was true that he had 'met the Christ'. Knowing full well that an affirmative answer would probably cost him the job, he responded levelly, 'I can no more deny the reality of what happened to me in Barkeley, Texas, than Saul of Tarsus could deny what happened to him on the road to Damascus.' Thankfully, his interviewer, Dr Wilfred Abse, the

University's Professor of Psychoanalysis and Analytical Psychotherapy, recognized and respected a man of integrity. As he told Ritchie years later: 'All of us . . . knew that you claimed to have had a out-of-the-body experience. If you'd pretended with me even for a moment that it hadn't happened, I'd have put you down as a deeply inscure person, and most probably an emotionally disturbed one who couldn't distinguish between fact and fancy.'[21]

So if that was the judgment of Dr Abse, a man who subsequently came to know Dr Ritchie directly as a working colleague and a good friend, where do we stand? Can we too accept Ritchie's 'fantastic' story as fact rather than fancy? For anyone of rational, critical, scientific mind that is understandably demanding a very great deal. But that is the goal we have now set ourselves. With Ritchie's whole story in mind, and also bearing in mind what we have learnt from other serious evidence for life after death, we will now, in part, do what we have criticized others for doing: examine the story's individual broad elements in relation to those individual elements reported by others and collected by researchers into near-death experience throughout the world.

The first element is that of being 'out of body'. For how can we be really sure that something of Ritchie, or of anyone else resuscitated from the dead, actually did separate from his or her body, and was truly able to move about in the manner claimed?

Chapter Five

But Can You Really Leave Your Body?

I was above, I don't know about *what*. But it was up . . . it
was like I didn't have a body! I was . . . but it was *me*.
Not a body, but me! . . . It was a *me inside*. The real me
was up there; not this here [*pointing to her physical body*].

American experient who 'died'
while undergoing tonsillectomy[1]

Just to recap the first part of Dr George Ritchie's experience
back in that December of 1943, we may recall that he fell
unconscious while being X-rayed, and then twenty-four
hours later exhibited every external appearance of being
dead. When checked twice by qualified medical personnel,
he had no pulse, no respiration, and no external signs of any
brain activity.

Yet he subsequently insisted that sometime during this
period something of himself surfaced into its own form of
consciousness. Although that something was invisible and
inaudible to anything of what we may call the normal living
world, in that guise he was able to see and hear everything
around him in apparently real time and real space. Defying
all existing scientific understanding, he was able to do that
seeing and hearing from a vantage-point that was not his
physical body's eyes and ears. He was able to move to
apparently real space locations, taking up positions that the
law of gravity makes impossible for any normal physical

body. He was able, as if with the effortlessness of thought, to travel long distances at immense speed. Of the three major senses, only that of touch and feeling seemed to be denied him, leaving him with neither the unwanted pains that had been ravaging his physical body, nor any feelings of tactile contact with wherever he found himself in the external world.

Now of course, so far as our present-day scientific understanding is concerned, all this is impossible nonsense. However, harking back to sentiments of Dr Michael Sabom's Florida night watchman quoted in Chapter 1 – 'I'm not telling you everything, doctor . . . Maybe later . . . when I know how serious you are' – we promised to treat such claims seriously. And the history of science ought to be sufficient warning of the folly of any one generation of scientists which insists that theirs is the one which has found out everything worth knowing.

So let us first of all consider the question of whether, quite aside from George Ritchie's claims, there is serious evidence for there being anything of a person that can be conscious, in the sense of 'awake' and 'aware', even when, so far as their reactivity to external stimuli is concerned, they may appear deeply unconscious, such as when under general anaesthetic, or in a coma.

With regard to general anaesthetics, although the vast majority of people on the receiving end of these drift blissfully off into full unconsciousness exactly as intended, there are quite definitely certain circumstances in which people can and do retain awareness, even though all else has been shut down. Mostly such cases have involved patients who have been given enough muscle relaxant to prevent them speaking or even blinking an eye, but not enough anaesthetic either to send them to sleep or to deaden all pain. And almost invariably these are horror stories.

These, for instance, are the words of one British woman who remained aware during a Caesarean operation:

> It was just like being trapped inside your body or being buried alive. I couldn't scream. I couldn't move a muscle. I couldn't do a thing. I felt as if I was going to die. I kept thinking 'I'll go to sleep in a minute' but they made the incision and it felt like a red-hot poker. I felt a lot of movement in my abdomen and I felt lighter as they lifted the baby out. There was scraping, then I felt the stitches going in and being pulled tight. It seemed to go on for ever.[2]

In the case of coma, it has also become increasingly recognized that patients can remain intelligently aware during such a state, even though this may be so deep and prolonged that they fail to respond to any non-mechanical stimuli, and may seem totally 'brain-dead'. When in the late 1980s a twenty-two-year-old British girl, Debbie Crowley, became profoundly comatose from appalling and clearly mortal injuries that she sustained in a road accident, her fiancé, as a token of his undying love, went through a ceremony of marriage with her as she lay hooked up to every instrument in the hospital ward. As observed by everyone present at the ceremony, at the very moment that the couple were pronounced man and wife, and the wedding ring was slipped on to Debbie's finger, her blood-pressure leaped dramatically, clearly indicating that something of her 'knew' what was going on.[3] Similarly, when in September 1979 the late Earl Spencer, father of Princess Diana, suffered a severe brain haemorrhage that sent him into deep coma for several months, his wife Raine determinedly kept talking to him at his bedside as if he could hear her, and playing him tapes of his favourite music. On his at last regaining consciousness (to the strains of his favourite operatic aria), he told her, 'I knew you were there, and I heard everything you said to me.'

Most significantly of all, there very recently came to light the case of a twenty-six-year-old English carpenter, Ian Doughty, who four years ago was effectively declared a complete vegetable after a horrific vehicle accident caused him to be on a ventilator for four weeks, followed by more than a year's deep coma from which even after 'waking' he showed no apparent responsiveness. Then, as a last resort, he was transferred to London's Royal Hospital for Neurodisability where specialist staff tried various stimuli, such as playing him recorded tapes of carpentry shop sounds, in an effort to try to 'reach' him. In the event, to their astonishment, their supplying him with a simple buzzer did the trick. In the words of his father Arthur Doughty, who despite the doctors' advice insisted that he had felt all along that his son had a continuing awareness:

He [Ian] is locked in a body he can't control, but his mind is there. He remembers all his friends and family and he can do mental arithmetic. We asked him if he wanted his picture taken by The Times and he agreed. It is one buzz for yes, two for no and four for swearing. He has a sense of humour. If you ask him would he like a big buxom blonde, he'll give a big long buzz.[4]

According to the Royal Hospital for Neurodisability specialists, possibly as many as 40 per cent of patients who are in the same 'persistent vegetative' state as Ian may similarly have still properly functioning minds imprisoned in bodies so severely disabled that their efforts to communicate have gone unrecognized.[5]

There is, then, some very serious evidence for a continuing intelligent awareness remaining even when the brain itself has been very seriously damaged. And this despite the difficulties such evidence poses for many of today's research psychologists, such as Dr Susan Blackmore, because it implies the existence of something beyond the physical brain, which they regard to be the be-all and end-all for all of us, with our consciousness simply being its by-product.

However, the further proposition that such sceptics really baulk at is that there could be circumstances, such as in George Ritchie's case, when the awareness persists despite all appearances of physical death, and even seems to detach itself from the physical body. The first objection here is that despite George Ritchie and others like him having been pronounced dead by competent medical personnel, they could not *actually* have died. According to this view, whenever anyone recovers from what appears to be death, and goes on to lead a full and active life, any pronouncement that they were dead, from however eminent a clinician, and whatever the sensitivity of the diagnostic instruments used, *must* be considered mistaken. By this definition true death is the state from which no one returns, and no special purpose seems to be served by objecting to this. In deference to this view we will therefore simply use quotation marks when referring to anyone believed to have 'died' and then been resuscitated.

For however we define true death, the phenomena we are looking at occur mostly specifically when a person has come within a whisker of it. This seemingly near-death state, as distinct from the anaesthetics and coma examples described earlier, acts as a trigger for their then leaving their physical bodies, and seeing these as if from an outsider's viewpoint.

At this point we confront the key issue, and the one provoking the fiercest opposition from any sceptic, that of whether there really is something of us which in those circumstances can and does leave our physical body. Obviously just one case like Dr George Ritchie's is not enough to determine such a major new understanding. Thankfully we already have more than enough examples in the cases reported through time across the world, and also collected by already mentioned major researchers such as the Americans Drs Raymond Moody, Kenneth Ring, Michael Sabom, Maurice Rawlings and Melvin Morse, the English psychiatrist Dr Peter Fenwick and the Australian Dr Cherie Sutherland. The hard task is to come to the right evaluation of these.

And here it is irrefutable that quite independently of Dr Ritchie's experience, universally, and for a very long time, people who have been in a state closely resembling death have described the sensation of seemingly leaving their body and looking down on it from a vantage-point impossible for their physical eyes and ears.

For instance, the Tibetan monks who wrote the *Bardo Thodol*, or *Book of the Dead*, back in the eighth century described the dead person staying around the place where they died, and watching relatives and friends making arrangements for their funeral, just as we noted in Chapter 3 of Emanuel Swedenborg and his account of his deceased friend Christopher Polhem's telling him of seeing his own funeral. In 1825 the American folklorist Henry Rowe Schoolcraft, in making a study of native American Indians of the Mississippi, wrote how a resuscitated Chippewa warrior chief described being 'killed' on the battlefield, and watching his warriors prop his 'corpse' up against a tree, totally frustrated at being unable to make them understand he was still alive.[6] In the 1860s an American Mormon likewise told how, having been very badly injured in an accident: 'His spirit left his body and stood, as it were, in the air above. He could see his body and the men standing around and he heard their conversation.'[7]

Similarly, among present-day informants, a sixty-year-old Ohio housewife described to Dr Michael Sabom her viewing of the efforts to resuscitate her after she 'died' of a cardiac arrest while hospitalized in January 1978:

> I had left my body and was to the side . . . They called the express team and I could see them coming in, and all the doctors and nurses and all the confusion. They were punching my chest, putting IVs in me . . . I could see the little needle they were putting in my hand . . . I could see my face very clearly and they were lifting my eyelids. They were pulling my eyelids up to see where my eyes were, I guess . . . Then they were feeling around my neck where the pulse is . . . I saw this one girl grabbing everything [from my locker] because the doctor had said: 'We're going to have to get her up to ICU [the intensive care unit].' She was grabbing everything and dumping it into bags and suitcases.[8]

Englishman and former Church Army Captain Edmund Wilbourne, who has in his possession the actual signed certificate of his 'death' from pleurisy back in 1949, has described how he saw his body being prepared for the Manchester hospital mortuary in which he actually 'woke up': 'I saw myself lying on the bed. I saw a young nurse. She was preparing me for the mortuary. I remember thinking at the time how young she was to have to do such a thing as getting me ready and even shaving me.'[9]

An Australian experient, Robert, who was declared dead on the operating table after having earlier tried to commit suicide with a shotgun, described to Dr Cherie Sutherland his memory of this scene: 'The next thing I remember is looking down on my body, with the surgeons around, and I distinctly knew. I knew it was me. I thought: "That's me. They're wasting their time. I'm not going back."'[10]

Innumerable similar examples of this kind could be quoted. One feature worth noting in passing being that there can be some significant differences among experients' awareness concerning their actually being 'dead'. For instance the Australian suicide Robert, because he had quite deliberately attempted to take his own life, fully expected to die, and accordingly felt no surprise or confusion on finding himself in what seemed to be this state. However, for those who may have had absolutely no prior expectation of dying, there can be considerable confusion,[11] as in George Ritchie's disembodied attempt to get to Richmond, Virginia. There can also be realization accompanied by disbelief and outrage.

Again, examples can be cited from many centuries ago, as in the case of the Tibetan monks who wrote the *Bardo Thodol*: 'When the consciousness principle gets outside the body it says to itself "Am I dead or am I not dead?" It cannot determine, it sees its relatives and connections as it had been used to seeing them before, it even hears the wailings.'[12]

Likewise Emanuel Swedenborg, who wrote back in the eighteenth century: 'When a man comes into the other life he is not aware that he is in that life but supposes that he is still in the world, and even that he is still in the body.'[13]

Among modern experients, we find this from a young American woman among Dr Raymond Moody's informants:

I thought I was dead . . . but I just couldn't figure where I was supposed to go. My thoughts and my consciousness were just like they are in life, but I just couldn't figure all this out. I kept thinking, 'Where am I going to go? What am I going to do? and 'My God, I'm dead! I can't believe it!' Because you never really believe, I don't think, fully, that you're going to die.[14]

Likewise this from Englishwoman Gillian McKenzie of Eastbourne (see Chapter 3):

> I thought 'My God, I'm dead!' I was quite angry. I thought, 'It's not fair, I'm not even in the operating theatre yet and it's not going to be very easy for James [her new-born son] . . . if I'm dead. And anyway, I don't want to die.' I felt very annoyed about it . . .[15]

Absolutely apparent is that whatever state these individuals may be in (and whatever the semantics, they certainly perceive themselves as dead), their normal, self-questioning consciousness remains very much in play, causing them to have very much the same reaction as my own on experiencing the Abercrombie House ghost (see Chapter 3); literally, 'I can't believe this is happening to me'. In the same vein, such may be their confusion over the circumstances in which they find themselves that, exactly as in George Ritchie's case, they may initially completely fail to recognize their 'dead' bodies as their own because they have never seen themselves before as others have seen them. As one of Dr Raymond Moody's informants told him:

> Boy, I sure didn't realize that I looked like that! You know, I'm only used to seeing myself in pictures or from the front of a mirror, and both of those look *flat*. But all of a sudden there I – or my body – was and I could see it. I could definitely see it, full view, from about five feet away. *It took me a few moments to recognize myself* [italics mine].[16]

Among the many astonishing aspects of this opening phase of the experience is that in their observing of their body and the physical world around them, these individuals almost invariably find themselves, exactly as George Ritchie did, floating up free of gravity to locations that would normally be physically impossible for them, and viewing themselves in ways that would be quite impossible for their physical eyes. For instance, self-avowedly 'down-to-earth' retired British Army Major Derek Scull, who 'died' of a heart attack while in a hospital's intensive care unit, told Peter and Elizabeth Fenwick: 'I floated up to the top left-hand corner of the [hospital] room. I looked back and saw my own body, *lying there with its eyes closed* [italics mine] . . .'[17]

An American woman who 'died' of cardiac arrest while turning on to her side in her hospital bed told Dr Raymond Moody:

> I started rising upward, slowly . . . On my way up I saw . . .
> nurses come running into the room . . . I drifted on up past
> the light fixture – I saw it from the side and very distinctly –
> and then I stopped, floating right below the ceiling, looking
> down. I felt almost as though I were a piece of paper that
> someone had blown up to the ceiling.[18]

Even those who 'die' in the open air, such as from a traffic accident, report very much the same experience of floating over their body and viewing it at a normally impossible elevation, as in the case of a young American saleswoman struck by a car while hurrying across a pedestrian crossing, who told Dr Michael Sabom:

> I was above the whole scene viewing the accident . . . It was
> just like I floated up there . . . [up to the] rooftop or maybe
> a little higher . . . very detached . . . And I saw my body. My
> attention was called to my body when the attendants put it
> on the stretcher . . . I saw myself in profile. I was actually

towards the front and side of the car, viewing all of this . . .
I remember them looking at my eyes. I guess they were
checking my pupils.[19]

Consistent in essentially every case is that from whatever
'out-of-the-body' vantage-point the person's awareness may
seem to have taken up, he or she is able to see and mostly able
to hear[20] whatever is happening round about exactly as if they
were actually occupying that very point in space. In other
words, if an onlooker's head happens to be in the way, then
their line of sight is blocked, whatever their receiving 'eyes'
may be. As a fifty-seven-year-old American construction
worker who watched those trying to resuscitate him after a
cardiac arrest told Dr Michael Sabom: 'They were moving me
back and forth in the bed but I couldn't see what else they
were doing 'cause there were so many of them bent over me.'[21]

To this extent everything may seem 'natural', even lulling
the experient, as in George Ritchie's case, into believing
themselves still 'alive' – until they find, to their astonishment, that absolutely nothing of themselves, either in the
form of sight, sound or touch, seems perceptible to the living
people whom they are still able to see and hear around them.
As an American woman who, just like Dr Sabom's construction worker, 'died' in hospital and watched the procedures
to resuscitate her, told Dr Raymond Moody:

> It was really strange. I wasn't very high; it was almost like I was
> on a pedestal, but not above them to any great extent, just
> maybe looking over them. *I tried talking to them but nobody
> could hear me, nobody would listen to me* [italics mine].[22]

As Dr Michael Sabom's construction worker said of one
moment during the resuscitation team's attempts to revive
him:

One time a nurse I could see looked me [i.e. the aware 'me', rather than his physical body] right in the face just this far away [indicating one foot]. I tried to say something, but she didn't say nothing . . . She was like looking at a movie screen that can't talk back and that doesn't recognize you're there.[23]

An Australian, Hal, who as a fourteen-year-old schoolboy suffered a series of heart attacks while in the school playground, likewise told Dr Cherie Sutherland:

I was out of the body, and I thought to myself 'I must be dead'. So I went up to Miss Smith [one of his teachers] and told her not to bother, I was dead. She took no notice of me. I made a few more attempts to speak to her and to Miss Breen then gave up . . .[24]

For every experient the weirdest aspect of this is that it is the *living* world they observe that now has all the insubstantiality of so-called ghosts. Exactly as George Ritchie remarked of the man whose shoulder he tried to tap, and the telephone pole guy-wire he tried to lean against, Hal said of his attempt to make contact with his teacher Miss Smith:

I went to take her arm and my hand went right through her . . . I went to open the door but my hand went through the handle. I then tried the bricks beside the door, pushed with my hand, and then went straight through the bricks to the outside. I remember going through the bricks two or three times just to try it out.[25]

A US Army captain who had both his legs and an arm blown off while in action in Vietnam told Dr Michael Sabom of his 'seeing' the medical team's efforts to save him: 'I actually remember grabbing the doctor. Nothing [happened]. Absolutely nothing. It was almost like he wasn't there. I grabbed and he wasn't there or I just went through him or whatever.'[26]

With regard to getting around in this insubstantial state, just as George Ritchie found, without even realizing it, that merely thinking of getting outside the hospital duly transported him, so an American experient, Lisa, stumped at what to do next after finding herself floating on the ceiling, found the solution via the same process. As reported by her interviewers, researchers Barbara Walker, Dr William Serdahely and Lori Bechtel, 'the answer came to her immediately. She realized that all she needed to do was to let her mind tell her soul body where to move, and in doing so her soul would travel to that destination.'[27]

Likewise Dr Michael Sabom's night watchman informant (see Chapter 1) imparted:

> I could see anywhere I wanted to. I could see out in the parking lot, but I was still in the corridor . . . It was just like I said, 'OK, what's going on out in the parking lot?' and part of my brain would go over and take a look at what's going on over there.[28]

And just as distance was no object for George Ritchie, who was whisked as if in little more than a trice from Abilene, Texas to Vicksburg, Mississippi, en route to Richmond, Virginia, so in another example, American Professor Patrick Gallagher, an agnostic anthropologist who 'died' in an horrific car crash in (of all places) Death Valley, California, reported of his floating in the air above the body:

> I quickly discovered also that not only was I floating and hence free from gravity but free also from any of the other

restrictions that inhibit a flight . . . I could also fly at a terrific rate of speed with a kind of freedom that one normally doesn't experience in normal flight in airplanes, but perhaps experiences a little more in hang-gliding and things like that . . . But I noticed that I could fly at a phenomenal rate of speed and it seemed to produce a feeling of great joy and sense of actually flying in this total fashion.[29]

In another example, an Australian experient, Shana, told Dr Cherie Sutherland of her 'dying' from a surgical operation undergone while she and her mother were visiting England:

And then I was outside my body and I was watching everybody working on me . . . I could see my mother out in the hall of the hospital in Sussex, England, and I could see my father in Australia. I could see everybody I was connected to – it was just one big global thing – and the doctors and the nurses working on me.[30]

Inevitably of more than a little interest is what kind of body, or lack of it, these experients perceive themselves to be perceiving from. George Ritchie, it may be recalled, began looking for his clothes on first emerging from his body, and then unconcernedly went off on his cross-country trip to Vicksburg without ever finding them. He subsequently mentions nothing of his giving any further thought to what his out-of-the-body body might 'look' like. If this might seem odd, it is not. Other experients describe little, if anything at all, of their perceptions of their out-of-the-body bodies.

For instance, among English near-death experients, this is what housewife Ella Silver told Peter and Elizabeth Fenwick: 'I felt as if I didn't have a body, but was all mind.'[31] Likewise Mrs Frances Barshey: 'I seemed to be mind and emotions only.'[32]

An American experient told Dr Kenneth Ring: 'It seemed like I was up there in space and just my mind was active. No body feeling ... I had nothing but my mind.'[33] And Dr Michael Sabom's Florida saleswoman traffic accident victim imparted: 'It was as though I was pure intellect.'[34]

The only qualification to this comes from one of Dr Raymond Moody's informants who after remarking in similar vein, 'I got the feeling ... that this form ... wasn't a body, just a wisp of smoke or vapour ... almost like the clouds of cigarette smoke you can see when they are illuminated as they drift around a lamp,'[35] then went on: '... but it [i.e. that which he perceived of his form] had what I would call a hand ... I know this because ... I reached up ... with my hand.'

George Ritchie, it may be recalled from Chapter 4, had tried to tap the shoulder of the man entering the all-night café, implying at least that he did not 'feel' himself to be handless. Likewise, when the Australian experient Hal, tried to take his teacher's arm, and Dr Michael Sabom's US Army captain tried to 'grab' the doctor, none reported the problem being a lack of hands. Yet no one ever seems to 'see' anything of such out-of-the-body body parts, and there is a general consistency to this that is oddly impressive, irrespective of our inability to make sense of it in terms of the world that we think we know.

The question that now arises is: what do the sceptics make of all this? As we have already mentioned there are some, such as the English psychologist Dr Susan Blackmore, who have studied near-death experiences only to reject them as being evidence for anything separating from the body that might survive death. So what are their grounds for this?

Fraud, that great scourge of the spiritualist mediums, they do not attempt to allege, since the obvious sincerity of the great majority of near-death experients makes even the idea unworthy and unthinkable.[36] Nor can it easily be claimed that those who have the experiences are just self-deluded religious fanatics. Experients come from all persuasions and all walks of life, and a significant proportion have even been outright agnostics and atheists beforehand, finding their beliefs profoundly shaken and changed by the experience. One such, as we will see later, was atheist philosopher the late Sir Alfred Ayer.

Nor is the phenomenon one to be found predominantly among the old and senile. As we saw, George Ritchie was only twenty. The American paediatrician Dr Melvin Morse[37] and the Australian sociologist Dr Cherie Sutherland[38] have come across a significant number of cases among children of six years old and even younger, one case to be quoted later in this book even occurring when the child was only two and a half.

Accordingly the only serious alternatives are either that some form of awareness truly separates from experients' bodies during some close encounter with death, or that they hallucinate such a separation. If the latter is to be believed, then obviously some explanation is needed for such convincing-seeming hallucinations.

Here the sceptics' prime researcher and spokesperson is the already mentioned Dr Susan Blackmore, Senior Lecturer in Psychology at the University of the West of England, Bristol – it is a subject on which she feels able to speak with some authority because while a cannabis-smoking student at Oxford University she specifically had the experience of separating from her body on one occasion. As she has described, she was smoking in an Oxford college room, feeling 'terribly tired' and listening to music with two friends, Vicky and Kevin, when, in her own words:

> As I sat listening to the music, the voices of my friends seemed a long way off. If I thought about my own body it

did not seem to be firmly on the hard floor but rather indistinct, as though surrounded by cotton wool. In my tiredness my mind seemed to follow the music into a scene of a tree-lined avenue. The whole was like a tree-lined tunnel and I was hurtling through it . . . simultaneously I was aware of Vicky asking if I would like some coffee. Kevin answered but I did not . . . It is to Kevin's credit that he both initiated and helped me with the next stage. Quite out of the blue, and I have no idea why, he asked, 'Sue, where are you?' This simple question baffled me. I thought, struggled to reply; saw the road and leaves, tried to see my own body; and then did see it. There it was below me. The words came out: 'I'm on the ceiling.' With some surprise I watched the mouth – my mouth – down below, opening and closing and I marvelled at its control.

Kevin seemed quite calm at this pronouncement, and proceeded to question me in detail. What was it like up there? What could I see? What was 'I'? . . . Again, as I formulated answers, the mouth below spoke . . . From the ceiling I could apparently see the room quite clearly. I saw the desk, chairs, window, myself and my friends all from above. Then I saw a string or cord, silvery, faintly glowing and moving gently, running between the neck of my body below and the navel, or thereabouts, of a duplicate body above . . . With encouragement I moved out of the room, myself and my cord moving through the walls, another floor of rooms and the roof with ease. I clearly observed the red of the roofs and the row of chimneys before flying on to more distant places . . . I visited Paris and New York and flew over South America.[39]

Now, at first sight Dr Blackmore's cannabis trip exhibits some obvious similarities to the near-death experience, including her leaving of her body, her viewing herself from above, her passing through solid walls, and her 'thought-travelling' thousands of miles. And it begins to look particularly bad for the credibility of near-death experiencers actually leaving their bodies when, as Dr Blackmore determined beyond all doubt, her experience was quite definitely nothing more than a drug-induced hallucination. For instance, when the next day she studied the roofs of the houses over which she had theoretically 'flown' she found them to be in fact grey, instead of the red that she had 'seen'. Likewise she found that a whole floor of rooms that she 'saw' herself pass did not exist, nor did the row of chimneys.

In this light, and recognizing that it is quite definite that hallucinogenic drugs such as cannabis have not been directly taken by those reporting near-death experiences, one of Dr Blackmore's prime explanations for people having the sensation of leaving their bodies during near-death experiences has been that the brain may produce its own natural hallucinogens during the body's dying process. As this argument runs, when respiration stops, the lungs no longer supply oxygen for the brain, triggering a condition known as cerebral anoxia in which hallucinations can undoubtedly occur, as reported, for instance, by those who have climbed high mountains such as Everest without oxygen. However, as has been pointed out by Allan Pring, an English near-death experient who, as a former RAF pilot, encountered cerebral anoxia during training for sudden oxygen-loss emergencies, the disorientation associated with oxygen-loss hallucinations is quite different from the state of mind during a near-death experience. While in the former, pilots lose consciousness and try to land on clouds, his memory of his near-death experience is of a happening that was totally 'real', and has remained 'crystal clear' in his mind for over fifteen years.

Furthermore, when Dr Blackmore's cannabis hallucination is studied carefully, in actuality it has nothing of a true near-death experience. For instance, whereas everything seemed to her 'indistinct, as though surrounded by cotton wool', the true near-death experient almost invariably sees and hears everything in the 'real' world with great clarity, just as reported by Allan Pring. Whereas Susan Blackmore described herself as being able to communicate with Kevin from the ceiling, her physical body being seen to answer his 'Sue, where are you?' question, we have already seen how true near-death experients finds themselves immensely frustrated by seeming to be separated from the living world as if by one-way sound-proof glass, so they cannot be heard, seen or felt by those whom they can clearly see and hear on the 'other side'. And whereas Sue Blackmore says that her hallucinated out-of-the-body body resembled a 'duplicate' of her physical one, even possessing a navel connected to her physical body by a 'silvery' cord or string, the true near-death experient, as we have already seen, finds himself or herself quite unable to say anything about what kind of out-of-the-body body they might have.

While on this topic, it is worth noting that 'silvery cords' between the 'soul body' and the physical body have been regularly reported by fake spiritualist mediums for at least the last century, but have absolutely no equivalent place among the generality of near-death experience case histories. As but one example, had George Ritchie possessed any such 'silvery cord' in his out-of-the-body state he would surely have used this to find his way back to his body in the Camp Barkeley hospital. Yet neither he nor any other 'serious' near-death experiencer has reported anything of this kind.[40]

In short, the fact that under the influence of drugs someone can fantasize a separation from their physical body, as so clearly happened in Dr Susan Blackmore's drug-induced state, is no argument that some awareness element in us cannot make a true separation of this kind at the point of death.

Even so, we clearly need some pretty positive evidence to persuade us that such a separation truly does occur. As we saw in the case of Dr George Ritchie, his recognition that it had been Vicksburg, Mississippi that he had visited during his out-of-the-body flight to Memphis was very powerful evidence for him, but what else of this kind is there?

One example, cited by Peter and Elizabeth Fenwick, concerns their informant the English Army Major Derek Scull, who told them that while his out-of-body awareness was in its 'floating on the ceiling' position, he happened to look through his hospital room's high-set windows, immediately spotting that his wife was in the outside ward's reception area just about to make him a completely unexpected visit. As he told the Fenwicks:

> She [his wife] was wearing her red trouser suit. I thought, 'My God, what an inappropriate time to arrive. It's not visiting hours, I haven't shaved, I'm looking dreadful, and anyway I'm up here and she's down there, and there's the body. What's going to happen?' The next thing I was conscious of was being back in my bed, I opened my eyes and there sitting beside me was Joan in her red trouser suit. I wasn't a bit surprised, because I knew she'd arrived. I'd already seen her.[41]

As determined by Dr Peter Fenwick, it would have been quite impossible for Mrs Scull to have been seen by the major from his hospital bed, because his door was shut, and bodily at least he had been flat on his back throughout the previous forty-eight hours. Also the red trouser suit was not something his wife would have been normally expected to wear. Apparently she had chosen its vibrant colour specially to cheer him up. So clearly this was very convincing for Major Scull, and also for Dr Fenwick from his impressions of Major Scull as a reliable witness. But even so it would not satisfy a Dr Susan Blackmore, who would argue that everything rests on the major's own unsubstantiated and possibly faulty memory of having seen his wife in her red trouser suit prior to her arrival in his room.

A little more convincing from this same point of view is the case of Maria, an American woman who 'died' of cardiac arrest while she was being operated on in the University of Washington hospital in Seattle. On her telling hospital social worker Kimberly Clark that she had been 'out of her body' during her operation, Clark initially disbelieved her on the grounds that Maria had most likely made it up from simple observation and background knowledge. However she began to take a little more notice when Maria told her how, in 'out-of-the-body' wanderings very similar to George Ritchie's, she had 'thought herself' outside, over the hospital's emergency room driveway, and up to a window ledge at the third-floor level. As Maria insisted, there she had come 'eyeball to shoelace' with a tennis shoe, which she was able to describe in a high degree of detail. As Clark knew, Maria had been admitted at night and, just like Major Scull, had been flat on her back ever since. So if such a tennis shoe genuinely had been in the location described, it would have been quite impossible for Maria to have observed anything like this by normal means, and might still be found where she 'saw' it.

Accordingly, at Maria's urging, Clark took it upon herself to make a thorough search for the shoe, whereupon, in Clark's own words:

> With mixed emotions I went outside and looked up at the
> ledges but could not see much at all. I went up to the third

floor and began going in and out of patients' rooms and looking out their windows, which were so narrow that I had to press my face to the screen just to see the ledge at all. Finally, I found a room where I pressed my face to the glass and saw the tennis shoe! My vantage-point was very different from what Maria's had been for her to notice that the little toe had worn a place in the shoe, and that the lace was stuck under the heel and other details about the side of the shoe not visible to me. *The only way she would have had such a perspective was if she had been floating right outside and at very close range to the tennis shoe* [italics mine]. I retrieved the shoe and brought it back to Maria; it was very concrete evidence for me.[42]

Here we have then, in the case of a near-death experience, precisely the kind of corroboration that the experient had *genuinely* been out of her body that Dr Susan Blackmore's drug-induced out-of-the-body experience so palpably lacked. Yet even so, a single example like this is clearly not enough. We need more evidence of different varieties, for which it may be useful now to look at one aspect of near-death experience that we have so far only glanced at. This is that according to a wide cross-section of experients, their hearing and sight during the experience seem actually to be significantly clearer than in their normal physical bodies.

Concerning hearing, for instance, we are told by three of Dr Kenneth Ring's informants:

'My ears were very sensitive at that point.'

'I heard everything clearly and distinctly.'

'My hearing was clear . . . I felt I could have heard a pin drop.'[43]

Likewise concerning eyesight, we learn from the informant of Dr Kenneth Ring's who described her hearing as very sensitive that her 'vision also' was dramatically heightened.

Another said: 'My sight – everything was clear. I could specifically see myself or anything that I was looking at.'

Yet another said: 'It was as if my whole body had eyes and ears. I was just so aware of everything.'[44]

Importantly, we find no one ever saying of this phase of the experience, 'I blinked', or 'I closed my eyes' – despite the fact that so far as our physical eyes are concerned this is something we do mostly quite unconsciously almost every minute of the waking day, suggesting that the out-of-the-body state's 'eyes' and 'ears' are of a very different order from those of the physical body.

All of which gives rise to the question: what of people who *physically* are well known to have seriously impaired hearing and sight? If they suffer a near-death experience, are they able to hear and see clearly during the out-of-the-body phase? If so, surely this must represent very important evidence that they truly do leave their bodies and perceive these with a sight that is not of this world.

Conscious of the extreme importance of this question, Dr Kenneth Ring published in 1984 in his book *Heading towards Omega* the case of a particularly short-sighted Connecticut woman who described her normal vision as seeing 'at fifteen feet what most people see at four hundred', and who had her near-death experience on going into shock following post-surgical complications. In her words, on finding herself 'floating on the ceiling' of the operating theatre:

It was so vivid . . . They were hooking me up to a machine that was behind my head. And my first thought was, 'Jesus, I can see! I can't believe it, I can see!' I could read the numbers on the machine behind my head and I was so thrilled. And I thought, 'They gave me back my glasses.'[45]

As this woman told Ring, she quite deliberately tried to remember the numbers she read on the machine, and on her recovery was allowed to revisit her operating theatre to check if they were correct, which indeed they were. For Ring the frustration of this case was that although the woman told him she had shared her finding with her anaesthetist, this individual could no longer be traced for verification purposes, having moved to another state.

Undaunted, Ring decided to focus upon those blind from birth to determine if any of them might have suffered a near-death experience and been able to 'see' while in this state. At first he thought he had the perfect example when, on reading physician Larry Dossey's book *Recovering the Soul*, he came across Dossey's ostensibly factual account of a congenitally blind woman called Sarah who after 'dying' during a gall-stone operation, described 'seeing' not only herself while in her out-of-the-body state, but also:

> the operating room layout; the scribbles on the surgery schedule board in the hall outside; the colour of the sheets covering the operating table; the hairstyle of the head scrub nurse . . . and even the trivial fact that her anaesthiologist that day was wearing unmatched socks.[46]

In the event Dossey, on being approached by Ring for permission to interview this patient, was somewhat shame-facedly obliged to confess that 'Sarah' did not exist. He had invented her simply as a composite of what he thought ought to be true of blind near-death experients.

Still undaunted, Ring then turned his attention to organizations for the blind, explaining his research needs to them, and obtaining from them a small but significant list of individuals who claimed to have had near-death experiences.

On interviewing these, aided by then graduate student Sharon Cooper, Ring found one particularly interesting case, that of Vicki Umipeg of the western United States. As Vicki told him, she had been born in 1950 so prematurely that she was only twenty-two weeks in the womb, and due to the imperfect medical knowledge of the time had been permanently and irretrievably blinded when an excess of oxygen in her incubator destroyed her optic nerve. According to her own description of herself: 'I have never had any concept of light or of shadows, or anything, no colour, no nothing.'

Accordingly, of particular interest for Ring was the fact that in February 1973, when she was twenty-two years old, Vicki was involved in a horrific car accident. Her skull was fractured, causing her deep concussion, and her neck, back and legs all received serious injuries. Shortly after being taken to the nearest hospital she went into a classic near-death experience. She seemed to leave her body, and in her own words, as expressed during a short talk she gave in Seattle in 1994:

> I could move around so freely ... I had never known anything like it ... [It was] *the only time I could ever relate to seeing,*[47] *and to what light was, because I experienced it. I was able to see* ... They were talking about me, when I was brought in, *and I could see them working on me*, and I could hear them saying 'Well, if she comes out of this she may be in a vegetative state, the head injury is pretty severe, we do know that there is blood on the ear-drum, and they were talking about that. And I could hear them talking about that I might not be able to hear. And I kept trying to scream at them, and I kept trying to say, 'I'm right here, I'm fine, can't you hear me, I'm right here.' And I was shouting with every ounce of strength I had, and they couldn't hear me, but I could hear them. And it was very frustrating to me, and I

could not communicate with them, and I felt this terrible sense of desperation and frustration for a while about not being about to get through to them, like 'Why can't you guys understand me, I'm right here.' And they didn't. And then I went up through the roof . . . and that freaked me out. And objects were like nothing . . . *And I saw this light approaching me* [italics mine], or I was approaching it, maybe a little of both, I don't know.[48]

Inevitably the immediate and serious question this raises is: although we know that Vicki had been blind all her life, how can we be sure that she genuinely out-of-bodiedly 'saw' all that she said she saw? Keenly aware of the issue's importance, Ring questioned her carefully about every aspect of this. He asked her what was the first thing she positively remembered 'seeing' in the course of the experience. She told him: 'I was up on the ceiling and I heard these doctors talking, and I saw this body, and at first I wasn't sure it was my own.' Asked how she decided it was hers, she said this was chiefly by her waist-length hair, part of which had to be shaved off. She also recognized her rings:

I think I was wearing the plain gold band on my ring finger and my father's wedding next to it. But my wedding ring I definitely saw . . . That was the one I noticed the most because it's most unusual. It has orange blossoms on the corners of it.[49]

Asked about her going up through the roof, she described this as 'astounding . . . it was like the roof just melted'. Asked what she was aware of upon finding herself above this she responded: 'Lights and the streets below and everything. I was very confused about that.' Asked whether she could actually see the hospital's roof, she said, 'Yes'. Asked what else she could see around her, she said the city's lights and buildings, but everything seemed to happen extremely fast and before she knew it she was away and heading for the light.

Aware from his own psychological knowledge of the difficulties for those born blind adjusting to any circumstances in which they regain their sight, Ring questioned Vicki very carefully about her feelings upon so temporarily experiencing the world of the sighted, noting carefully the words she used of this: 'scary', 'frightening' and 'disorienting'. She also spoke of it as 'very foreign', like: 'hearing a foreign language when you just don't know the language at all. You know something meaningful is being said but you don't have any frame of reference for understanding it.'[50]

Whereas Larry Dossey's fictitious 'Sarah' had spoken of the 'colour' of sheets, and her anaesthiologist's 'unmatched socks', Ring was very impressed that Vicki did not report making any kind of colour identification during her experience, and on his directly questioning her about this, said that she could not discriminate colours, but could only suppose them to be what she perceived as 'different shades of brightness'. As Ring remarked on this and similar:

> It is these sorts of comments that Vicki made that lend her testimony a certain kind of plausible authenticity. It would make sense that she was somewhat disoriented and confused by the experience. It would make sense that colour would not be discriminated by her and could have only abstract meaning, and that persons and forms that she would have known in the past by tactile contact or by verbal construction were what she was able to discern.[51]

Equally important to Ring was his finding that Vicki's was by no means an isolated case. In his home state of

Connecticut on the other side of the United States he interviewed thirty-five-year-old Brad, who like Vicki had been blind since birth. Brad told him he had a near-death experience during the winter of 1968, when at the age of eight, and living at the Boston Center for Blind Children, he had 'died' after breathing difficulties from pneumonia that caused his heart to stop for at least four minutes. As he told Ring, he felt himself lifting up from the bed and floating towards the ceiling, from which vantage-point he *saw* his lifeless body, and he *saw* his blind room-mate get up and go for help, a fact which his room-mate independently confirmed. Like Vicki, he then went up through the ceiling, and *saw clearly* the world outside. It was around 6.30 in the morning, and he saw the sky to be cloudy and dark. There had been a snowstorm the night before, and he noted the streets were slushy. Snow was banked up at the sides of the road and he gave a detailed description of what this looked like. He saw a streetcar go by. He saw the playground used by the children of his blind school. Of all these things he said: 'I clearly visualized them. I could suddenly notice them and see them. I can remember being able to see quite clearly.'

Exactly as with Vicki, everything seemed to happen extremely fast, and within moments he was whisked into an other-worldly realm.

Now as Kenneth Ring points out, the cases of Vicki and Brad are not just isolated examples. Aided by Sharon Cooper, he was able to interview twenty-one blind near-death experients he studied in depth. Of these, no fewer than fifteen firmly claimed the sensation of sight during their experiences, another three said they could not be sure because the sensation was so unfamiliar to them, and only three said positively that they could not see. Among those who had known the sensation of sight before becoming blind, one woman blinded by a stroke at the age of twenty-two, and who had been very near-sighted even before then, said with absolute conviction: I know I could see [during the experience] and I was supposed to be blind . . . And I know I could see everything . . . It was very clear when I was out. I could see details and everything.'[52]

Kenneth Ring and Sharon Cooper reported of another case:

A forty-one-year-old woman underwent a biopsy in 1991 in connection with a possible cancerous chest tumour. During the procedure the surgeon inadvertently cut her superior vena cava [large vein leading into the heart], then compounded his error by sewing it closed, causing a variety of medical catastrophes including blindness – a condition that was discovered only shortly after surgery when she was examined in the recovery room.

At that time, she was rushed in a gurney down the corridor in order to have an angiogram. However, the attendants, in their haste, slammed her gurney into a closed elevator door at which point the woman had an out-of-the-body experience. She told us she floated above the gurney and could see her body below. However, she also said she could see down the hall two men – the father of her son and her current lover – both standing looking shocked.

In trying to corroborate her claims, we interviewed the two men. The first man could not recall the precise details of that particular incident, but the second witness – her lover – did and independently confirmed all the essential facts of this event. (It should be noted, by the way, that this witness had been separated from our participant for several years and they had not even communicated for at least a year before we interviewed him.)

Furthermore, even if she had not been blind at the time, the respirator on her face during this accident would have partially occluded her visual field and certainly would have prevented the kind of lateral vision necessary for her to view these men down the hall. But the fact is, according to indications in her medical records, and other evidence we have garnered, she appears already to have been completely blind when this event occurred.[53]

Kenneth Ring and Sharon Cooper have released these preliminary details in advance of a major monograph on their study of near-death experiences in the blind awaiting publication at the time of this book being prepared for press.

However, unless these people are involved in some conspiracy of liars (an idea which is both unworthy and inconceivable), it is already clearly apparent that some form of awareness carrying powers of sight, hearing and movement can and does separate from the physical body at the onset of death. Cases such as those of George Ritchie, and of those dying people who have appeared to their loved one, sometimes thousands of miles distant, add further weight to this view. Inevitably it takes a great deal of believing, and only continuing research of the kind being undertaken by Dr Kenneth Ring is going one day to bring this within the bounds of our present-day science.

But meanwhile a further demand upon our credulity is needed. For as we may recall, something of George Ritchie not only separated from his physical body, it also, if his story is to be believed, went on into another world . . .

Chapter Six

And Can You Really Reach a Realm of the Dead?

> God Appears and God is Light
> To those poor Souls who dwell in Night
> But does a Human Form Display
> To those who dwell in Realms of day?
>
> William Blake, 'Auguries of Innocence'

Recapping the phase of George Ritchie's experience that followed his floating out of his physical body, as described in Chapter 4, we may recall that on his eventual relocation of this he suddenly found himself in the presence of a Man of Light, a loving, all-knowing Being whom he seemingly instinctively 'knew' to be Jesus. As if in a trice, and with the Man of Light still beside him, he saw every moment of his life replayed before him, but from the perspective of that life's effects upon others. Then he found himself moving at immense speed towards a distant light, which at first appeared to be an ordinary city of the present day, except that his out-of-the-body 'eyes' could now discern many thousands of self-evidently 'dead' beings mingling with the living. Exactly as in the predicament in which he had earlier found himself, he saw that these dead beings could clearly hear and see people in the 'real' world, but seemed completely unable to make contact with them, or to make themselves seen, heard or felt. Before being returned to his body he also saw that while many of the dead beings seemed to be trapped in a dull, drab hell of their own basic emotions, there was also a dimension of brilliantly lit beings of whom he caught little more than a glimpse.

Now, if we try to relate this to the standard 'pattern' for a near-death experience as laid down in particular by Drs Raymond Moody and Kenneth Ring, we may initially suppose that it doesn't quite 'conform'. According to the Moody model, for instance, the 'floating above the body' phase is followed by the experient:

1. moving towards the Light, often with the accompanying sensation of hurtling through a long, dark tunnel;
2. upon reaching the Light, entering into a brightly lit realm peopled by transformed-looking dead relatives and other brilliantly lit beings;
3. sometimes but by no means always meeting a Being of Light, whom only some experients identify with Jesus;
4. only at this point being shown the life review, before being told to 'go back'.

Notably, for instance, George Ritchie's experience did not include any phase of meeting up with dead relatives (though this may have been the 'bright' realm which he glimpsed before rejoining his body). His encounter with the Man took place before the other phases, likewise his life review. He also had more of a 'hellish' experience than others have described. However, all this may simply serve to warn us, as Raymond Moody and others would endorse, that there is no one rigid 'pattern' or even sequence to which we should expect every near-death experience to conform. Every experience is different, and as some experients have pointed out, putting any of the elements into a logical order, however necessary this may be for descriptive purposes, can only distort something that in actuality had no 'before or after', nor any other limiting framework.

With this in mind we will initially follow the Moody model, beginning with that which is among the commonest and best-known of all phases of near-death experiences, the sensation of moving towards the Light as if through a long tunnel. As in so many other aspects of the near-death experience this is an image that has been around for a very long time – the Flemish painter Hieronymous Bosch, for instance, pictorially represented it almost exactly 500 years ago in his painting *The Ascent into the Empyrean* that hangs in the Palace of the Doges, Venice. Likewise, long before Raymond Moody, the American Roman Catholic priest Father Louis Tucker explicitly referred to it in describing the onset of his near death from ptomaine poisoning back in 1909:

> The sensation was not quite like anything earthly; the nearest familiar thing to it is passing through a short tunnel on a train. There was the same sense of hurrying, of blackness, of rapid transition, of confused noise, and multiform, swift readjustment.[1]

Among modern-day experients, an Australian, Olivia, who nearly died during childbirth, told researcher Dr Cherie Sutherland: 'I went into something that appeared to be like a tunnel and I was moving very fast. There was a roaring noise like a very high wind . . . There was light at the end of the tunnel . . .'[2]

Likewise Englishwoman Mrs S. A. P. Thirlwall, who had her experience during major dental surgery, told Peter and Elizabeth Fenwick: 'I started zooming down this really black tunnel at what seemed like 100 mph. Then I saw this enormous brilliant light at the end.'[3]

These are merely token cases among literally hundreds of very similar examples. But as part of our admonition against becoming too fixated upon any too concrete images, it is important to note that some experients point out that they did not necessarily pass through any actual tunnel so much as have the impression of being in a tunnel because of the speed with which they seemed to be moving through space (or whatever). Thus Australian experient Juliet, for instance, who 'died' during a bladder operation, remarked after describing the 'feeling of being pulled very quickly along':

> I've read that people go down a tunnel and there's a light at the end of the tunnel, but it wasn't actually a tunnel, it was more like just space. There was no enclosure, there was just a feeling of wholeness.[4]

Similarly, fellow-Australian Laurel Lloyd-Jones, who 'died' after reacting badly to anaesthetics administered for a hysterectomy operation, commented:

> I then felt myself moving off very fast, exceedingly fast, into what seemed like outer space. *I always felt it was the fact of going so fast that gave me the sense of being in a tunnel* [italics mine]. I was going towards a very bright light.[5]

This also accords well with Father Louis Tucker's description, 'the nearest familiar thing . . . is passing through a short tunnel on a train', and with George Ritchie's, who likewise never spoke of any actual tunnel, but rather of speeding 'high above the earth . . . toward a distant pinprick of light'.[6]

Of the approximately one in four experients who reach the light at the end of the tunnel, these mostly describe themselves as feeling enveloped by an overwhelming sense of peace that removes any lingering fear, in a realm that they may find near-impossible to express in words. Very commonly those images that they do mange to conjure are of a meadow, or of a garden filled with flowers. As Englishman David Whitmarsh described: 'Suddenly I found myself standing in a field of beautiful yellow corn. The sky on the horizon was the deepest of sky blues that I have ever seen and I felt even more at peace in this lovely tranquil place.'[7]

An Australian woman who nearly died during a difficult childbirth told Dr Cherie Sutherland: 'It was like there were gently rolling hills, no crags, no sharp edges, nothing that was cruel, nothing that was other than gentle. The sky was intense blue, the scene was gently rolling.'[8]

And an American woman who suffered respiratory failure told Dr Kenneth Ring: 'I was in a field, a large, empty field, and it had high, golden grass that was very soft, so bright. And my pain was gone and it was quiet, but it wasn't a morbid quiet, it was a peaceful quiet ... I was really happy in that place.'[9]

There may be accompanying music. In the words of an American woman who suffered cardiac failure at her home, and owing to some unusual circumstances lay comatose and undiscovered for three days: 'I could hear beautiful music; I can't tell you what kind because I never heard anything like it before ... It sounds – I could describe it as a combination of vibrations, many vibrations.'[10]

Likewise the blind-since-birth girl Vicki (see previous Chapter), who found she could 'see' during her experience, reported: 'I heard the sound of like wind chimes, which were from the lowest to the highest frequencies you can imagine, and it was just incredibly beautiful.'[11]

Whereas any sense of smell seemed to be completely absent during the out-of-the-body phase, now delightful odours may be experienced accompanying the pleasing sights and sounds, as in the case of Englishwoman Dawn

Gillott: 'a wonderful summery smell of flowers,'[12] also a seventy-year-old American accountant: 'The air smelled so fresh. I have never smelled anything like it.'[13]

If all this may sound more than a little too cliché-paradisical, and too good to be true, then the fact that it may indeed be more of a semblance than a true other-worldly actuality is borne out by comments of other informants, such as one of Dr Raymond Moody's, a middle-aged man who had his experience as a result of a cardiac arrest: 'I seemed to be in a countryside with streams, grass and trees, mountains. But when I looked round – if you want to put it that way – *they were not trees and things like we know them to be.*'[14]

Similarly English air-traffic controller Allan Pring spoke only of 'a landscape without form, composed only of light and colour' that he found 'impossible to describe.'[15]

This is also reinforced when we look closely at the next aspect of this phase of the experience, the meeting up with deceased relatives. As we have already noted, the phenomenon of dying people seemingly being 'met' by friends and relatives who have died before them has been around for a very long time. Back in AD 922 an Arab diplomat witnessing the funeral of a Viking chieftain recorded the words of a slave woman being sacrificed to join her dead master:

> The first time they lifted her up she said: 'Look! I see my father and mother!' The second time she said: 'Look, I see all my dead relatives sitting around.' The third time she said: 'Look, I see my master sitting in paradise, and paradise is beautiful and green . . .'[16]

Likewise at the end of the last century American physician Dr Wilson of New York set down this account of the dying moments of his long-term patient, the professional singer James Moore:

It was about four o'clock . . . when, as I bent over the bed, I noticed that his face was quite calm and his eyes clear . . . Then something which I shall never forget to my dying day happened, something which is utterly indescribable. While he appeared perfectly rational and as sane as any man I have ever seen . . . he said in a stronger voice than he had used since I had attended him: 'There is Mother! Why, Mother, have you come to see me? No, no, I'm coming to see you. Just wait, Mother, I am almost over. I can jump it. Wait, Mother.' On his face there was a look of inexpressible happiness, and the way he said the words impressed me as I have never been before, and I am as firmly convinced that he saw and talked with his mother as I am that I am sitting here. In order to preserve what I believed to be his conversation with his mother, and also to have a record of the strangest happening in my life, I immediately wrote down every word he had said.[17]

Among modern-day near-death experients, roughly one in four report similar encounters with deceased relatives and friends, with parents, grandparents and great-grandparents predominating among the former. In the case of the already mentioned American anthropologist Professor Patrick Gallagher, for instance, he remarked of his reaching what he described as 'an incredibly illuminating sort of place, in every sense of the word' at the end of 'some sort of tunnel': 'I saw my father there, who had been dead for some twenty-five years.'[18]

An American woman of Hungarian parentage told Dr Kenneth Ring:

. . . suddenly I saw mother, who had died about nine years ago. And she was sitting – she always used to sit in her rocker, you know – she was smiling and she just sat there looking at me and she said to me in Hungarian, 'Well, we've been waiting for you. We've been expecting you. Your father's here and we are going to help you.'[19]

Just as in the case of ghosts, such 'greeting' individuals may be seen wearing clothes, and more usually those they are known to have worn in life, rather than the misty white drapes so beloved of the makers of evangelically inspired American documentaries. This is how the American Roman Catholic priest Father Louis Tucker described the experience he had associated with his near-death ptomaine poisoning in 1909: 'Father was waiting for me. He looked exactly as he had in the last few years of his life and wore the last suit of clothes he had owned.'[20]

As in the case of true ghosts, greeting relatives may also appear as solid-looking as in life, just as we noted in Chapter 3 of Anne Allen's appearance to Canon Dominic Walker at the time of his ceremony of laying her to rest. Thus an Australian near-death experient Jennifer, who 'died' at age seven as a result of pneumonia, told Dr Cherie Sutherland: 'I saw Great-grandmother as solid as you.'

But just as we saw how the reports of perceived physical surroundings seemed over-idealized, so too (and in this instance there is a contrast to ghosts), the visual appearance of these perceived 'dead' human beings may often seem 'enhanced' and idealized by comparison with what may have been their true earthly appearance during their declining years. As an American retired labourer told Dr Michael Sabom of the deceased relatives he met during his experience:

My grandmother had been ninety-six. She never did look old. She looked perhaps forty or forty-five. My mother was sixty when she died and way overweight. And she looked trim and a good general-health look, happy and healthy. Everybody looked healthy, real, real healthy.[21]

Englishman David Ayre of Bristol, England, who had his experience as a result of a very determined attempt to commit suicide, told me of his meeting with his father who had died at the age of seventy-three, that he looked 'substantially younger and healthier, particularly in his complexion'.[22] On a mother's appearance to an American cardiac patient, the patient's remark, 'My mother was an amputee and yet that leg was now restored! She was walking on two legs!'[23] may remind us of Billy Graham's grandmother on her death-bed seeing her dead husband Ben, who had lost an eye and a leg in the American Civil War: 'There is Ben, and he has both of his eyes and both of his legs!' (see Chapter 3).

It needs to be stressed, however, that not everyone 'sees' their welcoming relatives and friends in such an explicitly visual way. As remarked by one of Dr Raymond Moody's informants:

A good friend of mine, Bob, had been killed. Now the moment I got out of my body I had *the feeling* Bob was standing there, right next to me. I could see him in my mind and felt like he was there, but it was strange. *I didn't see him as his physical body* [italics mine]. I could see things but not in the physical form, yet just as clearly. Does that make sense?[24]

Likewise Dr Michael Sabom's night watchman experient, referred to in Chapter 1, reported that he was unable to see, but otherwise felt himself in the presence of his long-deceased brother:

[With me was] my older brother, who had been dead since I was a young fella. I couldn't see, but I knew he was right by me, even patting me on the shoulder, saying, 'It's entirely up to you – you can do anything you want to do . . . I'll be right by your side and everything is going to be fine.'[25]

Another of Dr Michael Sabom's informants, the US Army serviceman 'killed' by a booby-trap bomb while serving in Vietnam (see previous chapter) similarly described himself as 'feeling' himself to be in the presence of all the fellow-soldiers of his company most recently killed in action:

. . . during the course of that month of May, my particular company lost forty-two dead. All forty-two of those guys were there. *They were not in the form we perceive the human body. I can't tell you what form they were in because I don't know, but they were there* [italics mine]. I felt their presence.[26]

Also needing to be stressed is that experients not uncommonly report of such encounters that they managed to recognize relatives who had died before they were born, even though they may never previously have seen photographs of them. Furthermore, these dead relatives also invariably recognized them, as if they had somehow been invisibly watching over them. This was certainly the case with the already mentioned Australian Jennifer, who reported of her meeting with her great-grandmother.

I saw this lovely lady . . . in a long white robe, and she had a beautiful face and I recognized her instantly. It makes me go goose bumps just to think of it even now. Anyhow she said, 'Don't be afraid, Jennifer.' And I said, 'I am not afraid,

Great-grandmother.' She said, 'You know me?' I said, 'Yes, Great-grandmother.'[27]

As Jennifer insisted:

The funny thing is, *I'd never known my great-grandmother*. When I was being brought into the house as a baby, she was being taken out on a stretcher because she was dying. They stopped the stretcher so she could cuddle me in her arms and hold me . . .

Although Jennifer was subsequently shown photographs of her great-grandmother in her younger years, she was quite sure she 'knew' who she was without these. Similarly, another Australian near-death experient, Grace, told Dr Cherie Sutherland,

There seemed to be figures . . . And as I looked one of the figures seemed to resolve itself, and . . . I thought, 'Oh God, it's my Aunty Hannah!' who died eleven years ago. *And then I saw my Uncle Abraham who died before I was born, and I knew them . . . They knew me even though they'd never met me . . . My granny who I'd never met, my grandfather, just all the people I've never known* [italics mine] and those I had known who'd died many years before, or who'd even died recently . . . then I turned and I looked at this figure standing next to me – it was my father. My dad died when I was sixteen . . .[28]

Closely parallel to this are instances of the blind seemingly visually 'recognizing' people they could never have seen with any physical eyes, and this despite these people's physical appearance being again apparently 'enhanced' in their other-worldly state. Thus the already reported blind-since-birth Vicki, after having made her approach to the Light, 'recognized' two of her fellow-pupils from blind school, Debbie and Diane, both of whom she had befriended and who had subsequently died. As Vicki knew, in life Debbie had been grossly fat and profoundly retarded, yet as she saw her in her 'other-worldly' state she was 'beautiful', 'brilliant', her face 'light, bright and happy' – 'perfected', as Vicki put it when summing up.

Furthermore, when Vicki was asked by Kenneth Ring how she could possibly have recognized her dead friend from such a profoundly changed appearance – particularly bearing in mind that she had never seen the girl in life – Vicki's explanation was not, as he expected, one relating to touch, or to any other of the remaining physical senses well known to be heightened in the blind. Instead she insisted that her recognition was 'intuitive'. Whereas during her out-of-bodily viewing of the world of the normally sighted she had experienced considerable confusion and disorientation, in the other-worldly realm everyone and everything seemed 'clear', 'immediate' and 'direct'. In a phrase that Ring found repeated by the similarly blind-since-birth Brad (even though the two lived on opposite sides of the States and did not know each other), Vicki described her perception of everything in this dimension as 'the way it's supposed to be'.

Accordingly, what we seem to be glimpsing in the case of the blind is the very converse of the experience of the sighted in respect of the out-of-the-body and other-worldly phases of the near-death experience. Whereas to the born-blind everything seems confusing during the out-of-the-body phase, because they are trying to make sense of a 'reality' they have never previously experienced, to the normally sighted everything in this phase seems unusually clear, because they are still seeing the same 'real' world that they have always been used to. And while for the blind all becomes clear in the other-worldly phase, because their interpretative apparatus is untrammelled by having experienced normal sight, for the sighted all becomes near-highly bewildering and impossible to put into words, because they are now experiencing something totally foreign to their normal five senses – indeed, as 'foreign' a language as that in which Vicki described her first sensation of sight. Effectively, the perceptions during the other-worldly phase are those of the 'eyes of the mind' which may supply images according to its own translation rather than ones of any concrete other-worldly reality.

In immediate support of this line of thinking – in particular that other-worldly sight and sound are very different from those of the normal physical dimension[29] – we learn from Father Louis Tucker how he understood and interpreted the apparent absurdity of 'seeing' his father in his after-life guise wearing the same suit of clothes that he had worn in life. In Father Tucker's own words: 'I knew that the clothes Father wore were assumed because they were familiar to me, so that I might feel no strangeness seeing him.' And as he continued by way of explanation:

> I knew all these things by contagion, because he did . . . I discovered that we were not talking, but thinking. I knew dozens of things that we did not mention because he knew them. He thought a question, I an answer, without speaking; the process was practically instantaneous.

Twelve centuries ago the Tibetan monks who wrote the *Bardo Thodol* already understood such things when they wrote of the images 'seen' in the realm of the dead: 'It is quite sufficient for you to know that these apparitions are [the reflections of] your own thought forms.'[30]

And when we look across the range of near-death experiences as reported right across the world we find exactly the same exchanges of thought as the common currency of communication between the living and the dead. Thus as remarked by the US serviceman who 'died' in Vietnam and found himself in the invisible presence of the forty-two fellow-soldiers of his unit recently killed in action: 'We communicated without talking with our voices.'

Likewise American blind-since-birth Vicki said of the dead people she met that their communication was 'not in the way that I am talking to you now, but by thought'.

Just as Father Louis Tucker, in Baton Rouge, Louisiana, in 1909, described communicating with his father as by thinking, not speaking, so the would-be suicide David Ayre of Bristol, England told me of his near-death experience meeting with his dead father in 1978: 'There was just compassionate communication ... just telepathic ... It was incredible, *as if he knew everything I knew, and I knew everything he knew*' [italics mine].

Englishwoman Audrey Organ likewise told Peter and Elizabeth Fenwick of her meeting with her dead father upon nearly dying during a surgical operation: 'Here I was in a tunnel of glorious light with my dad, who had died some years ago ... We were enormously happy, conversing but *without the usual verbal speech, all via the mind*' [italics mine].[31]

Australian experient Grace told Dr Cherie Sutherland of her near-death experience meeting again with her father with whom she had not been on speaking terms at the time of his unexpected death: 'And then Dad spoke to me, although there was no speaking – *his mind spoke to me* [italics mine].[32]

Likewise Grace's fellow-Australian Juliet remarked of her experience, in another example of nearly dying during a surgical operation:

These beautiful people were standing around ... And they kind of just looked at me. *There wasn't really any verbal interchange* [italics mine]. It didn't feel as though anyone really spoke to me, but the feeling was 'No, Juliet. You have to go back.'[33]

We may now recall from George Ritchie's vivid account of his experience in 1943, how upon his being shown that terrible scene of the unhappy dead, enslaved by their very own emotions, he reported:

> *Whatever anyone thought*, however fleetingly or unwillingly, *was instantly apparent to all around him, more completely than words could have expressed it* [italics mine], faster than sounds could have carried it.

Similarly, Ritchie reported that it was via exactly the same thought exchange that he communicated with the Man of Light. From the latter's very appearance, there simply came into his mind, accompanied by 'a kind of knowing, immediate and complete', the words, 'You are in the presence of the Son of God.' This extended through to the down-loading into his mind of all the scenes from his life, throughout which was the unspoken yet insistent question, 'What have you done with your life to show Me?'

Which leads us to other near-death experients' accounts of their encounters with the Man of Light. This was the experience of the previously mentioned air-traffic controller Allan Pring, who exactly as in the case of George Ritchie (Chapter 4), had no encounter with any deceased relatives (meeting the Man of Light instead), and was shown his life review before proceeding to 'the light'. In Pring's own words:

> I was met by a figure of light, and it was what can only be described as a 'Jesus' figure. But I *knew* that the appearance of the figure was to make me feel comfortable in this new

place. *We did not speak to one another because words were not necessary* [italics mine].[34]

Here we may recall both Ritchie's 'a kind of knowing, immediate and complete', and Father Louis Tucker's words: 'I knew that the clothes Father wore were assumed because they were familiar to me, so that I might feel no strangeness seeing him. I knew all these things by contagion, because he did.'

Allan Pring's fellow-Englishman James Carney, a man with none of either Pring's or Ritchie's education, likewise reported of his experience with the Man: 'I mentally asked the question . . . and it seemed that instantly I received a mental answer.'[35]

Occasionally experients have reported 'seeing' this Man, giving a description which may, as in the cases of the green fields images, be of prosaic Sunday School book quality, and thereby of the assumed, 'making me feel comfortable' variety. This, for instance, is a description by Englishwoman Mrs Holyoake, one of the few to unhesitatingly identify the Man with Jesus: 'Jesus came walking towards me with arms outstretched. He was dressed in a long white robe, his hair to his shoulders, ginger-auburn and he had a short beard.'[36]

Altogether more common and arguably far more powerful, however are those encounters in which either the Man is not 'seen' or in which considerations of what he may actually have looked like are seemingly completely incidental, exactly as in George Ritchie's account, which carries no physical description of Jesus's appearance (as, incidentally, in the Christian Gospels).

This, for instance, was how an American eighteen-year-old who unsuccessfully tried to commit suicide by jumping off a cliff, described what he understood of the Man's 'voice' to Kenneth Ring:

RING: Okay, let's focus on the voice then. You never saw anything?

EXPERIENT: No, it was still. The whole time it was in complete darkness.

RING: Even during the time that the voice was speaking to you?

EXPERIENT: Yeah.

RING: When you heard the voice, you heard it as a male voice. Did you actually hear the words or –

EXPERIENT: *It was like it was coming into my mind. It was like I didn't have any hearing or any sight or anything.* It was like it was projected into my mind.

RING: What you told me before – is that the gist of what the voice said? Or is it pretty much the actual words?

EXPERIENT: It was mostly thoughts, you know? It was mostly thoughts. It wasn't like somebody – you know, like you and I are communicating with words. It was mostly thoughts – like, I would picture in my mind my mother crying and my girlfriend crying and then there was the thought about a daughter, she [his girl-friend] was holding a baby. It was like – the more I think over it, the more it comes out as words, but *when it happened it was more like symbols* [italics mine] – symbolic, you know?

RING: So what you're doing now is trying to translate it into words?

EXPERIENT: I'm trying to change it into English, yeah.

Here a particularly interesting feature is that this young would-be suicide, exactly like Ritchie, 'saw' the feelings of those to whom his life was connected, except that while Ritchie re-experienced the hurts that he had caused others, the suicide saw via symbols his hurtful actions projected into the future, even upon a daughter not yet born. Anyone who has been in a crisis moment, and found a symbol float seemingly spontaneously into his or her mind, may well now see this in a new light.

But inevitably the question all this raises is how the honest sceptic is expected to believe it all. Where's the material evidence? Where is anything that is testable? Since it's 'all in the mind', how can anyone be sure it's not all just hallucinations?

What immediately needs to be said is that the published near-death experience literature may well include some accounts of 'other-worldly' experiences which are indeed hallucinations or even outright fabrications. Native American Indian Betty Eadie reportedly 'died' during a surgical operation in 1973, and in her book *Embraced by the Light*[37] she details an extensive 'other-worldly' phase that included meeting Jesus, being introduced by him to two of her friends who had died, seeing 'dead' people working on 'large, ancient-looking looms', being shown a bookless library containing 'every particle of knowledge', being greeted in a beautiful garden by beings 'wearing soft pastel gowns', and much more. Fellow-American Dannion Brinkley, resuscitated after being struck by lightning, has likewise given a vivid account in his *Saved by the Light* of his being out-of-bodily transported to 'a city of cathedrals made entirely of a crystalline substance that glowed with light', and being given knowledge in boxes which contained a tiny television picture by which he could glimpse future events. Neither book can be said to be in any way more 'fantastic' than George Ritchie's. Yet there is something about the concreteness of their imagery which fails to convince, and Eadie, for one, has been accused of switching her story several times, and not being altogether honest with the public about her religious agenda.[38]

But such aberrations should not be allowed to cloud our judgment on the general run of near-death experients. Most of these have made no attempt to publicize themselves in the way that Eadie and Brinkley have. And deserving emphasis is their repeated insistence that their experience was real. We may recall from Chapter 4 George Ritchie's words as a practising psychiatrist that his experience was 'the most entirely real thing that's ever happened to me . . . I've had a chance to study . . . hallucinations. I've had patients who were hallucinating. There's just no resemblance.' We hear similarly from English air-traffic controller Allan Pring, 'I had no doubt that everything I was experiencing was real.'[39] And fellow-Englishman Alf Rose: 'This was a true real experience, I'm fully satisfied about that.'

Nor again can those who have such experiences be dismissed in general as gullible religious cranks. Allan Pring, for instance, said of his beliefs prior to his experience in 1979: 'I had no knowledge whatsoever of near-death experiences. I did not believe in life after death. I was not religious. I did not believe in God.'[40]

Anthropologist Professor Patrick Gallagher, who had his experience in Death Valley, was a complete agnostic. Repeatedly, experients have stressed their healthy questioning of their own senses in the course of the experience, just as I found myself mentally repeating, 'I can't believe this is happening to me' during my wife's and my encounter with the ghost at Abercrombie House, described in Chapter 3. One twenty-three-year-old American college student told Dr Michael Sabom of her recollections of her other-worldly 'seeing' of her dead father upon nearly dying herself from complications following a kidney-removal operation: 'Even then my mind was saying, "But I can't be seeing Daddy and talking to him – he's dead" . . . Yet I could see him perfectly.'[41]

Australian experient Grace likewise said of her other-worldly meeting with her father from whom she had become estranged shortly before his death:

> Standing in that place, it went through my mind, '*Is this real or is it just my imagination* [italics mine] because it's what I want to have happen?' It's really peculiar, but I actually thought that: 'Am I doing this within myself because it's what I want?' And then Dad spoke to me, although there was no speaking – his mind spoke to me. And he said, 'No, honey' (because that was his name for me). He said, 'Honey, you're not imagining, it's not coming from you, you're with me and this is our time to talk.'[42]

Perhaps the most amusing example of this genre derives from Englishwoman Mrs Gillian McKenzie of Eastbourne, a highly articulate and down-to-earth individual of my direct acquaintance, who on discovering herself seeming 'dead' as a result of complications during childbirth, incredulously remarked of her becoming aware of the Man of Light seem-ingly next to her and familiarly addressing her as 'Gill': 'I thought, "Heavens! It's God! Surely I can't come before God straight away? Surely there should be a sort of reception place or something?'[43]

A fascinating element in its own right is that, quite unlike the case of dreams, which as we all know we almost invariably forget immediately upon waking up, one after another of those who claim near-death experiences have insisted that the memory of their experience has remained exceptionally sharp and vivid even after what may be several decades. As Englishwoman Mrs Jenny McMillan remarked, for instance:

Seventeen years on, the whole experience is still quite clear in my mind. Although it had a dream-like quality, the memory has faded far less than some very important events, both happy and sad, in my normal life, despite the fact that I have rarely discussed it and only written it down once and never read it since.[44]

If we turn to the reactions of a sceptic such as Dr Susan Blackmore, all that she seems able to offer, by way of explanation of all that we have seen, is yet again that these experiences are just hallucinations of the dying brain. Recently, under the influence of psychological concepts of the individual 'depersonalizing' during crises such as the imminence of death, she has argued for near-death experiences generally being the brain's self-perceived self breaking down in the process of the brain's dying. In her own words: 'My conclusion is that the near-death experience brings about a breakdown of the model of the self along with the breakdown of the brain's model processes.'[45]

But this hardly even begins to explain the apparent extreme clear-headedness and continued self-awareness of those selves whose brains are going through this supposed disintegration process. As for the so convincingly real encounters with deceased relatives, Dr Blackmore hardly addresses these at all. But even so, the question remains – where, from those who claim near-death experiences to be true contacts with the dead, is there anything that might be considered scientific proof? How can anyone be sure any near-death experient truly met up with a real dead relative during the other-worldly phase of their experience?

Here one difficulty is that when an adult obtains information about a dead relative as if from an 'other-worldly' source, they can always be accused of having discovered it by some normal means. Or they may have been told it when a child, then forgotten it, so far as their normal consciousness was concerned, only for it to be 'revived' with their physical body in the course of their near-death experience.

But what about children who have had near-death experiences? One intriguing example I came across in 1989 was that of the then five-year-old Amy Davis, daughter of Senior Aircraftsman Paul Davis of RAF Halton, near Aylesbury, Bucks, England, and his wife Pauline. As I learned from Mrs Davis, even though Amy was a perfectly healthy child, before she was two years old she had 'died' no fewer than four times – at six weeks, at eight weeks, at four months, and at twenty-four months – each time as the result of recurrent cot death syndrome, and each time being revived by her mother.

Then in 1988, when Amy began attending the local school at Halton, on returning home one day she asked Pauline: 'When we die, do we go to heaven?' Pauline told her that we did. 'Do we go to Jesus?' Amy asked. Pauline again agreed. 'Do we stay there for ever?' Amy went on. Yet again Pauline agreed, only to be quite astounded when Amy firmly contradicted her with the words, 'No, Mummy, that's wrong. When I met Jesus he told me, "Amy, you must go back because you're special."' As we will see later, this instruction to 'go back' is a persistent feature of near-death experiences and one which the five-year-old Amy – who had never been told even of her 'dying' – could hardly have known of.

Amy imparted one further clue that at least one of her 'deaths' seemingly included a near-death experience. Her maternal grandfather, who died when Amy was only eight months old, had always called Pauline 'Polly', the only member of the family to do so. From a very young age Amy had repeatedly spoken of someone called 'the man' – 'the man said . . .' – whom Pauline had simply assumed to be some imaginary companion of Amy's. But then one day Amy announced to her mother, 'The man said, "Hello, Polly!"'

From this Pauline realized with no little sensation of going cold, that during her experience Amy must have met not only Jesus, but also her dead grandfather.

Clearly this is a long way from proof of Amy having met her dead grandfather, but thankfully, it is not just a single isolated anecdote. From a quite different culture comes a considerably more detailed case, concerning Durdana Khan, younger daughter of physician Dr A. G. Khan. Today a graduate of University College, London, as a child Durdana lived on a Pakistani army base in Kashmir in the foothills of the Himalayas where her father was the army doctor, and where in 1968, when she was two years old, she began suffering alarming paralyses, vomitings and spells of blindness. Although tests proved inconclusive, her symptoms resembled those of a viral encephalitis that had already killed several children in the area.

Then one morning that same autumn, when Durdana was just two and a half, she gave every semblance of having died. Dr Khan, busy in his medical inspection room at the time the news was brought to him, rushed back to the garden of his living quarters where his wife was standing beside Durdana's cot. After a quick examination he sorrowfully confirmed, 'She's gone,' but following the regulations of the time, sent one of his staff hurrying for emergency resuscitation equipment. As he himself takes up the story:

> My wife carried the child to our bedroom and laid her down on my bed. After another examination I began to carry out the prescribed emergency procedures, rather half-heartedly, knowing that they were unlikely to have any effect. While doing so, I found myself repeating, half unconsciously, under my breath, 'Come back my child, come back.' As a last resort my wife poured into the child's mouth a few drops of the nikethamide – a respiratory stimulant – we had

given Durdana the night before. They trickled out of her lifeless mouth and down her cheek. We looked sadly on – and then, to our amazement, the child opened her eyes and, making a wry face, gravely informed us that the medicine was bitter. Then she closed her eyes again.[46]

Although, according to Dr Khan's best estimate, his daughter had been 'dead' about a quarter of an hour, her vital signs began to reappear, and during the ensuing days she gradually became stronger and able to talk to her parents. Dr Khan again takes up the story:

One day soon afterwards . . . mother and daughter were in the garden. 'Where did my little daughter go the other day?' asked my wife. 'Far, far away, to the stars,' came the surprising reply. Now Durdana was an intelligent and articulate child – and whatever she said had to be taken seriously, or she would become annoyed. 'Indeed, exclaimed my wife,' and what did my darling see there?'

'Gardens,' said Durdana.

'And what did she see in these gardens?'

'Apples and grapes and pomegranates.'

'And what else?'

'There were streams, a white stream, a brown stream, a blue stream and a green stream.'

And was anyone there?'

'Yes, my grandfather was there, and his mother, and another lady who looked like you.'

My wife was greatly intrigued. 'And what did they say?'

'Grandpa said he was glad to see me, and his mother took me in her lap and kissed me.'

'Then?'

'Then I heard my daddy calling me, "Come back my child, come back." I told Grandpa that Daddy was calling me and I must go back. He said we should have to ask God. So he went to God, and Grandpa told him that I wanted to go back. 'Do you want to go back?' God asked me. 'Yes,' I said. 'I must go back. My daddy is calling me. 'All right,' said God, 'go.' And down, down, down, I came from the stars, on to Daddy's bed.

Here must of course be noted the arguably symbolic paradisical 'garden' images remarked on earlier in this chapter, simply with slightly different features consistent with Durdana's Pakistani culture.[47] Also of particular fascination for Dr Khan was that Durdana described herself as having 'come to' his bed, when on her temporarily regaining consciousness 'she was in no state to know where she was', and she and her sister normally slept or played in their own or their mother's beds, never in his.

Yet more compelling was what was to come. Durdana's condition was diagnosed as caused by a brain tumour, requiring the Khans to take her to Karachi for an operation on her skull, following which, while Dr Khan returned to his army post Mrs Khan took Durdana to visit several relatives in Karachi as part of her convalescence. Dr Khan again takes up the story:

While visiting the house of one of my uncles, as they sat chatting over a cup of tea, Durdana wandered about the room . . . Suddenly she called out 'Mummy, Mummy!' My wife ran to her. 'Mummy,' said Durdana excitedly, pointing to an old photograph on a side table, 'this is my grandpa's mother. I met her in the stars. She took me in her lap and kissed me.' Durdana was quite right. *But my grandmother died long before Durdana was born; only two photographs of her exist, and both are in the possession of this uncle of mine. Durdana was visiting his house for the first time in her life, and in no way could she have seen this photograph before* [italics mine].[48]

All this, it should be stressed, took place some seven years before Raymond Moody had even brought near-death experiences to world attention. Inevitably it relies heavily upon the testimony of the Khan family, but although I do not know them personally I have the strongest attestation of their integrity from Peter Brookesmith, editor of *The Unexplained*, who kindly brought their case to my attention and has been a friend of theirs over several years. In his words: 'None of the family, in my opinion, would lie about this, least of all Durdana herself: she has been brought up to have a very powerful moral awareness.'[49]

Peter Brookesmith also added an intriguing footnote that he was told by Durdana's elder sister concerning her attendance on her mother, during the latter's final hours before her death in 1979. Apparently at one point Mrs Khan

> ... announced that her own father and an uncle, both since long dead, had arrived in the room. She actually introduced her [i.e. Durdana's sister] to these invisible personages. Mrs Khan then told them to go away as she wasn't ready for them yet, which they apparently did. She next gave her daughter a long lecture on her future duties to the family, and waited for her 'guides' to come back to collect her before finally expiring.

All this, of course, still cannot constitute 'proof' that anyone has truly 'met' the dead. But it may serve to convey that other-worldly encounters with deceased relatives, recounted by near-death experients, and those similar encounters reported by dying people who do not come back, seem to be different sides of the same coin. Either both are equally valid and convey something of the actuality of whatever form of existence continues beyond the grave, or both are equally hallucinatory.

And although again it cannot count as 'proof', there is one further aspect of these encounters with deceased relatives that deserves mention in passing: the fact that these sometimes involve family prophecy. As we may recall from the case in Chapter 3 of the dying Mrs Jane Charles, who 'saw' her long-dead husband together with her eponymous great-granddaughter of whose death she had not previously been aware, Mrs Charles *predicted* in her dying moments that her granddaughter Janet would 'get over' her loss, as indeed she did. Similarly consistent with a widespread folkloric tradition that dying persons have powers of seeing into the future, one case worthy of mention is that of the Australian near-death experient Grace, whose encounter with her dead father we mentioned a little earlier.

Grace had been married only a year when she found herself dying during an extremely difficult first labour. Her last memory of this was the words of one of the medical team, 'We're losing her', before she found herself launched straight into the other-worldly dimension in which she met her father. Up to that point she had no idea of the sex of her still unborn baby, nor whether it would survive, still less any inkling of the marital bombshell her father was about to drop upon her. As she imparted to Dr Cherie Sutherland:

> He [i.e. her father] said, 'You have to go . . . you must go back [i.e. to the land of the living]. *You're going to have a son,* and you'll have to bring this boy up, bring him up by yourself.' *Then Dad told me my marriage was going to break up* [italics mine]. . . . And I remember saying, 'Dad, I don't want this to happen. I always thought that when I got married, it wouldn't happen.'[50]

Does something of us leave our physical bodies at death?

The soul leaving the body, and floating over it after death, as conceived by the eighteenth century English visionary William Blake (1757-1827). From at least as far back as the days of ancient Egypt, peoples all over the world have claimed that something of us leaves the body when we die, and may temporarily hover over it before going on to an other-worldly realm.

Right: The modern-day German cancer specialist Dr. Josef Issels. One of his terminally-ill patients very convincingly described herself floating down the hospital ward, and able to see 'out-of-her-body', just moments before she died.

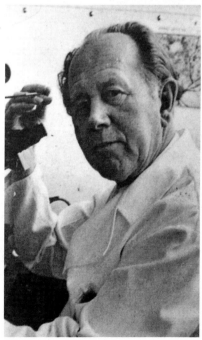

Emanuel Swedenborg – the 18th century Swedish scientist who found himself perceiving the newly dead

In 1751 the distinguished Swedish engineer Emanuel Swedenborg (*above left*), after attending the funeral of his equally scientific-minded fellow engineer Christopher Polhem (*above right*), described having unmistakably perceived the dead man's 'presence' in the course of the ceremony. According to Swedenborg, Polhem expressed his bewilderment at his being buried while he felt still very much 'alive', and felt obliged to contradict the officiating priest's assertion that he would not be resuscitated until the Last Judgement – as he knew he had already been 'resuscitated' for some while!

Below: Abercrombie House, near Bathurst, Australia, where the author and his wife together experienced a 'breathing' ghost in the January of 1994.

Eddie Burks – the present-day English engineer who now routinely perceives 'ghosts'

In the early 1980s, following the death of his wife, Eddie Burks of Lincoln (*above*), found himself with an uncanny ability to perceive 'ghosts'. As but one example, in August 1992, called in to advise on a ghostly figure in Elizabethan costume disturbing staff at Coutts' Bank in London's Strand, Eddie Burks found himself 'seeing' and 'talking to' an unhappy individual subsequently identified as Thomas Howard, 4th Duke of Norfolk (*right*), beheaded on the orders of Queen Elizabeth I in 1572.

Lord Jenkins of Hillhead, who when an M.P. was 'visited' by his dying friend via a dream

In February 1977, while at a hotel in Rome, the then English Labour MP Roy Jenkins (*above*), experienced an exceptionally vivid dream of his friend and fellow MP Anthony Crosland (*left*) appearing to him to tell him that he was 'perfectly all right' even though he was just about to die. Just over an hour later Jenkins was telephoned to say that Crosland had died more than a thousand miles away in Oxford.

Dr. George Ritchie, the American who could not believe he was 'dead'

Today a retired successful American psychiatrist (*right*), back in December 1942 the then twenty-year-old George Ritchie twice 'died' of double pneumonia while stationed with the U.S. army at Abilene, Texas. Preoccupied by a burning need to get to Richmond, Virginia, Ritchie found himself out-of-bodiedly 'flying' across country, only beginning to suspect he was 'dead' on stopping himself part-way at a city where he perceived a bridge crossing a wide river. As he discovered only some months after his successful recovery, the bridge he had out-of-bodiedly 'seen' was at Vicksburg, Mississippi (*below*), one which he had never visited before, yet parts of which he could describe accurately as a result of his near-death experience.

Vicki Umipeg, the born-blind American woman who experienced sight for the first and only time during her near-death experience

Blind from birth, Vicki Umipeg (*above*) found herself able to 'see' the earthly world for the first and only time during her near-death experience as a result of a car accident in February 1973. She also 'saw' friends of hers from blind school who had died. Her account of her experience matches that of some twenty other blind people who have had near-death experiences, and represents striking evidence that something of us may continue to 'see' after physical death without the use of physical eyes.

Howard Storm, the agnostic American art professor who tasted 'Hell'

Until he was 38 years old art Professor Howard Storm of Northern Kentucky University had always rejected the idea that there might be any form of life after death. Then in the summer of 1985 he collapsed from a perforated stomach while visiting Paris. Before being operated on, he 'died', thereupon experiencing a 'hellish' realm so real that it completely changed the course of his life. Such was the lasting effect of the experience that today he has become the Revd. Howard Storm of the Zion Uniting Church of Christ, Norwood, Ohio.

Right: A J Ayer – 'my thoughts became persons!' Like Howard Storm, atheist philosopher A J Ayer and others found 'thought' to be the automatic means of communication while in the 'other-worldly' state.

Edwin and Laurel Lloyd-Jones – the Australian couple who gave up everything after a near-death experience

Laurel Lloyd-Jones (*above*) and her husband Edwin, photographed near the group of elm trees which, together with an unusual rock formation (*right*), Laurel says she out-of-bodiedly saw from the air subsequent to her near-death experience from a cardiac arrest in April 1980. Laurel claims she was being shown the location where she and Edwin were directed to create a retreat house as 'a place of rest and solace for many'.

Below right: Laurel's great-grandmother Matilda Everingham, whom she insists visited her shortly after her near-death experience

Exactly as predicted, Grace's baby, eventually successfully born by Caesarean section, turned out to be a son. And the husband who Grace had confidently anticipated would be her life partner turned out to be a reckless spendthrift who ran up enormous debts, including clearing every penny that her father had left her, ending their marriage and necessitating that she raise her still-infant son on her own, exactly as her dead father had predicted.

Hallucination? Coincidence? Wishful thinking? There can be no easy answers when dealing with anything as non-material as near-death experiences. But in any case, our exploration of their myriad of intertwined features is by no means at an end. As we reminded ourselves at the very beginning of this chapter, George Ritchie had had a foretaste of a very hellish realm, quite different from the seemingly paradisical surroundings in which at least some of the deceased friends and relatives seemed to be dwelling. Indeed, such has been the persistence of the latter surroundings among most *reported and remembered* near-death experiences that several of the gurus of the subject have supposed that anything of the hellish variety must be illusory, leading, no doubt, to the comparative neglect of George Ritchie's story.

But as we are about to discover, one of the most telling indications of the veridicality of near-death experiences is that they are not mere wishfully invented intimations of what an afterlife might be like. Far more than anything of this kind, experients find themselves suddenly and irrevocably down-loaded with life values that may previously have never consciously occurred to them, yet which they learn to be of altogether more importance than anything they may previously have considered important in their entire lives. George Ritchie's seemingly medieval images of a hell of the experient's own making begins to appear not quite so archaic after all . . .

Chapter Seven

A Question of Judgment

*The whole period of my existence seemed to be placed before
me in a kind of panoramic review, and each act of it seemed
to be accompanied by a consciousness of right or wrong.*

Rear-Admiral Sir Francis Beaufort
on his near-death from drowning in 1795

The idea that some form of judgment awaits whatever
element of us leaves our physical body at death has been
around for a very long time. In the Egyptian Gallery in
London's British Museum is displayed a strip of papyrus
more than 3000 years old depicting the spirit of the dead
notable Hunefer being escorted into the judgment hall of
Osiris, the ancient Egyptians' equivalent of the Man of Light.
In the god's presence Hunefer is obliged to declare himself
innocent of a long list of sins: 'I have not lied . . . I have not
caused pain . . . I have not killed, I have not made suffering
for anyone.' Hunefer also has to allow his heart to be
solemnly weighed against a feather, the symbol of Ma'at, or
correct conduct. According to Egyptian belief, any failure on
his part could have meant his being cast down into an
Underworld of unhappy spirits.

Understandably, our modern mind baulks at anything so
theologically primitive. Indeed the Church of England,
which rejected the idea of a purgatory at its very inception,

as recently as July 1996 threw out the traditional Christian images of hell and damnation, declaring them 'a crudely sadistic notion',[1] and opting instead for the more comfortable prospect of just annihilation, or nothingness, even for a Hitler or a serial killer. And this might seem reasonable enough. For after all, even if we are prepared to accept the possibility of some form of life after death, who in today's scientific age is prepared any longer to believe in the Hieronymous Bosch-type images of devils with pitchforks and cloven hooves leading lost souls into fiery furnaces?

However, our concern in this book is neither with clinging to traditional beliefs for their own sake, nor with going along with whatever concepts today's Anglican hierarchy considers the most fashionable and the most comfortably defended. Instead, our objective has to be to determine impartially and clear-headedly whatever, in the light of near-death experience and related testimonies, best suits the available evidence. For as we have just seen, many near-death experients glimpse their dead relatives seemingly happy, and in paradisical-seeming surroundings. Yet as we also noted in Chapter 4, George Ritchie 'saw' a very different dimension, one of extremely unhappy dead beings. And my own and others' encounters with ghosts likewise seemed to suggest that some dead people may linger at least temporarily unhappily 'chained' to the earthly world. So where does the truth lie? Should 'hellish'-type experiences be taken seriously? And if so, what do these tell us about whatever may await each of us non-near-death experients when we die? This immediately leads us to an as yet unmentioned case which, like George Ritchie's, may at first sight seem incredible, yet which the credentials of the experient oblige us to treat with due seriousness.

In 1985 American Howard Storm might be considered to have been at the very peak of his career. At only thirty-eight years old he was Professor of the Department of Art at

Northern Kentucky University, Cincinnati. His wife Beverly was a lawyer who had borne him two fine children, and together they had created a beautiful home, with a half-acre flower garden in which Storm took great pride. So far as religion was concerned, he modernistically rejected anything and everything of this kind as just wishful thinking, even joking that he preferred to call himself an agnostic only because defending an outright atheist stance was too tiring. With regard to life after death, his view was 'absolute certainty that there was nothing beyond this life – because that is how the really smart people understand it'.[2]

Then in the early summer of 1985 Storm and his wife took a group of his students on an art tour of Europe. On the morning of Saturday, 1 June he showed them Paris's Sainte Chapelle, and the painter Delacroix's studio in the rue de Fürstemberg. He was beginning to feel oddly emotionally low when suddenly he collapsed with the most excruciating pain in his stomach, so severe and localized that at first he thought he had been shot. A hastily summoned doctor diagnosed a perforation of Storm's stomach and gave him a pain-killing injection, and he was then rushed to hospital where it was decided he needed an 'immediate' operation. However, 'immediate' in Parisian terms did not mean quite the same as in American, particularly over 'le weekend'. Despite Storm's escalating distress and his wife's impassioned pleas, the surgical team departed for the night, leaving him in a room with one other patient, and promising him an operation the next morning, a morning which so far as his pain threshold was concerned he did not feel he would have the strength to live to see. Shortly after 8.30 he bade his still-attendant wife an emotional farewell and lapsed into what he fully expected to be the oblivion of death.

The next morning he found himself in what we may now

recognize as a classic out-of-body phase of the near-death experience. In his own words:

> I opened my eyes and I was standing looking at my body in the bed, and I was standing right next to the bed. And there was my wife, and I started yelling and screaming at her, like, 'What's going on? How can I be standing up, looking at myself?' And I felt completely real, and she didn't respond to me. And I gestured wildly, and I started swearing and screaming, and no response . . . I figured that she was crazy or something, so I turned around to my room-mate and I started yelling at him. And the same thing, he was just like frozen. They did absolutely nothing, except that I knew that they were alive, and that my body was empty, and I had no interest in getting back into that body or having anything to do with that body.[3]

Exactly as we noted of other experients, Howard Storm immediately began questioning his own sanity:

> Obviously the first thing I thought about was, 'Is this a dream? Is it a hallucination?' Yet by every sensation of myself I knew that it wasn't a dream or a hallucination. It was actually more vividly real than normal consciousness. I had in my younger days taken hallucinogens, and they are real interesting. But they tend to narrow focus . . . You also have this real sense of loss of control . . . But this was . . . like I was more aware of *everything*. All my senses were heightened, and I kept saying to myself 'This is not possible! This can't be happening!'

For Storm the one source of relief to his confusion was that he seemed to be feeling somewhat better than only shortly before. Then began the most unbelievable part of his experience, a journey into a nightmare. To his astonishment he heard voices of people who had no French accent calling him by his Christian name, seemingly from outside his hospital room door. As he remarked, he felt very reluctant to leave his wife, but:

> nobody would respond to me, and I needed help and here were these people that knew me by name. There wasn't a soul in the French hospital that could say 'Howard'. It doesn't translate into French. So it was real strange that they spoke English and could say 'Howard'. So I thought, 'Well that's in their favour. They must really know me.' So I went to the doorway . . .

Outside his room, still in his 'out-of-body' guise, he found himself in a mist, in this instance quite different from the brilliant light and clarity reported by those claiming 'paradisical' experiences. Dimly perceptible were people inviting him to follow them.

> They were . . . like twenty, thirty, forty, feet away . . . and they were tall, and they were short, and they were male and they were female, because I could make out silhouettes. But every time I would approach somebody they would back off into the mist, and that bothered me. I asked them who they were and what they wanted, but they wouldn't answer anything directly. For example if I said 'Well, who are you?' they would say 'You'll find out'. . . . I couldn't get a straight answer, and that bothered me a lot.

Storm dutifully followed where these 'guides' were leading him, walking seemingly interminably, with the mist getting thicker and darker, and (in marked contrast to the 'paradisical' experiences), with renewed pain now very much back on the agenda. According to his own description:

> It felt like we walked for days and weeks, and many many times I got very reluctant but they would chorus me on. And then I started feeling very, very tired, and weary, and my stomach was burning. And I was feeling real cold, sick, and they were starting to make fun of me ... I was really beginning to feel paranoid, like everybody was in on something, and I didn't know what was going on ... The fog kept getting thicker and thicker, and darker and darker and we ended up like I couldn't see anything, not even see my hand in front of my face ... And the people around me kept moving in closer and closer and closer, so that now they were right just beyond my reach. I could tell by their voices where they were and I said, 'I'm not going any further, I don't like this at all. I don't like you. I don't want any part of it, and I want to go back.' I was swearing at them and they were swearing at me. And we started yelling and screaming. They started pushing and shoving ... and they started hitting me. And I would swing around and try and hit somebody, and every once in a while make contact. The thing that was strangest ... I was kicking and slugging and clobbering, and everything I did they laughed at! I'd make real contact, hitting so hard that I'd really hurt my hand, and the person I had hit would laugh hysterically. And meanwhile they were tearing at me, ... and it was incredibly painful. And I came to realize that the point of the whole game was simply to put pain on me, and that my pain gave them joy and pleasure.[4]

Unmistakably we may find ourselves reminded of the 'battlefield' of 'writhing, punching, gouging' individuals 'boxing the air' that George Ritchie had 'seen' – except that

Storm, instead of observing this from the sidelines, as Ritchie had, was right in the very thick of it. His torments lessened only when he lost his own will to fight his persecutors, but they still remained around him 'picking at me occasionally' as he lay exhausted and spent, 'full of hopelessness, despair and pain'.

Then the totally unexpected happened. In Storm's own words:

> I heard 'myself' coming from inside me, saying to my consciousness, 'Pray!' And I said to myself . . . to that little voice that I knew was me, but I didn't know where it was coming from, I said, 'Why? Why bother? I mean, that's like a cop-out. You know that's for children. I don't do that.' And the voice insisted. It said, 'Pray!' again. And the problem was that I didn't really know what that meant, because I hadn't done it since I was probably fifteen years old . . . And so I used little bits and pieces of things that I could remember . . . a few snatches of the 23rd Psalm and a little bit of the Lord's Prayer, all the formal stuff I could think of . . .

Of no little surprise and fascination for Storm was his tormentors' reaction to these prayers:

> They [the people around me] didn't like it at all . . . They were yelling and screaming at me to stop. [They told me] I was a fool. Nobody could hear me. What did I think I was doing? If I mentioned God they said there was no such thing as God. Why was I relying on all that superstition and nonsense? I liked the effect it was having on them . . . and I became more and more forceful as I said it. And I started swearing, mixing swears and prayers. And they got angrier and angrier. But they [also] got more and more distant until

eventually I realized that . . . they were all gone. There was no sense of them around. There was no sound of them around.

Then I felt very, very bad because I hadn't believed any of the stuff I was saying. I just did it, and it had an effect, so I just did it. But it wasn't real sincere or anything. And I'm lying there absolutely helpless, windless . . . [with] an incredible sense of sadness, aloneness. And that little voice that suggested prayer said to me, 'Jesus loves you', in the sense of the Sunday School song, 'Jesus loves me. Yes, I know.' And I screamed into the darkness 'Please Jesus save me.' *And I meant it.*

As Storm stresses, he really did not have a clue who Jesus was. His heartfelt cry was simply to his Sunday School perception of God, whom he saw as in any case synonymous with Jesus. But to whomsoever it was addressed, the cry did not fall on deaf ears:

In the darkness I became aware of a star or a small light. And it started getting very big very fast, and I realized that it was coming right at me . . . And it came right on me, and as it did I came back off the floor, and all of me came all back together . . . Like in *StarTrek* when . . . someone gets beamed aboard, I just became beamed whole again. And I was surrounded in this light, and I was aware that the light was a Being. And all these things I knew immediately. That the light *loved* me. That it *knew* me. That it was really powerful and good. And we went out of that place, and there was a real strong sense of moving upwards very rapidly. And we travelled together and I was in ecstasy . . . If you can imagine having orgasms of every sense and of your intellect . . . that's what I was into. It was wonderful. I wasn't talking. I wasn't thinking. It was . . . here's me and my buddy, and we're travelling through space, and this is really great.

As we may now recognize, Storm was being 'transported' in a manner now very strikingly reminiscent of the experience of Ritchie and others. As if travelling through space, he saw a great 'centre of light' with 'millions, trillions of small lights entering and leaving it at different rates and different directions'. As he got closer he was so intensely awed by this, and by the radiance he could feel from it, that in his own words:

> I thought to myself, 'I'm afraid'. And my fear was that it was too much, it was too intense. And then my Friend said to me in my mind – my Friend had a voice and it wasn't my voice – and he said to me, 'Oh, that's OK! We'll stop here. We don't want you to be afraid.'

Storm now found himself surrounded by several other Beings of Light, or as he called them, 'centres of radiance', each with slightly different characteristics and slightly different hues of 'a lot more colours than we can see'. Fascinatingly, particularly in the context of our earlier deductions concerning human appearance in the 'other-worldly' dimension, there formed in his mind the Beings' question, 'Do you want to see us in human form?' To which his mental reply was: 'Absolutely not, I've seen plenty of that. This is the most beautiful thing I've ever seen in the world, please don't show me you in human form, just be what I am seeing now, because it's incredibly beautiful.'

Thoroughly humbled at the 'incredible love and perfection and beauty' with which he found himself surrounded, Storm's initial reaction was one of an intense unworthiness, that perhaps these Beings had made some mistake whisking him from the gloomy realm of the gougers and punchers. In his words:

> I felt like a piece of filth, that's how I thought of myself. And they said that they don't make mistakes, and that I was exactly in the right place at the right time, and that *this was what it was supposed to be* [italics mine].

Here we may recall that the blind-since-birth Vicki and Brad in Chapter 5 both quite independently used that very same phrase when speaking of their other-worldly experience. As Storm went on:

> And I kind of argued a little bit. I said, 'Are you sure? Are you really sure?' And they said, 'Yes' . . . And every time I'd weaken . . . they'd kind of bolster me up with feelings of love, and then say things that I'd respond to . . . I said, 'Everything I think of, you respond to. Do you know what goes on in my mind?' And they said, 'Yes.' And I said, 'What if I have a thought that I don't want you to know about?' And they said, '*We know everything that you think about and we have always known everything that you have thought about* [italics mine].'

Here, then we again find ourselves in the same world of absolute total transparency of thoughts that we already came across in the case of George Ritchie, and of so many other experients. As Storm learned further of this process:

> They [i.e. the 'other-worldly' beings among whom he found himself] feel everything that we feel. So when we inflict pain and misery on other people, they feel that pain and misery. All the suffering that we inflict in this world, they feel it.

145

They also feel our joy and our happiness too. They feel everything. They feel our emotions. They know our thoughts. They in fact are not there and we here. *They are here.*

In passing we may also note that we heard the very same observation before, from the world's tribal peoples and others, that they could positively feel their dead relatives and other spirit beings around them. But for Storm perhaps the most extraordinary moment was when, in a manner strikingly similar to Ritchie's experience, the Beings showed him a holographic-type review of his life. As he recollected:

My life played out before me, maybe six or eight feet in front of me, from beginning to end . . . Some things they slowed down on, and zoomed in on, and other things they went right through. They showed me my life in a way that I had never thought of before. All the things that I had worked to achieve, the recognition that I had worked for, in elementary school, in high school, in college, and in my career, they meant nothing in this setting.

I could feel their feelings of sorrow and suffering, or joy, as my life's review unfolded. They didn't say that something was bad or good, but I could feel it. And I could sense all those things they were indifferent to. They didn't, for example, look down on my high school shot-put record. They just didn't feel anything towards it, nor towards other things which I had taken so much pride in.

What they responded to was how I had interacted with other people. That was the long and short of it. Unfortunately, most of my interactions with other people didn't measure up with how I should have interacted; which was, in a loving way.

Whenever I did react during my life in a loving way,

they rejoiced. Most of the time I found that my interactions with other people had been manipulative. During my professional career, for example, I saw myself sitting in my office, playing the college professor, while a student came to me with a personal problem. I sat there looking compassionate, and patient, and loving, while inside I was bored to death. I would check my watch under the desk as I anxiously waited for the student to finish . . .

When I was a teenager, my father's career put him in a high-stress, twelve-hour-a-day job. Out of my resentment towards his neglect of me, when he came home from work I would be cold and indifferent toward him. This would make him angry, and it would give me a further excuse to feel hatred toward him. He and I would fight, and my mother would get upset.

Most of my life I had felt that my father was a creep and I was the victim. When we reviewed my life I got to see how I had precipitated so much of that myself. Instead of greeting him happily at the end of the day, I was continually putting thorns in him – in order to justify my own hurt.

I got to see, when my sister had a bad night one night, how I went into her bedroom and put my arms around her. I didn't say anything. I just lay there with my arms around her. As it turned out, that experience was one of the biggest triumphs of my life.

I felt very strongly that the whole life's review would have been emotionally destructive, and would have left me a psychotic person, if it hadn't been for the fact that my Friend, and my Friend's Friends, while we watched the whole thing, were loving me . . . The therapy was their love, because my life's review kept tearing me down. It was pitiful to watch, just pitiful. I couldn't believe it. And the thing is, it got worse as it went on. My stupidity and selfishness as a teenager only magnified as I became an adult – all under the veneer of being a good husband, a good father, a good citizen. The hypocrisy of it all was just nauseating. But through it all was their love . . .[5]

In the course of his experience Storm felt the 'solid and real' body that he had still felt he had during his 'hellish' phase, 'becoming more and more transparent', leading him to suppose that the slate of his failings had been wiped clean and that he would be remaining with his new-found 'other-worldly' Friends. But they told him, 'You have to go back.' Although he mentally pleaded that if he did so he would be 'doomed to err', they assured him that it was all right for him to make as many mistakes as he wanted so long as he learned by them. When he then tried arguing that he simply could not bear to leave them, they told him:

> that they would be around, and that if I really needed them, sincerely needed them, they would let me know they were with me. I wasn't to worry or to fret, because they were right there with me all the time. And with everybody. And they always had been and always would be.

On Storm's finally asking what was expected of him on his return to life – was it to build cathedrals or to carve wonderful sculptures – this provoked some considerable other-worldly amusement:

> They laughed! They thought that was really funny, because it was pointless. They made it clear to me that it was exactly what I had done wrong, working with inanimate objects half my life rather than working with people. The art was fine, but don't focus on that. Focus on whatever people come into my life . . . *Loving people and living with people is what's really important . . .*

When Storm eventually reluctantly accepted that he was expected to return to life, seemingly the next moment he woke up to find his wife being hustled out of his hospital room, and nurses and orderlies preparing him for his operation. Once more he experienced unbelievable physical pain before going unconscious again under the general anaesthetic. When afterwards he told first his wife, then his family, of his experience, they initially regarded him as almost out of his mind for the complete volte-face that this had caused to his ideas on religion and the afterlife. Indeed, for a while he probably was almost insufferably 'over-the-top' in this-worldly terms. But just as he had to readjust to the everyday world, so likewise his family had to readjust to the very different Howard Storm that they now found as husband and father. For such was the profundity of the effect of the experience upon him that he sought a religious vocation, and today he is the Rev. Howard Storm of Zion United Church of Christ in Norwood, Ohio. He gives lectures on his experience, and when he does so the emotions that the vivid memories raise in his mind still often reduce him to tears.

But can we really believe that his glimpses of a 'hellish' dimension have some sort of reality? And can we really believe that each of us may one day have to undergo, in the presence of a Being or Beings of Light, something of the very same searching-out and evaluation of all our past actions that he, and Ritchie before him, say they went through?

Inevitably, with even the Church of England's hierarchy rejecting the idea of hell, the 'hellish' element is the most difficult to treat seriously. Because the great majority of reported near-death experiences are undeniably of the pleasant variety (and this seemingly regardless of what the individuals' earlier ethical standards may have been), there has been a tendency on the part even of leading researchers to be suspicious of anything different, which may well explain why Ritchie's experience has never previously been discussed in the depth we have attempted here.

However, even aside from Ritchie and Storm, the 'hellish' cases are there. One of Raymond Moody's subjects was a man who as a result of deep depression over his wife's death, shot himself and 'died', in the course of which he had his near-death experience, only to be successfully revived. He told Moody: 'I didn't go where [my wife] was. I went to an awful place. I immediately saw the mistake I had made. I thought: 'I wish I hadn't done it.'[6]

Alexandra, an Australian who 'died' at twenty-nine years old as a result of a blood infection following the removal of her left kidney, told Dr Cherie Sutherland of an experience with some striking parallels to Storm's:

> I felt myself falling into an abyss . . . this was out-of-control motion. It was very, very terrifying and seemed to go on for a long time . . . It was moist and dark and there were sort of nasty shapes and smells. I visualized I was falling into some awful pit, but it was quite large and there were no walls and there were no parameters and there was less and less light. And then it was just pitch-dark. I remember praying my heart out that I wasn't just going to be lost in space or the universe. I felt like I was falling into hell . . . That was one of the most frightening things I think that's ever happened to me. I was so alone . . . at that moment of what you would call absolute terror and despair . . . I cried out.[7]

Moments after crying out, according to Alexandra, she found herself being comfortingly held in two large arms and told she was 'a child of God'.

American cardiologist Dr Maurice Rawlings has described the case of a postman patient of his who had a cardiac arrest while undergoing tests, and who 'died', then revived again several times while Rawlings was carrying out resuscitation procedures that included the insertion of a pacemaker wire into the vein leading directly into the man's heart. For Rawlings, the astonishing feature was what the postman told him during his moments of recovery:

> Each time he regained heart-beat and respiration the patient screamed, 'I'm in hell!' He was terrified and pleaded with me to help him ... He then issued a very strange plea: 'Don't stop!' You see, the first thing most patients I resuscitate tell me as soon as they recover consciousness is, 'Take your hands of my chest; you're hurting me!' I am big and my method of external heart massage sometimes fractures ribs. But this patient was telling me, 'Don't stop!' But then I noticed a genuinely alarmed look on his face ... The patient had a grotesque look on his face, expressing sheer horror! His pupils were dilated, and he was perspiring and trembling – he looked as if his hair was 'on end'. Then still another strange thing happened. He said, 'Don't you understand? I am in hell. Each time you quit I go back to hell! Don't let me go back to hell!'[8]

A particularly significant feature of this postman's experience was that, as he subsequently told Rawlings after his recovery, he then went on to a paradisical 'other-worldly' dimension, just as Alexandra and Storm had done. But of the hellish phase that he had told Rawlings about while the latter was resuscitating him he could remember absolutely nothing. The implication here is that perhaps 'hellish' experiences may be more common than the statistics for them suggest, but unlike those relating to 'paradisical' states, those who have them very quickly blot them out from their normal consciousness, with just occasional exceptions such as Storm and Ritchie.

Indeed, in support of such selective amnesia, we have what appears to be a particularly notable example from arguably the last man who might have been expected to have a near-death experience, the late philosopher Sir Alfred Ayer, a lifelong atheist and supporter of the Humanist Association. In May 1988 the then seventy-seven-year-old Ayer choked on a piece of smoked salmon while recovering from pneumonia in the intensive care unit at University College Hospital, London. His heart stopped and he 'died' for some four minutes before the medical staff managed to resuscitate him, the fascinating aspect being that on his recovering consciousness a few hours afterwards, and finding a longstanding Frenchwoman friend sitting at his bedside, he very lucidly told her in his fluent French: 'Did you know that I was dead? The first time that I tried to cross the river I was frustrated, but my second attempt succeeded. It was most extraordinary. *My thoughts became persons* [italics mine].[9]

From his remark that he knew he had been dead, his reference to a river barrier, and above all his cryptic phrase, 'My thoughts became persons' (so redolent of the thought-based communication process during near-death experiences), it would seem fairly obvious that Ayer must have had some kind of near-death experience – except that on fully regaining consciousness he could remember nothing of what may have lain behind these remarks, hellish or otherwise. All he had been left with was something of the order of a dream about space and time, one sufficiently interesting in its own right to be considered in the next chapter, but clearly not the experience that gave rise to what he told the Frenchwoman.

Overall the clear implication, the Church of England's discomfort with the idea of a hell notwithstanding, seems to be that if there is anything serious in the idea of people living on in some 'paradisical' dimension, then there may well indeed be some form of 'hellish' dimension as well, even though those who experience it may prefer not to remember it. It is notable that in contrast to the brilliant light reported by those who have paradisical experiences, those who have the hellish ones describe being drawn into escalating darkness. Whereas the former report heightened clarity of sight and sound, the latter describe only dimness. Instead of the euphoria felt by the former, the latter feel only anxiety and unease. And rather than being overwhelmed by loving beings, the latter feel isolated in hostile surroundings and, to recall Storm's phrase, only 'hopelessness, despair and pain'.

Furthermore, if we are prepared to take seriously both the paradisical and hellish aspects of the near-death experience, there are even indications of some in-between dimension as well, exactly as we contemplated in our earlier discussion of ghosts. Not only have we already noted something of this indicated by George Ritchie's experience, we learn from the American blind-since-birth Vicki of what she 'saw' while in her 'tunnel'-like intermediate phase: 'There was one area I passed by where there was a group of drab, dull, unhappy people who were unable to move.'[10]

Likewise a female subject of Raymond Moody's who 'died' for fifteen minutes, reported seeing 'bewildered' people who seemed 'trapped' and unable to release themselves from the earthly world, again using the world 'dull':

I don't know exactly where I saw them . . . but as I was going by, there was this area that was dull – this is in contrast to all the brilliant light. The figures were more humanized than the rest of them were, if you stop to think about it in that respect, but neither were they in quite human form as we are. What you would think of as their head was bent downward; they had sad, depressed looks;

they seemed to shuffle, as someone on a chain gang. I don't know why I say this because I don't remember noticing feet. I don't know what they were, but they looked washed out, dull, grey. And they seemed to be forever shuffling and moving around, not knowing where they were going, and not knowing who to follow, or what to look for. As I went by they didn't even raise their heads to see what was happening. They seemed to be thinking, 'Well, it's all over with. What am I doing? What's it all about?' Just this absolute, crushed, hopeless demeanour – not knowing what to do or where to go or who they were or anything else . . . They didn't seem to be aware of anything . . . they seemed to be caught in between somewhere. Something is tying them down, because they all seemed to be bent over and looking downward, maybe into the physical world . . . maybe watching something they hadn't done or should do. They couldn't make up their minds what to do, because they had the most woebegone expressions, there was no colour of life . . . this was something that was maybe like a black and white movie. Just the different tones of grey – dingy, washed out. They were not aware of me. They showed no sign of being aware that I was there . . . *They . . . reminded me of what I have read of as descriptions of ghosts* [italics mine] . . . There seems to have been a great huge array of them around.[11]

Unmistakably, this description resembles some of the best-attested sightings of ghosts. As but one example, to quote from reports of a ghostly Roman army in the cellar of the Treasurer's House, York, England as witnessed by now-retired policeman Harry Martindale and by former curator Joan Mawson: 'I couldn't see the legs of anybody. Nobody had legs, from about the knees. You didn't see any feet . . .

They were so tired-looking . . . No definite colour. They sort of shuffled along, dispiritedly.'[12]

Heaven? Hell? Purgatory? Understandably the modern mind may sill baulk at the notion that such ideas could continue to have any validity as we approach the twenty-first century. But nothing could be a clearer indication of a link between this kind of 'beyond-the-grave' evidence and the way we conduct our lives than another commonly reported element of near-death experiences, that of the so-called 'life review'. As we have seen, both George Ritchie and Howard Storm were shown behaviour-assessing 'reviews' in the company of the other-worldly 'Being' or 'Beings'. Such reviews are not only common to around a quarter of all near-death experiences, it is also clear that, as with so many other aspects of the near-death experience, people have been experiencing them for a very long time.

For instance, in 1795, when he was just twenty-one years old and serving as a midshipman in Nelson's navy, the noted hydrographer Rear-Admiral Sir Francis Beaufort very narrowly escaped drowning in Portsmouth Harbour. In his subsequent recollections of this he reported:

Though the senses were . . . deadened, not so the mind; its activity seemed to be invigorated, in a ration which defies all description, for thought rose above thought with a rapidity of succession that is not only indescribable, but probably inconceivable by anyone who has not himself been in a similar situation. The course of those thoughts I can even now in a great measure retrace . . . a thousand other circumstances minutely associated with home, were the first series of reflections that occurred. They took then a wider range – our last cruise – a former voyage, and shipwreck – my school – the progress I had made there, and the time I had misspent – and even all my boyish pursuits and adventures. Thus, travelling backwards, every past incident of my life seemed to glance across my recollection in retrograde succession; not, however, in mere outline, as here stated, but the picture filled up with every minute and collateral feature. In short, the whole period of my existence seemed to be placed before me in a kind of panoramic review, *and each act of it seemed to be accompanied by a consciousness of right or wrong, or by some reflection on its cause or its consequencesf* [italics mine].[13]

Among modern cases, one of the closest to Beaufort's is that of a young American who nearly drowned in a boating accident, and who told Dr Kenneth Ring:

It was amazing. I could see in the back of my head an array, just [an] innumerable array of thoughts, memories, things I had dreamt, thoughts and recollections from the past, just raced in front of me, in less than thirty seconds . . . It felt like this frame, millions of frames, just flashed through. It was thoughts and images of people. And a lot of thoughts just raced in split seconds. I had my eyes closed under water, but I could still see these images . . . A lot of them were very emotional . . . I saw . . . [my grandmother] as not wanting me to die. I saw what my drowning would do to her . . . There were thoughts of my brother. Just silly . . . nitpicking things I thought I'd forgotten. It was like . . . my whole memory was retaping. I was in reverse and everything was backtracking so I could go over it again like a tape recorder. But it wasn't in sequence.[14]

Just as Ritchie, Storm and Beaufort all described the perceived re-run of their past actions as being accompanied by what Beaufort called 'a consciousness of right or wrong, or by some reflection on its cause or its consequences', so too we hear from one of Raymond Moody's experients:

> Then it seemed there was a display all around me, and everything in my life just went by for review, you might say. I was really very, very ashamed of a lot of the things that I experienced because it seemed that I had a different knowledge, that the [Being of] light was showing me what was wrong, what I did wrong. And it was very real. It seemed like this flashback, or memory or whatever, was directed primarily at ascertaining the extent of my life. It was like there was a judgment being made, and then all of a sudden, the light became dimmer and *there was a conversation, not in words, but in thoughts.* When I would see something, when I would experience a past event, it was like I was seeing it through eyes with (I guess you would say) omnipotent knowledge, guiding me, and helping me to see. That's the part that has stuck with me, because it showed me not only what I had done but *even how what I had done had affected other people.* And it wasn't like I was looking at a movie projector because I could *feel* these things; there was feeling, and particularly since I was with this knowledge . . . *I found out that not even your thoughts are lost . . . Every thought was there . . . Your thoughts are not lost* [italics mine].[15]

English air-traffic controller Allan Pring remarked likewise:

> My life passed before me in a momentary flash, but it was entire, even my thoughts were included . . . I knew that . . . whatever came next would be a direct consequence of not only what I had done in my life, but *what I had thought and what had been my true feeling at the time* [italics mine].[16]

This very same perception was reported by Swedish anaesthiologist Dr Goren Grip, who had his near-death experience
as a result of an anaesthetist's bungle during a surgical
operation when he was five years old. Despite his young age,
not only did he retain the memory with great vividness, it
also profoundly affected the whole direction of his life, in
particular his choosing to become a doctor. In his case the
Being of Light, irradiating immense love, appeared to him as
he lay on the operating table and showed him the triumphs
and failings even of his five tender years. In his own words:

> I re-experienced everything that had happened in my life
> and watched it as a spectator with the Being. Most of what
> I saw was about me and my brother, of whom I was very
> jealous. My attention was focused on our exchanges of
> emotions, my jealousy, my feelings of triumph when I hit
> him, his surprise when I hit him for no reason, his anger
> and resentment, and later his triumph when he got back at
> me ... When I did something loving to him, I experienced
> my love, my brother's surprise, as well as his love and
> happiness. *I experienced his feelings as clearly as my own,
> making this a fantastic lesson on the consequences of my own
> actions* [italics mine].[17]

Note Dr Grip's words, 'I watched it [i.e. the life review] as
a spectator'. If we look back to Rear-Admiral Beaufort's
account of his experience, we may note his remark: 'The
whole period of my existence seemed to be placed before
me.' George Ritchie, in his description of his life review,
likewise kept repeating, 'I saw myself ...' Storm said, 'We
watched my life.' And Allan Pring said, 'My life passed before
me.' In each case, as in essentially all life reviews, we find the
experient seeing himself or herself throughout his life as if

observing from out of the body, whether as if floating a few feet away in physical space, or as if from the perspective of someone else's feelings.

And consistently this observing is mostly not done alone. Just from the examples we chose for illustrative purposes, we may note how George Ritchie spoke of his watching his life in the company of the Being. As did Pring. As did Grip. As did Raymond Moody's experient. As did Storm, the only distinction in the latter case being the presence of others besides the main Being.

But now comes one of the many mysteries. While in the light of general Christian belief, and also of most other creeds, going back to ancient Egypt, it might surely be expected that it would be the Being who would make the judgment on each individual's past actions and sentiments, we consistently find this being done by the experient himself or herself. Thus as Australian Laurel Lloyd-Jones told Dr Cherie Sutherland: 'Then there was a review of my whole life. I can remember looking at it and assessing it and really judging it myself. I felt no one else judged me – *I judged myself* [italics mine].[18]

As an American who tried to commit suicide told Dr Kenneth Ring:

The only thing I felt judged by would be myself. Like in the very beginning, when I thought about these things, all these terrible things, then I thought about the good things . . . and I'd think about all the stupid things, all the mistakes I've made. *I think the judging was mainly myself judging myself* [italics mine].[19]

As Allan Pring told Peter and Elizabeth Fenwick: 'I did not feel that I had been judged *except by myself* [italics mine].'[20]

Likewise George Ritchie: 'I realized that *it was I who was judging the events* [italics mine] around us so harshly it was I who saw them as trivial, self-centred, unimportant.'

Furthermore, as Ritchie specifically made clear: 'No such condemnation came from the Glory [i.e. the Being] shining round me. He was not blaming or reproaching. He was simply . . . loving me.'[21]

Likewise Grip said: 'It was the love from the Being of Light that gave me the strength to see my life exactly as it was, without making it better or worse.'

In the case of Howard Storm, he not only agreed with this, he even regarded the Being or Beings as saving him from what might otherwise have been some very destructive effects of his own self-censure.

> I felt very strongly that the whole life's review would have been emotionally destructive, and would have left me a psychotic person, if it hadn't been for the fact that my Friend, and my Friend's Friends, while we watched the whole thing, were loving me.

Which raises the very crucial issue: how on earth can all these people have been so dramatically changed – as if in the twinkling of an eye – from the ordinary, self-centred and mostly atheistic individuals they had previously been, into individuals *judging themselves* (there is no other way of describing it), and often extremely harshly, from the perspective of 'other-worldly' life values that they had mostly not even begun to consider before? We may recall how the Raymond Moody life review experient expressed it: 'It was like I was seeing it through eyes with (I guess you would say) omnipotent knowledge, guiding me and helping me to see . . . even how what I had done had affected other people.'

Now, as we will be going on to see, one of the most

fascinating aspects of those 'eyes' is that they are not just a transient accessory only while the near-death experient is in the 'other-worldly' state undergoing the review. In many cases they seem actually to remain with the experient, fundamentally helping direct the rest of his or her life. But first, given the continuing difficulties to belief in any heaven, hell or purgatory (for all that we have seen), we need at least to try to conceptualize what sort of dimension they might exist in, along with the dead relatives, the preserved thoughts, and so much else, given that this has so far completely eluded detection by our present-day science . . .

Chapter 8

On Time, Space and 'Reality'

[I believe] that the answers to many of the questions that are posed by near-death experiences lie in a better understanding of the nature of time and what we term reality.

Near-death experient Allan Pring

As we already noted from the reports by George Ritchie, Howard Storm and others, whatever the 'after-death' realm that they may have experienced, it is one in which everyone's thoughts are as perceptible and as 'real' as physical objects are to our five physical senses. As George Ritchie said of his encounter with the Man, this Being knew 'every . . . thing about me . . . every . . . thought and action since the day I was born'. He also said of the more ordinary beings in the 'hell' that he glimpsed: 'Whatever anyone thought, however fleetingly or unwillingly, was instantly apparent to all around him, more completely than words could have expressed it, faster than sound waves could have carried it.' We have noted how American Father Louis Tucker, Englishman David Ayre and others all communicated with their dead relatives via exchanges of thoughts. Sir Alfred Ayer remarked in his experience's immediate aftermath: 'It was most extraordinary. My thoughts became persons.' Howard Storm was told by the Beings he encountered: 'We know everything that you think about and we have always known everything that you have thought about.' He was also assured that the Beings had always been watching over him, and would continue to do so.

Now, just how much we are prepared to accept any of this inevitably depends on our continued willingness to be receptive to whatever near-death experients relate. For if we accept their insistence that one mind can communicate with another via thought alone, then we have already strayed far beyond anything that Dr Susan Blackmore and 'the brain is all there is to us' school can explain away via psychological theory. We can either go along with the Blackmore school and regard near-death experiences as no more than hallucinations, in which case we have simply been wasting our time. Or we can continue to take them seriously, in which case we are obliged to wander further and further into a world in which the normal bounds of what we may fondly *suppose* to be reality seem no longer to apply, and in which everything is almost literally mind-blowing.

For the clear implication of the near-death experients' claims is that everything that we have ever thought or felt throughout our lives is, and always has been, stark staringly naked to those in the other-worldly dimension. Just as George Ritchie remarked of those punching, writhing gouging individuals whom he saw in the 'hellish' realm that they had no 'private corners' to hide themselves in, so we ourselves are similarly exposed, even as I write these words and you the reader read them. To anyone who likes their own privacy it may seem the ultimate nightmare that George Orwell envisaged, albeit in this-worldly terms, in *1984*. But if we are to believe the near-death experients, then 'thought-police' of a kind are among us, and always have been and always will be.

Yet how can we possibly conceive of any such dimension in which everyone's thoughts are instantly apparent to everyone else, or one in which our own 'in-life' thoughts are also purportedly readily readable to those on the 'other side' despite the 'screen' of our physical bodies? Obviously there are no easy answers – except that as one near-death experient after another insists, whatever this realm may be, the normally accepted rules governing time and space simply do not seem to apply to it.

Thus, for instance, speaking as I type this, only last night I was told by Pat Venn, a sharp-witted Brisbanian who 'died' after adversely reacting to anaesthetics used for a routine operation she underwent back in 1981, that she had 'absolutely no conception of time' during her experience. Likewise, Dr Cherie Sutherland told me how during her 'dying in childbirth' experience in 1971 the idea of her dying and leaving behind her young husband and new baby – something to which her 'normal' self would have reacted with absolute horror – seemed from the perspective of her 'otherworldly' self to be almost entirely of no consequence, because this part of her 'knew' that they would be together again in what she literally regarded as 'no time'. Fellow-Australian Laurel Lloyd-Jones, who 'died' in near-identical circumstances, told me that she felt exactly the same, again being amazed at 'herself' for thinking this way.

And right across the world, one near-death experient after another has repeated much the same theme. Thus Raymond Moody, in his book *Reflections*, the follow-up to *Life after Life*, wrote of an American man who found himself seemingly floating above his body after an explosion:

> his physical surroundings seemed to disappear entirely and a review of his entire life came before him, while he 'discussed' it in the presence of 'Christ'. When asked how long the review seemed to take, he remarked that if he were forced to put it in temporal terms he would have to say that it took an

hour at the very least. Yet when he was told he must return [to life] and the review disappeared, he again saw his physical surroundings. *The persons he saw coming to rescue him seemed frozen in stop motion, in the same positions they had been just as the review started* [italics mine]. When he seemed to be returning to his body, the action speeded up again.[1]

Englishwoman Avon Pailthorpe, who had her near-death experience during the mere seconds that it took for a following car to slam into hers as it lay across the fast lane of a motorway, told Peter and Elizabeth Fenwick that the experience included a full-blown journey through a 'tunnel; and a lengthy and unflurried debate with other-worldly Beings concerning whether she should live or die following the terrible injuries that she would sustain. As she 'woke', calmly watching the oncoming car still speeding relentlessly towards her, she even had 'time' not only to 'know' that she would survive the impact, but also to reflect she had been away from her body for so long that she felt 'strange to be in it – almost as though I had to reacquaint myself with it'.[2]

Likewise the English air-traffic controller Allan Pring said of his life review, which he described as 'entire' with 'even my thoughts included': 'Although it took but a moment to complete, literally a flash, there was still time to stop and wonder over separate incidents.'[3]

Accompanying and still consistent with near-death experients' talk of the apparent absence of time is their repeated insistence that the showings of their lives often lacked the spatializations before or after, forward or backward, that we normally regard as so essential for our 'conceiving' of time. Some, it is true, have loosely described their lives as moving either 'backwards' (as in Rear-Admiral Beaufort's case in the previous chapter), or forwards as they flashed before them. But when their descriptions are examined carefully, this is usually one of the instances of words failing them, since they may also speak of nothing being in sequence, and of everything of their past being present at one and the same time. As George Ritchie, for instance, described the opening moments of his encounter with the Being in the tiny Camp Barkeley hospital room:

> Into that room . . . *simultaneously*, though in telling about it I have to describe them one by one . . . also entered every single episode of my entire life. Everything that had ever happened to me was simply there, in full view, contemporary and current, *all seemingly taking place at that moment* [italics mine].[4]

Likewise Patrick, the Australian who had his near-death experience at the age of twenty-three while serving with the British Army during the Second World War, told Dr Cherie Sutherland: 'there was no concept of time either backward or forward. I could encompass the whole lot, and I could encompass the whole universe.'[5]

And American experient Frank, recalling the Being's comment upon his life review, 'You really blew it this time, Frank', stressed during his interview with Dr Kenneth Ring that he simply could not be sure whether the Being said this before or afterwards:

> I couldn't tell you if this was said before the whole movie thing or after it. Because somehow, even though I feel it was at the end, it could have just as well have been at the beginning. In other words, that statement referred to the whole thing, before and after.[6]

And if time is out of joint in this other-worldly dimension, then so is space, along with whatever feelings of assurance and hard factuality that gravity and the world of so-called 'hard' reality may hold for us. For implicit in so many near-death experients reporting of their 'floating on the ceiling' during the out-of-body phase was that their thought-body was free of gravity, able to pass through solid walls and ceilings, and to 'be' anywhere simply by thought alone.

Thus George Ritchie, after his talk of re-experiencing everything in his life taking place at one and the same moment, specifically went on: 'I had never before experienced the kind of space we seemed to be in. The little one-bed [hospital] room was still visible, *but it no longer confined us* [italics mine].[7]

Englishman David Ayre of Bristol, who had his near-death experience trying to kill himself with bottled gas, whisky and a pill overdose after sealing himself up in 'the smallest room in the house', told me how on finding his thought-body up in the top corner of the room looking down on his crumpled body, one of his first thoughts was that he had not left himself any means of getting out of this room. After a fleeting panic that this might mean he would have to remain earthbound as a ghost, the next moment he was 'through the wall' and in free flight towards the 'other-worldly' dimension.

We may also recall how George Ritchie, besides 'thinking' himself cross-country a large portion of the way from Abilene, Texas to Richmond, Virginia, with the Being as 'guide', almost literally 'dropped-in' on big industrial cities, finding himself 'seeing' through the fabric of the buildings into offices and homes. Shana, the Australian who found herself out of her body after 'dying' following a kidney operation in England, told Dr Cherie Sutherland: 'I could see my mother out in the hall of the hospital in Sussex, England, and I could see my father in Australia. I could see everybody I was connected to.'[8]

In the words of American experient Frank while telling Dr Kenneth Ring of his other-worldly encounter: 'It *has* to be out of time and space. It *must* be.'[9]

Furthermore, if we are treating seriously this idea that the other-worldly dimension is one in which time and space are simply not part of the equation, then it follows, even if this dimension doesn't particularly conform to our normal rules of logic, that there can be absolutely nothing anywhere which is not *known* once tapped into it. And indeed a significant number of near-death experients claim to have glimpsed this 'total' knowledge, even though, in contrast to the rest of their experience, they leave it behind when they return. For instance, as one American woman experient told Raymond Moody:

> [After my life review] it seemed that all of a sudden, all knowledge – of all that had started from the very beginning, that would go on without end – that for a second I knew all the secrets of all ages, all the meanings of the universe, the stars, the moon – of everything. But after I chose to return, this knowledge escaped, and I can't remember any of it.[10]

George Ritchie, it may be recalled, 'saw' all this same knowledge via the imagery of an enormous library 'the size of the whole University of Richmond', containing all 'the important books of the universe'. But he likewise returned without it. Dr Cherie Sutherland's Hal, the fourteen-year-old Australian who had his near-death experience on suffering a succession of cardiac arrests in his school playground, reported the same. He described his being shown around the other-worldly dimension by his deceased friend Tom:

> We went first into a big room and there was a corridor in front of us. It only seemed to be about twenty feet long,

but as we walked along there still seemed to be twenty feet to go. We kept on going and going. This corridor was alive – it was a living room. It had walls that went up about ten feet and then there were upper wall panels that leaned in towards us. These panels seemed to be beaming knowledge down on to me. As I went through, all this knowledge was coming to me. Everything that was known to mankind was in these archives and it was coming down into my mind. By the time I got to the end I felt I knew everything. But now I can't remember it!! When we finally were ready to leave, Tom said, 'Now I'm going to take all this knowledge away from you. You're not allowed to take that back.' I said, 'You can't take it away from me – it's all here in my mind.' I knew all languages, everything. He said to me, 'What's the word they use in Afghanistan for red?' I told him quite readily what the word was. Then he did something and I forget.[11]

With regard to languages, Cherie Sutherland has pointed out how one of Kenneth Ring's experients similarly described knowing all languages during his experience. In his words: 'I could hear languages. All languages. Languages that I had never heard before and I could understand them.'[12]

To which Sutherland has pertinently added:

I came across another interesting example of 'knowing everything' quite recently in an interview I did with a teenager who had her experience as a four-year-old child during a tonsillectomy. She described how, while she observed the operation, she felt such compassion for their ignorance. She felt that she, as the spirit of a four-year-old child, was so much wiser, knew so much more than they did.[13]

Now, if we may find this elusive all-knowingness even more difficult to believe than anything else that we have come across so far, we should immediately be made aware that there are in fact some surprisingly supportive indications that both near-death experients and those otherwise close to dying really do somehow 'see' into the future, and otherwise possess exceptional knowledge.

For instance, we noted in a much earlier chapter how tribal witch-doctors would 'call up' the dead to find out about future events. Of non-Westernized Australian aboriginals the anthropologist Ronald Rose wrote back in 1957, nearly two decades before Raymond Moody brought the phenomenon of near-death experience to public knowledge:

> Some strange beliefs have developed around the fact of dying. One, for example, is that the dying man becomes suddenly invested *with clairvoyant ability of the most extraordinary kind* [italics mine]. His last hours are likely to be filled by intense cross-examination on a wide variety of subjects.[14]

Many other tribal peoples around the world share the same beliefs, and that this is not all just superstitious nonsense finds the most authoritative confirmation in a major study of terminal illness in the elderly that was carried out in the early 1960s by the British physicians A. N. Exton-Smith and M. D. Cantaub. As they commented in the highly reputable medical journal *The Lancet*:

> Seven patients had a premonition of death and this was communicated to nurses by such remarks as 'Goodbye, I'm going' an hour before death. Another thanked the staff nurse who was doing the medicine rounds for all she had done, and said that she would not need tablets anymore after tomorrow. A man with congestive heart failure thanked all the nurses for their attention the day before his death, and a woman with rheumatoid arthritis, half an hour

before she died, asked that her friend should be summoned. *There is no doubt that these patients became aware that they were about to die, but the manner in which this knowledge was imparted to them could not be ascertained* [italics mine].[15]

Across the other side of the Atlantic very similar experiences have been reported by Dr John Hunter Phillips, professor of medicine at Tulane University in the United States. As he wrote in *Caring for the Dying Patient and his Family*:

I became interested in the mechanism of death in the elderly while serving in the nursing home, particularly in those patients who predicted that their death was imminent. They would say, 'I'm ready to die' and there was very little the physician could do to prevent it. There was usually no obvious lethal disease process evident at the time, the electrocardiogram might be normal, the chest X-ray normal, the screening blood tests all normal, and yet death would occur, usually within 24–48 hours once the positive statement was made. This made me very uneasy, and continues to make me uneasy when I sign the death certificate under the 'cause of death'.[16]

Although Phillips went on to say that he did not know '*why* they died', he might more accurately have phrased this that he did not know why the patients knew with such assurance *when* they would die.

And if we object that these were mostly elderly people to whom it would have been quite obvious that their allotted life-span was already running very short, the American paediatrician Dr Melvin Morse of the Children's Orthopaedic Hospital, Seattle, has noted what a senior nurse, Rosemarie Guadagnini, told him of a three-year-old child patient of hers named Toby:

When ... checked into the hospital where Rosemarie worked in New York City [Toby] was in remission from leukaemia and was in the hospital [just] for a check-up. One day in the playroom he began to tell Rosemarie about a recent dream. The dream, he said, told a story about a trip. Curious, she asked him to draw a picture of it. With crayons he drew a picture that was dark blue and grey on the left side. On the right he drew pictures of yellow and white flowers, bright birds, and a variety of pets. 'Pretty soon I am going to a special place,' he said when the drawing was finished. On his way to the special place, Toby said, he would first have to pass through a world of darkness, which he pointed to in the left-hand side of his drawing. It wasn't scary, though, he told Rosemarie, especially since he knew the beauty that was waiting on the other side. 'When are you going there?' asked Rosemarie. 'I don't know for sure,' he told her. 'But it's going to be soon, and I'll like it there.' Within a week Toby died.[17]

Notable here is that the vehicle of Toby's premonition was a dream, reminding us of what we learned earlier of the importance that ancient and tribal peoples ascribed to communications of this kind. And if it might still be objected that as a leukaemia sufferer, even in remission, Toby might have expected to die very young, then this was most certainly not so in the case of ten-year-old Eryl Jones, youngest daughter of Trevor and Megan Jones of Aberfan, South Wales, in whose case no illness of any kind was involved, and a premonitory dream was again the vehicle by which she learned of her fate.

For Eryl was a pupil at Aberfan's Pantglas Junior School when on the morning of 21 October 1966 a huge coal tip that overhung the whole village suddenly shifted due to an undetected build-up of underground water. As this crashed down on to the school, Eryl and 127 of her fellow-pupils, together with sixteen adults, were all crushed and suffocated to death beneath a forty-foot depth of black rubble. In Eryl's case the particularly extraordinary circumstance was that she 'saw' the disaster, and her own death, via premonitory dreams. As subsequently attested by her parents in a signed statement prepared by their local minister, the Revd Glannant Jones:

> She [Eryl] was an attractive, dependable child, not given to imagination. A fortnight before the disaster she said to her mother, 'Mummy, I am not afraid to die.' Her mother replied: 'Why do you talk of dying, and you so young; do you want a lollipop?' 'No,' she said, 'but I shall be with Peter and June [her schoolmates].' The day before the disaster she said to her mother, 'Mummy, let me tell you about my dream last night.' Her mother answered gently, 'Darling, I've no time now. Tell me again later.' The child replied, 'No, Mummy, you *must* listen. I dreamt I went to school and there was no school there. Something black had come down over it!' The next day off to school went her daughter as happy as ever. In the communal grave she was buried with Peter on one side and June on the other.[18]

With regard to such clairvoyance among near-death experients, we noted in an earlier chapter how the Australian experient Grace told Dr Cherie Sutherland how she learned from her dead father that her not yet born baby would be a boy, and that her husband would leave her while the baby was still in his infancy, both of which predictions were duly fulfilled. From the USA Dr Kenneth Ring has quoted a strikingly similar case of a woman who temporarily 'died' during a difficult childbirth, and was told by a 'Voice' not only the baby's sex (again a boy), but also that he had a heart condition, from which he would recover.[19] When her doctor, still in the course of trying to deliver the baby, urged that he needed 'to hurry this thing up because this little thing is starting to do strange things', she was able to tell him that the problem was the baby's heart but, in her own words, 'that he [the baby] was going to be all right, that he was going to have the problem but he wasn't going to die'.[20]

As Kenneth Ring commented:

Her son did [indeed] have a heart problem, which cleared up spontaneously to the surprise of her physician. The presence [i.e. the Voice] also informed the mother that her son would be an unusual child, gifted with rare talents, and that her relationship with him would be especially close and different from that with her other children (she now has three). She has since informed me that all these things have come about.[21]

In another case quoted by the paediatrician Dr Melvin Morse of Seattle, a twenty-year-old Californian woman called Carla, undergoing investigative surgery for what became revealed as an extremely aggressive and most usually fatal cancerous tumour, had a near-death experience in which she was told by 'the Light': 'You will not die, Carla. You will live at least forty-five more years.' In the event, the tumour did indeed respond to the treatment and eventually disappeared, though only time can tell whether Carla's predicted lifespan of at least forty-five years will hold true.[22]

There are many similar examples indicating an 'all-knowledge' time-and-space-transcending facility to whatever 'thought'-self is reached during the near-death experience. It is as if this 'self' exists at a level of our being normally reached only at crisis moments such as the imminence of death, which can and does transcend time and space. And a fascinating feature here is that this still hypothetical level may well help explain a little better a particularly well-observed yet baffling phenomenon normally supposed to be quite unrelated – that of so-called 'telepathy' between twins.

As is well known, there are numerous well-attested stories of one twin uncannily feeling the other's pain if the latter has been involved in an accident at perhaps hundreds of miles' distance. To take just one example, in his book *Parallels – A Look at Twins*, Ted Wolfner noted the case of one of twin girls rushed to hospital suffering from acute appendicitis. When her family returned home, they found the other twin writhing in agony, even though in her case there was no physical cause.

Now while in this instance adherents of the Susan Blackmore-type 'the brain is all there is to us' hypothesis can always argue that since the second twin knew of the first twin's plight, some degree of sympathetic shamming cannot be ruled out, this explanation is totally inadequate for the now well-documented cases of twins and even triplets who have been separated at birth, who have never been told that they were a twin, let alone of each other's existence, yet between whom there has continued a most uncanny *knowledge* of each other, albeit at a level quite different from that of the normal consciousness.

In one particularly spectacular example, boy triplets were born in 1961 to the same North American mother, and were immediately separated for adoption purposes, growing up in three separate families, totally unknown to each other, as Bobby Shafran, Eddy Galland and David Kellman.[23] In 1977 and 1978, and still quite unknown to each other, all three underwent psychiatric treatment because each felt that there was something missing in his life, without having any idea what this could be. Neither they nor their adoptive families had been told that they were separated triplets, and the respective psychiatrists each put it down to the fact of their having been adopted, even though all three boys had been brought up in loving and supportive families.

Then in September 1980 Bobby began attending a college in New York State, to find himself repeatedly mistaken for a mysterious someone called Eddy, who he learned had been a student at the same college the previous year. When another student who had known Eddy arranged for him and Bobby to meet, the moment of revelation came. As Bobby recalled of the moment, after a three-hour drive, as Eddy opened the door to him:

> I said, 'Oh, my God' – and simultaneously saw myself saying, 'Oh, my God.' I scratched my head – and saw myself scratching my head. I turned away, and saw myself turning away. Everything in unison, as though professional mimes were doing this. We started shaking hands, and wound up hugging.[24]

Subsequent newspaper publicity brought to light the third triplet, David, with whom there was a similarly extraordinary reunion. All three said in unison, 'I can't believe this!' followed by the equally simultaneous, 'I can't believe you said that!' before falling into each other's arms.

Typically, David, Bobby and Eddy were found to share a whole series of characteristics, from smoking the same brand of cigarettes to enjoying wrestling, Italian food and the company of older women. But for us the really significant feature is that *something* of each of them *knew* of the others' existence across physical space, and pined for this bond to be realized in their lives.

That this was no one-off freak occurrence is demonstrated by another example, this time from the UK, concerning twin sisters Bridget Harrison and Dorothy Lowe, who again were separated only weeks after their birth in 1945, and who knew absolutely nothing of each other's existence for the first thirty-four years of their lives. Then when they were reunited in 1979, not only did they each quite independently turn up to the meeting with seven rings on their hands, and two bracelets on one wrist and a watch and a bracelet on the other, in addition it emerged that:

Both women took piano studies to the same grade, then stopped after the same exam.
Both had had meningitis.
Both had cats called Tiger.
Both collected soft, cuddly toys (both gave each other teddy bears at their reunion).
Both are avid readers of historical novels, Dorothy of Catherine Cookson, Bridget of Caroline Marchant (Catherine Cookson's other pen name).
Dorothy named her son Richard Andrew. Bridget called hers Andrew Richard.
Dorothy called her daughter Catherine Louise. Bridget called hers Karen Louise (Bridget had actually wanted to call her daughter Catherine but changed it to Karen to please a relative).
Both wore almost identical wedding dresses and carried the same flowers.
Both chose the same perfume.
Both were anxious about their legs being too thin.
Both described themselves as short-tempered, strict with their children, impulsive.
Both liked hockey and netball at school.
Both chose the same make of washing machine.
Both described themselves as snobby.[25]

Most extraordinary of all, both twins had started a diary for the very first time in 1960, had purchased the very same make, type and colour of diary, and had filled in entries (which were inevitably different), for the very same days, leaving the identical others blank.

What cannot be stressed enough here is that mostly such parallels cannot be explained by genetics. The inference must be that there is some mental level, beyond the normal consciousness, in which the two minds *are linked as if there is no spatial distance between them*. And arguably it is exactly this same level that is tapped more consciously by the near-death experient and by the truly dying person when he or she, during the 'other-worldly' phase, 'sees' backwards and forwards in time, and effortlessly makes contact with someone spatially at perhaps many thousands of miles' distance.

Does any of this even remotely make scientific sense? Certainly not so long ago it would have all seemed totally incompatible with the so-called 'immutable' laws of physics as they were then understood, which held that there could be nothing 'outside' time and space. Time was something that was real and precisely measurable. It always ran 'forwards' in a straight line, and the universe was confined to what could be detected by scientific instruments.

All this has changed with the recent concepts of 'black holes', 'worm holes' in space, backwards causality, positive entropy, negative mass, imaginary mass, and much else that I do not personally even begin to comprehend, (thankfully, nor, it would seem, do even the experts). Such is the uncertainty, particularly in the light of recent findings that the fabric of the universe is around twice as old as other calculations suggest it to be, that there is now increased cogency to remarks such as Professor Stephen Hawking's that there may be much to be learned from the mathematical concept of notably directionless 'imaginary time' in which the normal distinctions between time and space disappear. In Hawking's words, it is a real possibility that:

so-called imaginary time is really real time, and . . . what we call time is just a figment of our imaginations. In real time, the universe has a beginning and an end at singularities that form a boundary to space-time and at which the laws of science break down. But in imaginary time, there are no singularities or boundaries. So maybe what we call imaginary time is really more basic, and *what we call real is just an idea that we invent to help us describe what we think the universe is like* [italics mine].[26]

However difficult this may be to take in, it finds echoes in many of the near-death experients' remarks that the 'reality' that they glimpsed during their 'other-worldly' state was actually 'realer' than the 'living' world that those of us in it so confidently call reality. Which leads us to the one part of philosopher Sir Alfred Ayer's near-death experience that he managed to bring back to normal waking consciousness, a part more in the nature of a parabolic dream than anything familiar from the normal run of near-death experiences. As Ayer began: 'I was confronted by a red light, exceedingly bright and also very painful even when I turned away from it. I was aware that this light was responsible for the government of the universe.'

Notably this cannot be the same 'light' reported by the general run of near-death experients, which is never normally described as red and most certainly never causes pain to whatever 'eyes' may observe it. Ayer continued:

Among its [the light's] ministers were two creatures who had been in charge of space. These ministers periodically inspected space and had recently carried out such an inspection. They had, however, failed to do their work properly, with the result that space, like a badly fitting jigsaw puzzle, was slightly out of joint. A further consequence was that the laws of nature had ceased to function as they should. I felt that it was up to me to put things right. I also had the motive of finding a way to extinguish the painful light. I assumed that it was signalling that space was awry and that it would switch itself off when order was restored. Unfortunately, I had no idea where the guardians of space had gone and feared that even if I found them I should not be able to communicate with them. It then occurred to me that whereas, until the present century, physicists accepted the Newtonian severance of space and time, it had become customary, since the vindication of Einstein's general theory of relativity, to treat space-time as a single whole. Accordingly I thought I could cure space by operating upon time. I was vaguely aware that the ministers who had been given charge of time were in my neighbour-hood and I proceeded to hail them. Either they did not hear me, or they chose to ignore me. I then hit upon the expedient of walking up and down, waving my watch, in the hope of drawing their attention not to my watch itself but to the time which it measured. This elicited no response. I became more and more desperate, until the experience suddenly came to an end.[27]

The fascinating aspect of all this is that if anyone wants to look for evidence of a sense of humour in the other-worldly dimension, then this seems to be it. Here we have the English-speaking world's arguably number one atheist philosopher finding himself, in the one 'vivid' memory of his near-death experience that he was left with, in a universe of an order completely alien to what he supposes this should be. Accordingly the only interpretation that he can come to is that everything must have gone wrong with time and space, and that it is up to him, Sir Alfred Ayer, to put it right.

So, upon his clearly perceiving that these poor dumb

Beings do not even have the power of speech, we find Sir Alfred heroically taking it upon himself to walk up and down among them waving his watch, rather like a pin-stripe-suited businessman trying to hail a London taxi amidst a tribe of naked Amazonian Indians. Except that he simply could not convey to these poor dumb 'savages' that the fine scientific instrument he was holding was the key to the universe, and that they really needed to try to understand this in order to get their lives back on to ordered, 'civilized' lines. So was the laugh really upon the 'savages', or upon Sir Freddy? The sad irony is that so far as anyone can tell of the few months that subsequently remained of his life following his near-death experience, his proud conviction of his own superior intelligence blinded him from seeing the correct interpretation of his own 'dream'.

All this, however, has been but an aside to help us try to gain at least some glimpse of the 'out-of-time', 'out-of-space' backdrop against which the thought-dimension we have been postulating should be viewed. Altogether more important is what the near-death experience is really all about – seemingly the most powerful lesson from the timeless, spaceless other-worldly level concerning how life in *this* world should be conducted, a lesson which the near-death experient is expected to take back and apply to whatever remains of his or her earthly life.

Not least of the many paradoxes concerning this level is that in one respect at least it exhibits a very strong awareness of earthly time. Almost to a man or woman, every experient who has had a foretaste of the 'other-worldly' dimension, reports either being told, or hearing from within themselves, words along the lines of 'You must go back. It is not your time yet . . .'

Altogether more fascinating, however, is what has changed about them when they do indeed 'go back' . . .

181

Chapter 9

A Transforming Experience

There is one common element in near-death experiences: they transform the people who have them.

Dr Raymond Moody

It is part and parcel of near-death experiences that those who undergo them return to life to tell their tales. Indeed, this is what distinguishes them from those who show signs of having much the same experience during their true dying moments.

As the pivot for their returning to life, some experients specifically describe having reached a barrier beyond which, they are given to understand, there can be no 'going back'. Sometimes, even for them to touch or take the hand of someone from the 'other side' can be understood to be a point of no return. But where the barrier takes the form of a visual image the variations by which experients 'see' this one compared to another clearly indicate, as in the case of every other 'other-worldly' image that we have come across, that it is merely a convenient symbol rather than the barrier's 'real' appearance.

Thus for Englishwoman Eleanor Cleator, the barrier was 'a low green trellis fence' with a gap in it which she could 'so

easily have gone through' into a beautiful landscape.[1] Likewise, one of Dr Michael Sabom's American cardiac arrest
patients saw a fence separating 'this side's' parched scrubland
from the 'other side's' 'beautiful pasture ... with in the
distance ... beautiful trees, beautiful grass and horses'.[2]
Australian experient Patrick saw a wall which some people
seemed to 'sshhooo straight through',[3] but which seemed to
act as a barrier for him, while Englishman W. C. Ball saw a
wall with a gate in it beyond which he could see, in his
words, 'my late grandparents on my father's side and an
uncle who died before I was born'.[4]

Rivers and streams are another commonly imaged 'barrier', as in the case of the Australian experient Hal who saw a
stream the other side of which were some of his deceased
relatives encouraging him to cross, something he found he
was unable to do – apparently, it seemed to him, because he
'was in another dimension'.[5] Likewise an American widow
told Dr Michael Sabom that she saw her deceased husband
wading across a stream to meet her, and felt that she only
had to take his hand to join him.[6] Sir Alfred Ayer, it will be
recalled from the previous chapter, spoke of trying 'to cross
the river'. And to anyone with a knowledge of classical
mythology this will inevitably call to mind the ancient
Greeks and their belief that the River Styx, with its ferryman
Charon, represented the border between this world and the
next. This river image is also equally strong among modern-
day Japanese.[7]

Doors are yet another common 'barrier' image, as in the
case of a young Englishman, D. M. Cook, 'killed' in a motor-
cycle accident in the former Rhodesia, who described being
offered a choice of going through either of two doors, one to
his right temptingly having 'the white light' behind it, the
other to his left being that by which he knew he would
return to earthly life.[8] The barrier can even be represented by

buttons. An American girl, Michelle, was offered the choice of pushing either a red or a green button, the latter being the one that would bring her out of a diabetic coma.[9] For Englishwoman Gillian McKenzie, the buttons were none other than those on the old-style coin boxes once used in British public telephone boxes. In her own words:

> I saw an old-fashioned phone-box. I thought, if I press Button B I will get my money back, but I will have to stay with Grandpa. So I pressed Button A and I heard Hamish [Gillian's husband] saying 'Hello, hello' and then I came round.[10]

Even from just this last example it ought to be evident that the visual aspect of the 'barrier' is at best only a symbol by which each experient makes his or her seemingly free decision between either going on into full and final death, or returning to life. And here the emphasis needs to be on *seemingly* a free decision, since the decision-making process itself, and determining who it is who makes the choice, can be a very subtle one from any 'this-worldly' point of view. Thus Avon Pailthorpe, the Englishwoman who had her near-death experience when her car crashed in the fast lane of a motorway (see previous chapter), felt herself to be the focus of a very lively debate between other-worldly presences, with the outcome of this one completely beyond her control. In her words:

> They [other-worldly Beings] were debating whether I should go back. I knew that I had absolutely no responsibility to make any decision. This was an almost unknown situation for me, and it was wonderfully liberating. I also knew that I could not influence what decision I made, but that whatever it should be it would be right.[11]

More commonly, however, the experient feels himself or herself to have a choice of sorts, with the 'other-worldly' stance, whether this may come from the Being or Beings, or from deceased relatives, ranging from one very gently in favour of their staying on in the 'other-worldly' dimension, to one very firmly against their doing so, depending on individual circumstances. As an example of the former, English nurse Mrs M. D. Drury, who 'died' from terrible head injuries after being completely unexpectedly attacked by her husband with a seven-pound lump hammer, told Peter and Elizabeth Fenwick:

> These people [i.e. the other-worldly beings] . . . wanted me to stop fighting and stay with them; I had achieved what I was sent to do. They recalled many of the good things I had done through my life and informed me of the comfort I had given to many of the patients who had died whilst in my care. They also mentioned the wrong things I had done in my life. When I insisted that I must return and gave my reasons they assured me that all I had to do would be done from where I was. At one point they told me to look down at myself. I was warned of the disabilities I would have to overcome as well as the pain I would have to endure, which would be worse than I had ever experienced. I said I still wished to return. They assured me that they would give me as much support as possible but the recovery was up to me and that I would have to live with what I achieved . . . Although it sounds as though I was arguing with these other people . . . I was not and neither were they. We were all very calm and talked very peacefully.[12]

As another example, Gillian McKenzie's deceased grand-father, we may recall, seemed to be expecting Gillian to stay with him, until told by her with her characteristic forthrightness: 'Grandpa, I can't . . . I've just had a son and Hamish has just got a new job and he won't be able to cope with the new baby.'[13] Likewise Dr Cherie Sutherland's informant Jennifer, upon being greeted by her great-grandmother with 'Take my hand, I've come to show you the way . . .' felt obliged firmly to respond 'Oh, I'd love to come with you, Great-grand-mother, but I can't go now, because Mum needs me and she's got no one to look after her but me.'[14]

From the opposite viewpoint, among the many examples of those positively told to go back – a return generally agreed to only with extreme reluctance – may be cited that of Dr Cherie Sutherland's Grace, who said of her 'debate' with her dead father: 'I said "Dad, I don't want to go!" He said, "You have to go. You must go back. You're going to have a son, and you have to bring this boy up by yourself."'[15]

Likewise a seventeen-year-old American girl, Cindi, told Dr Melvin Morse: 'My dead grandfather . . . came to help me. He was a very religious man. He took me by the hand and said, "Go back to your body. You have work to do."'[16]

And another American experient told Dr Raymond Moody: 'Instantly from the other side appeared my Uncle Carl, who had died many years earlier. He blocked my path, saying, "Go back. Your work has not been completed. Go back now."'[17]

By now the percipient reader may well be already suspecting some significance in the repetitious 'I have things I still want to do' from those who opt to go back, and 'You have work to do' to those who would have preferred to stay in the 'other-worldly' dimension. However, even more self-evident as an illustration of what seems to be going on here is a case quoted in unusual fullness by Raymond Moody, in his first book *Life after Life*.

This concerned an American called Jack whose violent coughing from bronchial asthma and emphysema had ruptured a disc in his lower spine, requiring surgery to alleviate his pain. This was highly risky, however, because of the effect of the anaesthetics upon his already badly damaged lungs. While desperately awaiting this operation, Jack had a most 'vivid and real' visitation by 'the Light', warning him that the operation would indeed prove fatal but that he was not to be afraid. (Here we may be reminded of the pre-death premonitions described in the last chapter, see pages 170–74.

Trying his best to adjust to this as calmly as possible, Jack nevertheless felt extremely worried about leaving his wife to soldier on alone with the burden of a problematic young nephew whom they had adopted. Accordingly, the day before his operation he decided to write them both farewell letters explaining his concerns, intending that they should find these only after his death. Then, in his own words:

After I had written two pages of the letter to my wife, it was just as if the floodgates had opened. All at once, I broke into tears, sobbing. I felt a presence, and at first I thought maybe I had cried so loud that I had disturbed one of the nurses, and that they had come in to see what was the matter with me. But I hadn't heard the door open. And again I felt this presence, but I didn't see any Light this time. And thoughts or words came to me, just as before. And he said, 'Jack, why are you crying? I thought you would be pleased to be with me.' I thought, 'Yes, I am, I want to go very much.' And the Voice said, 'Then why are you crying?' I said, 'We've had trouble with our nephew, you know, and I'm afraid my wife won't know how to raise him. I'm trying to put into words how I feel, and what I want her to try to do for him. I'm concerned, too, because I feel that maybe my presence could have settled him down some.' Then the thoughts came to me, from this presence, 'Since you are asking for someone else, and thinking of others [italics mine], not Jack, I will grant what you want. You will live until you see your nephew become a man.' And just like that, it was gone.[18]

To the amazement of his doctors, Jack got through his operation without any difficulties, and was still very much alive three years later when interviewed by Raymond Moody. However, the real fascination of his case is that what had seemingly been a cut-and-dried 'other-worldly' decision that he should die was reversed specifically because his concerns about his dying were for its effects upon others, rather than upon himself.

If we may be inclined to discard this as just a one-off instance of unusual selflessness, in fact, when we look at other near-death experients, we find time and again that their reasons for 'going back' are either because of work that they themselves have wanted to continue to do for others in the land of the living, or because of their being instructed, perhaps because of being still very young, that they had such work still to do.

Thus as we replay in our minds some of the sentiments that we have heard from experients, we hear:

Australian 'Jennifer': 'Oh, I'd love to come with you, Great-grandmother, but I can't now *because Mum needs me* and she's got no one to look after her but me.'
Englishwoman Gillian McKenzie: 'Grandpa, I can't stay here. I've got to get back. I've just had a son and Hamish has just got a new job and *he won't be able to cope* with a new baby.'
Australian 'Grace's deceased father: 'You have to go, you must go back, you're going to have a son, and *you have to bring this boy up by yourself.*'

American Cindi's deceased grandfather: 'Go back to your body. *You have work to do.*'

Right across the world, we find a quite overwhelming proportion of near-death experients expressing their binding commitment to much the same loving concern for others in a way that is often quite 'out of character' with the person they had been previously. Thus Australian Shana, who had her experience when a kidney operation went wrong, told Dr Cherie Sutherland: 'The one thing I got when I was up there was that my task was to serve, that the only purpose for humans is to serve the planet and to live life absolutely to the fullest.'[19]

Likewise fellow-Australian Laurel Lloyd-Jones: 'I noticed that there's been a change in me. There was a complete change in my attitude to the people looking after me. I'd brought back a touch of that love, and it's stayed with me.'[20]

And Englishwoman Mrs Audrey Quinn: 'Since my near-death experience I find I have become more sympathetic to other people's problems. I have become a Samaritan, hoping to help others in some small way.'[21]

From among Dr Kenneth Ring's American experients we hear: 'I try to help people more than I ever did before. That might always have been part of my nature, but now I realize that I *want* to help.'[22] And: 'It [the near-death experience] has given me tolerance. It's made me less judgmental.'[23]

Likewise an Illinois salesman told Dr Michael Sabom: 'I feel that we are measured a great deal by what we do for others. That we're all put here to help one another . . . The greatest law that we have is love.'[24]

Expressed in statistics that can only offer the crudest guide, no fewer than twenty-nine out of a sample of thirty-seven Australians interviewed by Dr Cherie Sutherland expressed a markedly increased desire to help others in the wake of their near-death experience.[25] And twenty-three out of a sample of twenty-six American experients interviewed by Dr Kenneth Ring felt the same.

But these are just the headlines, however, to far more in-depth 'radically altered life values' stories within each individual that comparatively few near-death experience researchers have sufficiently recognized or explored in proper depth, with the notable exception of Australia's Dr Cherie Sutherland.

Of these, one frequently recurring expression, for instance, is the experient's very marked sloughing-off of any concern for external appearances, for 'what people may think', and for future security. Thus Michael, the Australian who had his near-death experience on very nearly drowning in a surfing accident when he was fifteen, told Dr Cherie Sutherland:

> I used to worry a lot. I used to have to wear the right clothes, puff out my chest for the girls, all that sort of thing. But I don't now. Vanity's gone out of the window completely . . . I don't dress up or anything. I have a pretty laid-back attitude. I just sort of think that where I am now and what I am doing now is just sort of a passing moment of time, so impressing someone else doesn't really matter.[26]

Likewise an American fireman, who had his experience at the age of thirty-five, told Dr Michael Sabom:

> I used to worry about life and living it and trying to get ahead, trying to make life easier by working harder to make more money to make life easier. I don't do that no more . . . I just live from day to day . . . You can't live a day in advance or a day behind. You can only live for the day you're living.[27]

Almost invariably accompanying such abandonment of worrying about everyday living is a proportionate confident abandonment of any concerns about dying. As another Australian, Christina, told Dr Cherie Sutherland, 'Now I have no fear of death! Now I know that I'm not the body ... When you die it's not the whole of you that dies.'[28]

As one American told Dr Raymond Moody, 'Since this experience, I don't fear death. Those feelings vanished. I don't feel bad at funerals any more. I kind of rejoice at them . . .'[29]

And Englishwoman Eleanor Cleator told Peter and Elizabeth Fenwick: 'If that [her near-death experience] was "near death" I have no fear when my time for dying comes. I look forward to it with expectation of that wonderful joy and peace.'[30]

Cherie Sutherland has estimated that some 98 per cent of the experients she interviewed had lost their fear of dying, and although other researchers found slightly lower percentages, undoubtedly the proportion among all cases is extremely high.

Closely related to this may be a marked drop-off in what may previously have been strong enthusiasm for the pursuit of success and the acquisition of material goods and possessions that is so often considered the norm in developed Western society. For instance, a formerly acquisitive American woman experient told Dr Kenneth Ring: 'I feel totally different about home, house – material things. They're so unimportant to me.'[31]

Australian Shana told Dr Cherie Sutherland: 'I'm not at all motivated by material success now – it doesn't worry me at all. Sometimes I have it and sometimes I don't have it, and I don't care which way it is.'[32]

Englishman John Hunt, former general secretary of the

Institute of Incorporated Photographers, said of the aftermath of his experience, following a cardiac arrest:

> My sense of values has altered completely . . . Materialism
> to me is an evil thing. I see the evils of the expense account.
> I'm not the slightest bit impressed by the £40,000 car.
> Things like Rolls-Royces don't mean a thing.[33]

Instead, it is appreciation of the natural world and its wonders that experients find greatly enhanced. As John Hunt
specifically went on to say: '[Now] I enjoy the trees and being
by the sea – things Nature has to offer which before I'd never
even noticed.'[34]

Likewise, from among Cherie Sutherland's Australian
informants, Patrick remarked: '[Now] I really appreciate
nature. It's wonderful! Even the smallest bug, the way it's
painted, the way it moves – it's incredible!'[35]

Part and parcel of this greater appreciation of nature may
involve the experient now preferring his or her own company; of getting away from crowds and being on their own.
As an American who had previously looked to be with his
friends at any opportunity told Dr Kenneth Ring: 'I enjoy my
solitude a lot more now. I enjoy being alone. I've learned to
respect my time alone and get something out of it. Life is
very valuable.'[36]

And Australian Alexandra, who had formerly been a
doctor, told Dr Cherie Sutherland:

> I wanted more solitude [following my near-death experi-
> ence], I didn't want to rush back into medicine . . . I never
> bought that whole medical trip again . . . And that was
> pretty dramatic because I was then a very loyalist dyed-in-
> the-wool doctor. I withdrew from everyone, even from my
> mother for a time.[37]

If all these changes may have seemed ones 'for the good', it immediately needs to be stressed that such after-effects have not necessarily always been welcomed by those who were the experients' previous nearest and dearest. Despite the experients' very sincere new greater lovingness towards all humanity, this can not uncommonly put the severest strain on closer family relationships.

Thus Howard Storm's wife, it may be recalled from Chapter 7, very nearly left him after his experience because the entirely new 'I've found God' individual whom he had become was virtually a stranger to her. Dr Cherie Sutherland told me very frankly regarding her own personal near-death experience that she was so profoundly changed by this that her then husband felt she was no longer the same woman he had married, and she regards this as having contributed significantly to their subsequent divorce. American experient Barbara Harris, pointing out how the experient's loss of interest in material possessions can come extremely hard for any non-experient partner, admitted: 'My new sense of oneness and love for the planet became a wall in my marriage.'[38]

Although by no means all marriages are blighted in this way, nevertheless Dr Cherie Sutherland found that of her married Australian experients, some 36 per cent went on to divorce their partners sometime following their near-death experience, a statistic which is certainly no better than the average divorce rate throughout Australia.[39] And there is every likelihood that this pattern also holds good in other developed societies in which near-death experiences occur.

Nor is it only marital relationships that can come under such strains. Parents, too, may find themselves quite unable to relate to their offspring's changed values, as in the case of an American woman called Sue who had her near-death experience as a result of attempting suicide. As she told researcher Mori Insinger of the University of Michigan:

> My parents – my dad – you can't talk to him anyway. He's got three subjects: golf, money and Florida. They're retired, but that's all he's lived for. So I have never tried to talk to him about my near-death experience, and I won't ever try, and my mum, she doesn't even believe in it . . . [40]

Similarly Englishwoman Jane Dyson, who 'died' in intensive care following a very serious car accident, found anyone but her most immediate family almost unbearable. As she told Peter and Elizabeth Fenwick:

> Since recovering from my injuries I have found it very difficult to relate to people apart from my daughters and grandchildren. The rest irritate me so much I could shout at them. They all seem so concerned with trivial matters, which to me are not important. I have almost a feeling of disdain, which I know is unfair. [41]

Yet to attribute such profound changes in near-death experients' life values simply to their having 'found religion' would be very wide of the mark. While many experients would describe the change in them as 'spiritual', this does not necessarily mean their having become drawn towards the world of organized religion as such: indeed, rather the reverse. Thus as we hear from Anthea, an Australian interviewed by Dr Cherie Sutherland:

> Before I would have seen myself as a Protestant, but now I feel less that organized religion has the answers. Today I believe more in spirituality, and I don't feel it has to be

labelled. I feel more that the answers come from within your own being.[42]

And likewise from two American experients interviewed by Dr Kenneth Ring:

[Before I was] fairly religious, but in a superficial way. I was more or less caught up in the ritual and the trappings of religion. And afterwards, for the short period after, I realized that the ritual and all that really meant nothing. It was the faith and the deep down meaning that was of importance.[43]
I'm not such a follower of the church anymore. Like they say, 'You have to do this; you have to do that.' I don't do that. Because I have to do what *I* think is right now. I rely more on my feelings than on their commands. I don't believe in their commands.[44]

Nor can it seriously be maintained that this is just a fleeting change of outlook that quickly returns to normal, as in the case of those 'saved' in the heat of Billy Graham-style evangelical meetings, who all too often relapse to their old ways very quickly afterwards. In fact, near-death experients only comparatively rarely relinquish their new-found life values, more usually vividly retaining both the memory of their experience and their adherence to all that went with it, throughout the rest of their lives.

So the root questions arise: What can have 'got into' near-death experients that they have been so profoundly changed? How could they so suddenly and so completely about-turn on all the beliefs that they have previously held about the way they should conduct their lives? And most particularly, where on earth should such radically different life values have sprung from?

Oddly, while to the best of my knowledge no writer on near-death experiences has ever explicitly pointed it out before, the answer ought to be blindingly obvious. For where before have we heard those life values as expressed by Dr Michael Sabom's salesman experient from Illinois (and also before him by George Ritchie), that the purpose of our lives is to help and serve others, and that the greatest law is love? Are we not reminded of a certain Galilean Jew who told the parable of the Good Samaritan (Luke 10: 29–37)? Who insisted on washing his disciples' dirty feet? And who taught men to love even their enemies (Matthew 5: 44)?

Recalling the lessons that George Ritchie and other life-review experients learned so painfully regarding their passing judgments on others and adopting 'holier-than-thou' attitudes, may we not find more than a faint echo of that same Galilean Jew's words, as given in his Sermon on the Mount? 'Do not judge, and you will not be judged; because the judgments you give are the judgments you will get, and the amount you measure is the amount you will be given' (Matthew 7: 1–2). Also: 'Take the plank out of your own eye first and then you will see clearly enough to take the splinter out of your brother's eye' (Matthew 7: 5).

Mindful of the acquisitive American woman's so markedly revised sentiments regarding material possessions, are we not reminded of some more words from the Sermon on the Mount? 'Do not store up treasures for yourselves on earth, where moths and woodworms destroy them and thieves can break in and steal' (Matthew 6: 19)?

Remembering that American fireman's sentiments concerning living for the day rather than worrying about tomorrow, do these also not seem to be but a paraphrase of yet more words from the same source? 'Do not worry about tomorrow. Tomorrow will take care of itself. Each day has enough trouble of its own' (Matthew 6: 34).

And with regard to the young Australian surfer's avowed lack of further concern about wearing the right clothing to impress his friends and girlfriends, can we not again hear from the Sermon on the Mount, 'Why worry about clothing?' (Matthew 6: 28). Immediately following this in the same Sermon, we may note, is the exhortation: 'Think of the flowers growing in the fields; they never have to work or spin; yet I assure you that not even Solomon in all his regalia was robed like one of these' (Matthew 6: 28–30). Does not this bring back to mind English photographer John Hunt's remarks concerning his profound new love for all the things that Nature has to offer?

In short, it is as if every near-death experient, to a greater or lesser degree, has been 'down-loaded' (to use modern-day computer parlance) with every facet of the 'way to live' message that Jesus encapsulated in the Sermon on the Mount. Given this thinking, we may find it no surprise that Jesus, however much he was accredited with loving mankind, was also described as seeking out solitude at any opportunity (for example, Mark 1: 12; 1: 45; 9: 2; 14: 39), exactly like our modern-day near-death experients.

We might also suspect it to be rather more than coincidence that, just like the Being and others whom near-death experients encountered during their 'other-worldly' phase, Jesus is represented in the Gospels as being able to read thoughts. In the Gospel according to St Luke, for instance, when Jesus comes upon his disciples arguing amongst themselves concerning which of them is the greatest, he is specifically described as 'knowing what thoughts were going through their minds' (Luke 9: 47). Likewise, mindful of George Ritchie and Howard Storm's astonishment, if not horror, at the Being's reading of all their thoughts, we are specifically told that Jesus insisted that a man who harboured lustful thoughts for a woman was just as guilty of adultery as one who had actually committed the deed (Matthew 5: 28).

We may even find that the very same pressures undergone by experients in their subsequent relations with their nearest and dearest were ones that Jesus himself anticipated with his words that if anyone was forced to choose between living this message and staying on in his own household, then he, Jesus, had 'come to set a man against his father, a daughter against her mother, [and] a daughter-in-law against her mother-in-law' (Matthew 10: 35–6).

Yet the extraordinary paradox here is that only a surprisingly tiny minority of near-death experients have actually made the very equation that we have just done. In the course of their 'dying' they have seen themselves through different eyes. They have 'felt' all the hurt that their thoughts and actions (or lack of these) have inflicted upon others. And they have often very radically remodelled their lives accordingly. In doing so they have very dutifully followed Jesus's words: 'Always treat others as you would like them to treat you' (Luke 7: 12). Yet in terms of their actually attributing this whole new timbre to their 'new lives' as coming from him personally, this is not so. Just as many of those who encounter the Being find themselves extremely unsure whether he should be identified with Jesus, with God, or with someone else, so Jesus may go completely unrecognized as the author of their new values. Instead they may surprisingly commonly regard these as having come from 'within' themselves without any other agency, because to them the values seem so *instinctively* right, and that is all that now matters. This was clearly the case with the earlier quoted Kenneth Ring experient: 'I have to do what *I* think is right now. I rely more on my feelings than on their [any established church's] commands.'

It immediately needs to be stressed that for all anyone

knows, there may be nothing wrong with this lack of recognition, this disinclination to put an author's name to the newfound set of life values. After all, if the values in question are universal, why should they *belong* to any one historical individual, even to a Jesus of Nazareth? If the individual is following what he or she feels to be right in their heart, then why worry about from whom that voice in the heart might be coming?

But for us, trying to look at all this from the perspective of anyone still finding it extremely difficult to grapple with the idea that there might actually be life after death, it is supremely important. For upon a near-death experient's 'dying' it surely cannot be an accident that his or her whole mental perspective may become seemingly so instantaneously and so overwhelmingly fused with the life values of a Galilean Jew who in agnostic terms died once and for all nearly two thousand years ago. For so dramatic a transformation to happen to individuals who may previously have had no shred of religious belief, as in the case of Howard Storm, can surely only mean that someone, and from an order clearly not of this world, has been communicating with them. And if so, *who*?

Here we confront an issue inseparable from this book, and yet in a very real sense beyond it. For trying to tackle the question of whether or not there might be life after death is quite complicated enough already, without bringing in even bigger questions such as the existence of any deity. Even Sir Alfred Ayer, on his gracefully conceding (much to the chagrin of his fellow-humanists), that his near-death experience had 'slightly weakened' his previous conviction that there is no life after death, made clear his feeling that the two issues could and should be kept apart when he went on to stress that his 'conviction that there is no God' continued undiminished.

Yet to regard near-death experiences as *just* evidence for life after death, and hardly overwhelming evidence at that, is to miss the point of so much about them, a point that has all too often been glossed over in all previous serious books on the subject. That is, as we may be reminded from the cases of George Ritchie and Howard Storm, that if they are valid at all, then they are also demonstrations of contact with some dimension way beyond that of our earthly order – a dimension so sensational in its import, that it exceeds even the wildest schoolboy's dreams of meeting aliens from outer space.

So dare we bring the word 'God' into this? For one Australian couple who experienced their own extraordinary brush with the dimension in question, we would be more than failing in our duty if we even attempted to leave Him out . . .

Chapter 10

On Not Leaving God Out

George, God has entrusted you with enormous truths.
Mary Skeen Ritchie, stepmother of near-death experient
George Ritchie

Two decades ago, had anyone told Edwin and Laurel Lloyd-Jones that they would come to believe in life after death and the existence of God, and that they would dramatically change their lives for these reasons, they would have been laughed out of court. They had quite enough to occupy their lives bringing up their two children, looking after their very comfortable house in Beacon Hill, Sydney, keeping it up to date with all the latest technological gadgetries, and managing their flourishing dry-cleaning business.

So far as Laurel was concerned, even as a schoolgirl she had lost interest in anything that her former Sunday School religious instruction had taught her. When she was sixteen, and her sister, who was four years younger, lay critically ill, she had tried a prayer: 'If there's a God, please save my sister.' But when the sister died, in Laurel's words, 'The clanger came down. There is no God. There is nothing to believe in.' Edwin, for his part, had been almost totally repelled by his encountering the Welsh Methodist Church when he was only fourteen. 'Extremely hypocritical, quite negative and quite frightening,' are the adjectives he still uses of this. While he collected the usual offbeat magazine article as if nurturing a flicker that there just *might* be something, Laurel was more sanguine, admitting to 'delight in arguing against there being a God' whenever the topic came up during chatter with their more Christian-minded Sydney neighbours.

Then in April 1980 Laurel went into West Court private hospital in Sydney for a seemingly routine hysterectomy operation. She reacted badly to the anaesthetic, and went into cardiac arrest while still on the operating table. As the surgeons worked frantically to restart her heart she had the to us now familiar experience of looking down on her body and coming to the realization that she was 'dead'. Except this was not quite the shock that she might have expected. Although the moment she thought about Edwin and her children she found herself clearly able to 'see' them, to her surprise at 'herself' she felt no grief or sadness at the prospect of being separate from them. Because the very moment that the thought came to her she somehow equally swiftly 'knew' that she was *not* separate from them. In her words, so redolent of our deductions concerning 'time and space' and of all we learned from tribal peoples concerning their certainty of the proximity of their dead relatives:

> Time didn't exist [and] in that space there was no separation. It is only here that we are separate. And so my not wanting to come back did not seem to make me fearful or anything because I knew that there was no separation and that we would be together in no time.[1]

Next Laurel went into the now equally familiar 'tunnel' phase – except that to her it seemed more like going 'very fast' into 'a vast space' with 'a lot of coloured lights', rather than into any tunnel. Inexorably drawn to 'the Light', she stopped before this, feeling an 'immense sense of love, so huge that I can't even begin to describe it', combined with telepathically hearing the voice of someone whom, in her own words:

> I connected very much with my Creator, like a Christ-Being, though I couldn't say that it was Jesus. It was an instant recognition on some level. Not that I *saw* anyone to recognize. But it was a knowing on a heart level: Yes, I'm back with my God. Back with my Creator. Back with all love. Back with everything that's real. In a sense that *was* the real world.

As in the case of George Ritchie, Howard Storm and others, Laurel 'saw' her whole life replayed before her 'like running a video'. In her own words, she:

> saw lots of little things. But the thing that sticks out so clearly for me was *when I was denying God*. I was so shocked and horrified that I could have denied God's existence. Because in the presence of that love, in the presence of God, *there was just no doubting that God was real* [italics mine]. And yet in looking back at all the times that I had doubted that, and had long arguments [about it], there came up this total shame. And it was my deepest grief to think that I had denied God.

Just as we have found described by other experients, so Laurel, in her turn, felt the same 'all-knowing'. And amidst all this there came a simple message from the Being:

> *Now you'll believe in me* . . . I made you a woman, I created you. I know everything about you and I'm now going to send you back, because it's not your time to come over. You still have your life's work to do.

As Laurel was further told, she would have to wait to discover whatever this 'life's work' was going to be, though in the interim she should share her experience with Edwin and her children.

Meanwhile, Edwin was about to have an 'experience' of his own. Upon his visiting the hospital, the surgeon who had operated on Laurel was not available, and so he was not even told that she had temporarily 'died' during the operation. But he saw for himself that things had gone badly wrong. On his being allowed to Laurel's bedside she was still deeply unconscious, and as he recalled, 'She really looked like a corpse. And her hair, which was long at the time, was plastered down on her cheeks.' Very seriously concerned that he was about to lose her, he returned home to attend to the children, and then took a much-needed shower. And it was while he was doing so, washing his hair, with his eyes closed, and dejectedly replaying in his mind the corpse-like image that he had just seen of his wife, that in his words: 'I cracked up, and just wept. Deep, deep grief.'

The next moment he did something so out of character that it didn't even seem to come from himself at all. In his words:

I clenched my fist and struck it three times in the air. And I said, 'I believe! I believe! I believe!' And then the grief just lifted off me. And I had a very deep inner knowledge that she [Laurel] was OK. And I went to bed and had a good night's sleep. I rang the hospital and they said, 'Come in any time.'

As he went on:

The interesting thing – and it's beyond my comprehension – is that there was no early pre-pleading 'If there's a God, help, help, help!' It was just a clenched fist. And I *had* to say 'I believe! I believe! I believe!'

Along with Edwin himself, we will learn later the true meaning and significance of this episode, but meanwhile he duly hurried back to the hospital and was actually at Laurel's bedside when she recovered consciousness. As she has recollected this:

> I said to him, 'I died, didn't I?' At that stage he still hadn't spoken to the surgeon and he was quite startled to hear me say that. Not long after, the surgeon came in and said, 'You're very lucky to be with us. We nearly lost you. We did lose you for a while.' And I said, 'Yes, I know. I died, didn't I?' And he said, 'Yes, but how do you know?' I explained to him what I'd seen and heard.[2]

Particularly intriguingly to the surgeon, Laurel correctly described to him the dropping of a syringe during the time that her heart had stopped, so impressing him that he specially recommended her to read Raymond Moody's *Life after Life*.

As Laurel gradually recovered she shared more of her experience with Edwin and their children, and he shared his with her. Even so, the recuperation months were ones that she calls a 'twilight' time during which her old agnostic self-questioning kept resurfacing. In April 1982 she told one of the few friends in whom she confided at that time:

> I [now] really do believe in God. I have absolute faith that there is a purpose for us. But I don't relate to what the churches are telling us. I'm almost getting to the point of doubting that it even happened. Because what was the point of it?[3]

Two days later she received the answer. She was standing in the kitchen stirring a sauce for the family meal, and thinking to herself, 'What is it, God, that you want me to do?', when in her words:

> I just heard the same inner Voice that I'd been confronted with when I left my body during the near-death experience. That Presence of love came back and said, 'Pick up a pen and write down what you hear.' I thought I was going crazy, but after the third time of hearing it – 'Pick up the pen and write down what you hear' – I did it. And I started to ask questions. 'What is it that we are to do?' I was told that same afternoon that we were to go to the mountains in the south and make a place of rest and solace for many in the future.[4]

Underlining the reality of the whole experience was that it was just as if she was now hooked up to some 'hot-line' with the Being whom she had encountered when she had 'died'. In her words:

> It was incredible! Every time I wanted to ask something, there was the answer. I knew it was coming from something external to myself, but within myself, if you can understand. I had answers of a spiritual depth *that I knew wasn't me* [italics mine].[5]

Not without more than a few qualms about being believed, Laurel again shared her experience with Edwin. And while many a husband, told by his wife that a voice had told her that they had to sell everything and go to the mountains, might have begun dialling up the nearest psychiatrist, Edwin, mindful of his 'I believe!' experience in the shower, took her seriously. Although neither as yet knew exactly what was expected of them, nor where they were to go and when, this soon began to unfold.

First, one sunny Sunday afternoon that August, when they had been sitting together reading in the garden, Edwin asked Laurel to go inside and get the writing pad which she had begun using to write down whatever messages came to her. Edwin joined her and for a reason they still cannot account for both sat together on their staircase. The next moment, as recalled by Laurel:

> A spiral of energy . . . came boom into my heart area. I thought I was having a heart attack, it was so powerful . . . [as if] right through my body . . . Edwin looked at me. And he could see tears down my face. And he heard in his mind: 'Put your head on her shoulder.' And he did. He put his head on my shoulder, and felt this incredible energy coming through. And it was again just unadulterated love, pure love just pouring through. And it seemed as though it was opening up something in both of us, linking us. Because afterwards Edwin said, 'I said to myself, "Is this God?"' And at that moment he said he saw in his mind's eye: 'Edwin, Yes!' . . . And as we sat there, we both heard exactly the same message . . . *'You are as my disciples. I have called you to go to this place in the mountains'* . . . [Then], as we opened our eyes, there in front of us, in the corner of the room was this column of light. Sheer white light. We both saw it, and I remember saying to Edwin, 'I'll never ever doubt again.'

But as both admit, even then they did doubt again. And still there remained the nagging question of where and in what mountains they were supposed to go and when, to which Laurel, in her mental dialogues with the Being, initially only received the answer 'Don't worry ... you'll know soon enough.' Then she heard, 'Don't worry, it will all be different after you've seen the play.' As she instinctively enquired, 'What play?' she heard: 'It's a play with a man in it with a moustache, by the name of William. And there's also another man, who is a man of God. He will have a message for you, which will change your whole life.'

Three months later Laurel was serving on her own at the Lloyd-Joneses' dry-cleaning shop, attending to Rona Coleman, a professional actress who was one of their regular customers, when Rona mentioned that she was appearing in a musical being staged that week at Sydney's Ensemble Theatre. She urged Laurel to get tickets for herself and Edwin to see it. Initially Laurel made no connection between this musical and the play she had been 'told' about, and so her immediate, near-unthinking response was that she would 'talk to Edwin about it'. Then, moments after the actress had left the shop, Laurel heard her now familiar inner Voice telling her very clearly, 'Go and get the tickets!' Catching up with Rona in the car park, she arranged seats for herself and Edwin for the following Saturday evening.

Even before the show, however, a further extraordinary development took place. Laurel and Edwin were both at home, she upstairs in their kitchen, and he downstairs washing his hands, when suddenly he began to see something very strange happening to his hands. They began to turn a deep brownish colour. And as he looked at his fingers he seemed to be able to see the lines of all the veins and sinews and tendons, just as if he was looking at some form of colour X-ray. He called Laurel, only to find her already beside him. She had almost simultaneously heard her Voice telling her, 'Go downstairs, Edwin wants you.' And as the pair looked at Edwin's hands together, she recalls:

All the little veins and sinews were standing out. It was like looking through a high-powered magnifying glass. I just looked in amazement. Mine were perfectly normal. Then I just felt as though someone standing next to me gently took hold of my right hand and looked at it and put it under Edwin's hand. We both heard the same thing: 'Don't look at your hands, look at Edwin's.' Well, we both had goose bumps by this time, and his hands returned to normal before our eyes, and we just cuddled each other and we said, 'What on earth is all this about?'[6]

They did not have to wait for the answer for long. Because of visiting a sick friend, they were very nearly late getting to the theatre for Rona Coleman's play, and arrived only moments before curtain up. In Laurel's words: 'They handed me a programme as we rushed to our seats. As I opened the programme I said to Edwin, "You won't believe this, but this is about a man called William."'

Indeed it was. The production was *The Ballad of Billy Lane*, by George Hutchinson, based on the true story of William Lane, born in a gardener's hut in Bristol, England, who in July 1893 sailed from Sydney with 239 others to found a communist-style community in Paraguay, South America. And even while Laurel was settling into her seat there seemed something about the very air around her that convinced her that this was the play of which she had been told. As she whispered to Edwin: 'Can you feel the energy in the place? *It's so full of more than just the people here . . .*'

Seconds later the curtain rose to singing, and shortly after, there on the stage, played by actor Bill Conn, was 'William Lane', sporting a huge, handlebar moustache, just as Laurel had been 'told' by her Voice. At the same time as his entrance, the narrator described him as having 'heard an inner voice

209

which spoke to him', words that Laurel vividly remembers as having given her 'quite a jolt'. As she recalls of *The Ballad*'s story as performed before her and Edwin by Bill Conn, Rona Coleman and their fellow-actors:

> William Lane heard a voice. He wanted to go and set up a new form of community, which he did. And he was talking to people: 'We'll do it through sharing, and brotherly love and caring about each other.' And out into this window box above the stage came someone dressed as a priest depicted as a guardian angel. And he said: 'You'll fail, Billy. *You're leaving God out of it.*'

As Laurel remarked, 'By this time Edwin and I were both listening!' She went on:

> As it turned out, it [i.e. William Lane's brotherly love experiment] did fail. And the priest came out again and said, 'I told you you'd fail, Billy. You left God out of it.' In essence he was setting up a community very similar to what we were being told to do. William got really angry and said, 'Get out of my mind. You know I don't even believe in God. I can do it. I don't need you.' And the priest said, 'How can you *not* believe in God, who created you? Look at the universe. Look at the planets. And look at the stars. Look at nature. Look at a leaf. Look at a flower. And look at the beauty of it all.' And then he boomed out to Billy '*Look at your own hands! Look at the colour, look at the lines, look at the veins, look at the sinews! Who do you think made them?*'[7]

By then, as Laurel recalls, Edwin was already almost under his seat. But even more was to follow. For at this very point in George Hutchinson's play 'William Lane' very forcefully bangs his clenched fist three times, saying: 'I believe! I believe! I believe!' At that very moment Laurel and Edwin simultaneously came to understand why Edwin had said those very words that night of Laurel's 'death', upon his succumbing to such desolation and despair in the shower . . .

Indeed, for both Laurel and Edwin the play's realization of all that they had mentally 'heard' was near mind-blowing. In Laurel's words:

> I *think* we walked out of the theatre, I don't know. We went into the park next door to the theatre and stood and looked up at the sky and we just said, 'All right, God, we're prepared to listen. We realize now that you are talking to us.' And that was our definite one-hundred-per-cent proof. We knew that it solved something for us. Because we knew there was no logical reason why I should have been told about something that came out of an actor's mouth on the stage. *And it was all pre-planned.* And when we shared what'd happened with Rona, she said that the whole cast had been affected in doing that play. They felt they were being overlighted in what they did, and they got us to come back and talk to the cast about that experience. So that was the big clincher for us that made us commit our lives totally.[8]

And commit their lives totally Laurel and Edwin did. That very same night, while they were still reeling from the shock of it all, Laurel was suffering from a sore throat, and asked Edwin to pray on her behalf to the God who now seemed to be so near to them for some relief from this. Edwin comfortingly put his hands on her shoulders, and suddenly felt these quite involuntarily moved upwards to inscribe a circle a few centimetres above her head.

The next moment Laurel felt herself spiralling through her head and out of her body, just as she had during her near-death experience. Except that this time she was no longer in the same room as her body. Just as George Ritchie had found himself 'flying' over parts of the southern United States that he did not recognize, so she found herself 'flying' over hilly countryside that seemed quite unfamiliar to her. Below her there suddenly loomed into view a 'huge cliff-face' and a large expanse of water, like a lake or reservoir. As she came in closer she seemed to home into a valley through which ran a beautiful small river intermittently checked by gentle rapids. There were woods with many familiar Australian eucalyptus or gum trees. But there was also a grove of very European-looking trees. So where was she? And for that matter, how was she ever going to return to her body back in Beacon Hill, Sydney? As she recalls:

> Just when I started to get really afraid . . . I was *zoom* back in. As soon as the fear set in, that limited the whole experience and I was back in my body really fast. And I said to Edwin, 'I don't know where this place is, *but I'm sure I've just been shown the place we're going to.*'

Laurel recalls how during the following weeks she 'nagged God' for more information about the location of the place that she had been shown. Then, during one of her dialogue sessions, she was 'very clearly' given the name 'Tumut'. She was told 'It is out of Tumut, close to Tumut, yet it is remote.' So if it was so remote, she asked, was there even a house there, or would they have to build one? She heard: 'Yes, there's a little house on the top of a hill. The back of the house is to the east. The house looks down. There is a river, and a heavily wooded area on the other side.'

Laurel had never before even heard of Tumut, but she discovered from Edwin that it was a small town on the approaches to Australia's Snowy Mountains and Kosciusko National Park, over two hours' driving distance from Canberra, and a full day from their home in Sydney. He told her he had once briefly passed through it before they were married, but that was all he knew about it. Because of the demands of their dry-cleaning business they were unable to make any immediate visit. However, they decided to do this over the Christmas break, closing their shop from Christmas Day to the New Year, and leaving their children in the care of Laurel's mother, who made no bones about her opinion of their venture as being 'quite mad'.

So it was that on Boxing Day 1982 they arrived in Tumut and booked themselves into one of the town's motels. They tried looking at the notices of local properties for sale displayed in estate agents' windows, but because the agents' businesses were closed for the Christmas break there seemed little point. The only place that was open was the tourist office. Behind the counter the local tourism guide, Vera Roddy, initially looked completely blankly at them when they said that they were looking for some form of house in the mountains that might be suitable for converting into a retreat house. But then, as Laurel takes up the story again:

> I said to her: 'Look, a "friend" told me about this place near here. It's in a small valley. The hills come close around. And there are a lot of European trees, and a river flowing through it.' And I am trying to describe all this, and feeling very stupid . . . when at that very moment Vera said to me: 'What you are describing sounds like a place that I call "My Little Bit of Heaven". But I know the place is not for sale.' So we dismissed that one. But she said, 'Come back in the morning. I'll ring the people at the trout farm up in Goobarragandra Valley. Because it's a small enclosed valley, they might know of something for sale. I'll ring them tonight. You come back in the morning.'

That night, feeling very vulnerable and that Laurel's mother was probably absolutely right that their venture was 'quite mad', Laurel and Edwin prayed for guidance. According to Laurel the only words that came to her were: 'Just follow the signposts and you'll be shown the right place.'

The next morning, when they walked into the tourist office, Vera Roddy was beaming. She told them that Sandra Brown from the trout farm had walked into her office only ten minutes after they had left, saying that she had 'a funny feeling' that Vera was wanting to contact her. When Vera told her what Laurel and Edwin were looking for she recommended that they try driving along her Goobarragandra Valley road as there were indeed some properties for sale. For Laurel, even Sandra Brown's 'funny feeling' seemed a signpost, but this was as nothing compared to what followed. As Edwin drove along the only road leading through the valley, one bordered by fields and quaint farmsteads that might have come straight from his native Wales, they came to a large bend. From this Laurel, sitting in the passenger seat, found herself looking down over a large and very distinctive-looking cliff-face. She recognized it instantly as the one she had been 'shown' in her second out-of-the-body experience. Consulting the map they had been given by Vera, she also saw that the expanse of water she had 'seen from on high' must have been the Blowering Reservoir, with its Dam, though this was out of sight from their on-ground vantage-point. This seemed to be a second 'signpost' that they were heading in the right direction.

Driving on further, and now on to what had become a gravel road, they arrived at the Triton Trout Farm, where Sandra Brown greeted them and helpfully told them of a dairy farm that was for sale. Even from the meagrest details, however, this was clearly not what they were looking for. So Laurel again tried her story about the 'friend' who had told her 'about this place with European trees'. Just like Vera, Sandra recognized the description immediately. But again just like Vera, she assured them that there was absolutely no hope of the owners wanting to sell. She knew that they had only just won the right to develop the place as a holiday farm, having taken the local Council to the Supreme Court and won their case to do it. However she suggested that they at least go and see it anyway, as it was 'a really nice drive'.

Needing no further encouragement, Edwin and Laurel drove on, reaching a cattle-grid at the end of a rise, at which point Edwin quite unpromptedly stopped the car and turning to Laurel said to her very quietly, 'This is it, isn't it?' He insists that he could 'feel' that they had reached the right place. She assured him: 'Yes, I can feel it too.' And indeed as they drove on they came into the very same grove of 'European-looking' trees that Laurel had out-of-bodiedly 'seen'. There were some campers under the trees, and on Edwin and Laurel then asking where they could find the site's owners they were told: 'There's a little house at the top of the hill, up there.' Sure enough, partially hidden by all the trees, was what could only be that very same 'little house at the top of a hill' of which Laurel had been told when she was given the name 'Tumut'. Because it was indeed set up high, at the crown of a steep side-track, they had passed it by without noticing it. As Laurel takes up the story again:

> We got back in the car, drove it up the top of the hill, and got out. And I said to the owner, who was working outside, 'Excuse me. We are from Sydney, and we were just wondering if you were interested in selling this property?' And his mouth dropped open at that point. He said, '*Only my wife and I and God know that we want to sell it.*' And I said, 'Well, I think we are talking to the same Boss! Can we come in and talk to you about it?' So he took us in and sat us down, and

215

so it unfolded. He told us that he had felt called to go into the [Seventh Day Adventist] ministry. And he had said to God, 'If this is what you want then you'll have to give us a definite sign.' *And the sign was that someone would come along and ask to buy the place.* Because at that time he knew that he had to be at the theological college by February. It was late in the year. There was a huge real estate slump at that time. There had been drought. It was a depressed market. Nothing was selling. So he had virtually left it up to God: 'If this is what you want, create a miracle and I'll believe you.' And he said [to us], '*I think you're the miracle*' [italics mine] . . .

But of course, while this might be all very well in theory, there were not a few practical difficulties to be overcome. Not least of these was whether Laurel and Edwin could even afford to buy the property. As the owners, whose names were Trevor and Helen Oliver, showed them around, Trevor's doubts began to surface when Laurel explained that they had a house and business in Sydney, but neither of these was even on the market yet. However, Laurel assured him, 'If it is God's plan, then we don't have to worry about it. We'll go back and put them on the market, and all will be well.'

Leaving Trevor and Helen by no means convinced, Laurel and Edwin returned to Sydney, where a yet further extraordinary set of events unfolded. They did indeed sell their dry-cleaning business very quickly. As described by Laurel:

We were 'told' [i.e. by the Voice] that the business would be purchased by 'the man with the windows'. This was fairly obscure. It was only after the sale that we asked the purchaser what it was that he did prior to taking the redundancy package with which he was financing the purchase. He told us that he worked for Australian Consolidated Industries as Sales Manager of Shop Windows. His name was Bill Crawford.

Equally quickly their estate agent found them willing buyers for their house – Greg and Gwen O'Connor, Baptists who had their own story of a 'call from God'. Greg had been an out-and-out atheist car salesman, always rubbishing his wife about her belief in God, until he was on a flight with her to New Zealand, and heard 'a Voice' telling him that it was to be his mission 'to take God's word to the countries where it was not allowed'. He had heeded the voice to the extent of giving up his car salesmanship, and his motive for buying Laurel and Edwin's house was to free himself financially to go Bible-smuggling in Russia and China by getting rid of the mortgage that he had on his much bigger house. His difficulty, however, was this had already been on the market for a year without a sniff of a buyer. And when Laurel and Edwin's estate agent found them alternative buyers in a Chinese couple offering them cash at their asking price, the only sensible course seemed to be accept this and turn the O'Connors down – except that Laurel's 'dialogues' had 'told' her that the O'Connors were the true buyers.

Laurel and Edwin insist that quite independently of each other they now consulted 'the Voice' for what they should do, only afterwards swapping notes to find out what each had heard. Incredulously, they found that they had both received exactly the same message: 'You are to put up the price a thousand dollars to stall the sale. Within twenty-four hours your house will be sold to the O'Connors. Someone will buy their house.' Although it took courage for them even to give their estate agent the appropriate instructions, when they did so the incredible happened yet again. During that very twenty-four hours a buyer did indeed turn up out of the blue for the O'Connors' house, enabling them to buy Laurel and

Edwin's, including paying them the $1000 extra. Laurel and Edwin were therefore able to purchase Trevor and Helen Oliver's Goobarragandra property – and just in time for Trevor Oliver to join his theological college. Three different couples, one Baptist, one Seventh Day Adventist and one Christian but as yet uncommitted to any one denomination, had all had seemingly quite independent 'calls to God' duly answered. On 28 February 1983, Laurel's birthday, Laurel and Edwin actually moved into 'the place in the mountains in the south' to which she had begun to be directed almost exactly nine months before.

Today Laurel and Edwin Lloyd-Jones are still there at what is now known as the Elm Grove Sanctuary. They named it 'Elm Grove' because of that very same grove of 'European-looking' trees – which they subsequently learned to be elms brought over from England – that Laurel 'saw' as if from the air during her out-of-body flight that night she and her husband attended *The Ballad of Billy Lane*. And they called it a Sanctuary because again in precise accord with what Laurel was 'told' the day she first started 'penning' what she was 'hearing', it has been lovingly designed by her and Edwin as 'a place of rest and solace for many'.

For if there is any validity to our earlier argument that near-death experients return consciously or otherwise 'downloaded' with the ethics of Jesus's Sermon on the Mount, then Laurel and Edwin are the perfect examplars of this. As a couple who had formerly denied God, and who had no religious convictions, they are now professed Franciscans who have literally given up everything for the way of life that Laurel felt herself bound to follow as a result of her near-death experience. In Elm Grove's grounds they have built a simple but comfortable retreat house as an accommodation for up to nine guests who share it as a community. There is no set charge for those they receive here. Each is simply expected to make a donation according to his or her means. They have also built simple Franciscan-style outdoor and indoor chapels for private meditations and for prayers belonging to no one denomination. Although firmly ecumenical, their community's rule is under the active and enthusiastic joint protection of both the Roman Catholic Archbishop and the Anglican Bishop of the dioceses of Canberra and Goulburn before whom they made formal professions in April 1994.

Because of the Sanctuary's remoteness and tranquillity amidst the mountains and trees of the Kosciusko National Park, every corner is thus provided with the perfect conditions for the very same 'listening to the inner voice that is God' that is so often lacking in modern-day lives, and that Laurel and Edwin only found for themselves following Laurel's near-death experience. And as a perfect expression of their trusting totally in the God that they once denied, Laurel and Edwin no longer even own Elm Grove. Having purchased it, they made it into a trust upon which they can draw for their simple day-to-day needs, but which does not represent any source of capital that they can pass on to their children. As this effectively disinherited their now adult son and daughter, they sought and obtained their approval of this, thereby demonstrating that following the way of the near-death experience does not have to split families.

As the reader needs to be firmly aware, all this is no anecdote. We have used no pseudonyms for Laurel and Edwin Lloyd-Jones's story, and they are no 'holier-than-thou', 'heads-in-the-clouds' religious cranks. They are a real-life, good-humoured, down-to-earth couple with as many 'making-ends-meet' concerns as the rest of us, and fully aware of the incredibility of their own story. Yet as they insist, it happened, and the way that they have changed their lives is in its own way a testimony of this. If we might have supposed that near-death experiences are at best no more than evidence for life after death, then on the basis of Laurel and Edwin's story, following as it has upon the similarly in-depth ones of George Ritchie and Howard Storm, we need to think again. As their story demonstrates, the Being whom near-death experients report meeting upon their dying is not merely around just at the time of their deaths. He is also very much present in our everyday lives. And rather than the encounter with him being just of interest in terms of evidence for life after death, it is of arguably rather greater significance for how we should conduct the rest of our lives.

But if, in accordance with this book's theme, our quest still remains to seek out the best available evidence of life after death, then just as we found George Ritchie, when he was in the Being's company, to have been able to 'see' dead persons alongside the living, so we find glimpses of much the same phenomenon even in the subsequent everyday lives of Laurel and other near-death experients. We may recall how George Ritchie, unlike a proportion of near-death experients, did not actually 'meet up' directly with any of his own deceased relatives in the course of his experience. And this was likewise the case with Laurel, who when she 'died' merely felt very loving and familiar presences around her, rather than being able to identify them with anyone specifically related to her.

However, strange things began to happen to her, and continue to do so. Thus at around the very time that she was first told that she and Edwin would go to the mountains, when she was beginning to devote a little time each day to her 'listening to God', she was on her own when, in her own description, she got 'an almighty fright':

> There was a clear face right in front of me. It seemed to come right up to my face, really close, look at me, then step

back from me again. I saw this face so clearly in my mind's eye. She was a woman who appeared to be short-sighted, peering at me. She didn't smile at me or anything, and she gave me a bit of a fright. At the same time I heard the name 'Matilda'. And I had a sense that she was in some way connected to me.

Anyway, it kept puzzling me. I told Edwin about it. Also my mother. And I asked Mum, was there a relative of ours called Matilda? (Because with Australia and 'Waltzing Matilda', you start to wonder . . .!) And she said, 'Your great-grandmother was Matilda Everingham.' I asked her, 'Was she short-sighted?' And she said 'Oh yes, she used to squint.' And I was able to describe this person. She had quite dark skin, and she didn't look Australian. In fact she looked really mean. According to my mother, this was spot-on, even though I had never ever seen her, because she died before I was born. Anyway, my mother eventually went to her mother who was still alive and got an old photograph, and indeed this was the same woman whom I had seen.

Laurel showed me this photograph, of an indisputably very unsmiling-looking elderly lady, and Laurel's feeling is that as a maternal ancestor Matilda was perhaps 'checking up on her' following her becoming more 'in tune' with the dimension of which she had a foretaste during her near-death experience.

As another example, during Edwin and Laurel's first year at Elm Grove they were visited by old friends from Sydney, Trevor Scott (a senior geologist working for a mining company), and his wife Sheila. As Laurel recalled:

As we sat speaking, I became aware of an elderly woman, wearing a pair of gold-rimmed spectacles, standing immediately behind Trevor. She said to me, 'This one will "take flight" in the near future, and there will be no stopping him.'

While Laurel was still puzzling over the meaning of the woman's words, Sheila, seeing the astonished look on her face, asked her what she had 'seen'. Guardedly, Laurel told her. Then, still concerned to clarify what she had 'heard', she asked them, 'Are you going overseas, or making some big changes in your lives soon?' They responded enthusiastically that indeed they were. Because of Trevor's job they were shortly to move to Indonesia, where he was to take charge of a mining operation. As Laurel continues her recollections:

Somehow this was not what I had felt it was all about. Even so, I was more than happy to assume and hope that this was so, in order to feel more comfortable. Trevor asked me to describe the woman I had seen. As I did so, she again appeared behind him, telling me that she was his grand-mother, and that he had always enjoyed playing in her garden when he was a child. When I repeated this to Trevor and Sheila, Trevor confirmed everything that I had told him. His deceased grandmother had indeed worn gold-rimmed spectacles. And yes, when he was a child he really had loved her garden.

The tragic upshot of the story, however, is that just one month later Trevor Scott was rushed to Sydney's Royal North Shore Hospital, where he died completely unexpectedly of cardiomyopathy, a degeneration of the heart muscle, of which he had previously been completely unaware. For his widow Sheila there could be no doubting that the appearance of the dead grandmother to Laurel must have been a harbin-ger of Trevor's death, a realization which, although it took time for her and her two daughters to come to terms with their grief, gave her a hitherto unprecedented assurance that 'something exists beyond this life'. Indeed, although she is now living back in England, she has developed a particularly close bond with Laurel and Edwin, and has become one of the Trustees of their Sanctuary.

In yet another strange happening, one evening Laurel and Edwin had been out to dinner with a couple who were regular customers of theirs at their dry-cleaning business. The couple, Carol Dickson and her husband Bruce, had invited them back for coffee and Laurel was just making a 'call of nature' visit to the bathroom when, in her words:

> Out of the corner of my eye I caught this image. I was not even sure if it was not just my imagination. I simply saw this woman sitting on the edge of the bath, holding what I thought to be a doll. It was just a flash experience, but I also felt really uncomfortable being there in that part of the house.
>
> [When I went back to the living room] the conversation came round to Carol and her husband's house. I hadn't said anything to them [about what I had 'seen' in the bathroom]. They were simply talking about the house and extension, and said that they liked living there – *except that they hated the bathroom*. Carol said, 'I don't know what it is, but I always feel that there's someone looking at me.' So I told her of my experience, and she pushed me to tell her what I had seen. I said I had seen a woman holding a doll, sitting on the edge of the bath, looking at me almost accusingly, like, 'What are you doing in my bathroom?'
>
> Carol said, 'We hated that end of the house so much after we bought it that we went and spoke to the neigh-

bours and asked them about the house. We found out that *the woman who had lived in the house prior to our purchase had committed suicide. And she was pregnant'* [italics mine].

Furthermore, just as it will be recalled that I had felt impelled to 'do something' about the ghost encountered by my wife and I at Abercrombie House (see Chapter 3), so, speaking of that moment when she had been quite unaware of this experience of mine, Laurel went on:

> Suddenly I knew that I had to do something about that poor soul in the bathroom. I couldn't leave it alone. So I said to Carol (and I really didn't know what she would think of me), 'I'm going to try and take her with me tonight. And I'm going to pray for her.' And I went back into the bathroom. And I couldn't see anything. I couldn't feel anything. But I just sat in there and asked that Jesus would be with me, and get her to come with me. I knew that somehow I had to take her out of the house. And afterwards Edwin and I got in our car and again just prayed for her. A couple of days later, Carol and her husband rushed in [to the dry cleaners] to see us. Carol said 'The house feels so different. She's gone.' And literally, it had happened only by prayer.

And as reassurance that this is not a case of just one woman being 'over the top', this greatly enhanced acuity to ghosts is one quite definitely not peculiar to Laurel alone among near-death experients. Among Dr Cherie Sutherland's other Australian informants, only one-fifth had had some form of ghost experience before their brush with death. But some two-thirds of them reported one or more such experiences during the months and years following.

It may be recalled also how much earlier in this book we

came across Englishman Eddie Burks and his extraordinary perceptions of ghosts, perceptions that it is now very difficult not to ascribe, just as we suspected back in Chapter 3, to the near-death experience that Eddie suffered at the age of five. We may recall how Eddie now makes it his special calling to lay such ghosts to rest, helping them directly towards what he calls 'the Light'. Here we find further direct corroboration of the insights into ghosts as 'seen' during George Ritchie's so memorable near-death experience.

Furthermore, there is evidence that this acuity to ghosts is just one part of a general greater psychic perceptiveness triggered among near-death experients as yet another aspect of their so extraordinary 'transformation' as outlined in the last chapter. In keeping with the 'tuning into others' thoughts' that we have already noted of the near-death experience itself, one of Raymond Moody's American experients told him, 'It seems that [in my everyday life] I am more in tune with people now, that I can pick up things about them faster.'

Laurel, during my interview with her and Edwin at Goobarragandra, correctly told me that she was 'picking up' about my wife, whom she had never met, and who was then more than 600 miles away in Brisbane, something about patchwork quilts. Judith was indeed working on making a patchwork quilt at that very time. D. M. Cook, the Englishman who, as mentioned in the previous chapter, had his near-death experience as a result of a motor-cycle accident in Rhodesia, remarked: 'On two occasions since the accident I have awoken out of a deep sleep knowing respectively that my son had been born and that my mother had died. Both times were subsequently confirmed.'[9]

There are many other examples of such telepathic-type insights among experients from all countries. In keeping with the apparent timeless, spaceless character of whatever dimension it is that near-death experients tap into, these 'tuning-in' insights can also sometimes contain insights into the future.

Gillian McKenzie, the very down-to-earth Englishwoman who as seen in the previous chapter had pressed Button B for her return back to the living, told me:

> Sometimes I know things in advance. I know when people are going to telephone me, or I'll know when they are in trouble and I'll phone them. Sometimes it's just before, sometimes days in advance. That used to worry me, but I've got used to it now.[10]

Australian experient Pat Venn told me essentially exactly the same. Peter and Elizabeth Fenwick have quoted several examples of seeing the future cited among English experients. Both George Ritchie and Howard Storm were also given insights into the future.

Accordingly it is quite clear that if a near-death experience truly is, from all that we have seen so far, the best available evidence for life after death, then it is also very far from being *only* this, despite the fact that this is the way it has been treated by virtually every other writer on the subject. Quite inseparable from it are the huge questions still demanding answers. Is there a God? Are we more than just our physical bodies? Is it possible to read others' thoughts? Is it possible to 'see' into the future? Does it matter how we behave to those with whom we cross paths in life? Also quite clear is that the ancient and tribal peoples' beliefs in a realm of Beings and deceased ancestors just beyond that of our immediate senses should no longer be dismissed as mere primitive superstition. If near-death experiences have any validity, and are treated seriously to the furthest limits of what experients claim, then they seem to offer at least a glimpse of common ground between their insights, the beliefs of ancient peoples, and the basics of the teachings of Jesus of Nazareth and others of his ilk.

So can we really now put all these different threads together and come up with something that might be some form of sensible blueprint for our so material-minded scientific age? Inevitably this represents our greatest challenge of all . . .

Chapter 11

Conceiving the Inconceivable

> *They told me that the night & day were all that I could see;*
> *They told me that I had five senses to inclose me up,*
> *And they inclos'd my infinite brain into a narrow circle,*
> *And sunk my heart into the Abyss, a red, round globe, hot*
> * burning*
> *Till from all life I was obliterated and erased . . .*
> William Blake, 'Visions of the Daughters of Albion'

There is a famous Chinese legend about a community of frogs living at the bottom of a well. To them the sky was only as big as the round opening at the top of their well. Our scientific age, of course, has no such blinkered vision. It *knows* that the sky is vast – stretching for millions upon millions of what we call 'miles' in every possible direction. It also *knows* that the galaxies swirling around in that sky have been around for millions upon millions of what we call 'years'. So well-established and mind-boggling are these vast distances and time-scales that even the possibility that there might be something else, and that this modern-day scientific view of this universe could be as limited as that of the frogs at the bottom of the well might seem inconceivable. Yet conceive of it we must try.

If we begin by reconsidering some of the more universal of the patterns that we have learned from near-death cases from across the world, then one reasonable inference is that we seem to be able to distinguish three distinctly different though not necessarily separate levels to the experience.

The first of these is the altogether down-to-earth level of the physical body and brain, with its five senses, and with all the limitations associated with its various individual imperfections – possibly impaired mobility, eyesight, hearing, etc. At this level the observing consciousness, firmly rooted as it is 'inside' its physical body, perceives the physical world's solid objects as solid. It recognizes the existence of anything less solid from what its instruments tell it. And it feels any kind of physical injury as painful. In a different way, it may also feel intense and potentially painful emotional attachments to family and friends, to chosen career and to recreation activities, likewise to the possession of physical items such as a house, furniture, clothes and money. Earth time, earth space, earth gravity, all seem to it to be the only reality by which all else should be measured. This is the level that the ancient Egyptian knew as that of the *het*, or physical body. It is also the level of essentially all that is known and understood by our present-day science.

The second level is that at which the experient's observing 'self' seemingly vacates his or her physical body, and hovers temporarily over this in what appears to be physical space. At this point this 'self' or consciousness appears to have lost many of the limitations that it had when it was confined 'inside' its physical body. It is now apparently weightless, as if in zero gravity, and is able seemingly to move to wherever thought may take it. Whatever may have been the quality of the physical body's eyesight and hearing, its vision and hearing are now crystal-clear. Physical pain is now absent, and emotional pain surprisingly dulled. The three senses most associated with 'material' pleasure – touch, taste and smell – also now appear to be absent, with objects and living things that would normally feel 'solid' now feeling to be without substance, and presenting no barrier to movement through them. Although self-awareness, with accompanying memory, knowledge and feelings all may seem unchanged from level one, there can be confusion and uncertainty, particularly in the face of the realization of this apparent 'death'. There may also be vestigial concern about separation from family, missed appointments, ruined clothing, etc. although these rapidly give way to feelings of peace and well-being. Although modern science is already crying 'Hallucination,' for the ancient Egyptian most of this corresponds readily enough with what he would have identified as the dimension or level of his *ka*.

But the real departure point from everything that we may consider 'rational' occurs on the third level, which we earlier noted to have both 'heavenly' and 'hellish' variants, our focus, for present purposes, centring on the 'heavenly' one. Although a necessary preliminary to entering this level seems to be what a number of experients describe as whirling or floating through a tunnel, we have already noted, as suggested by Laurel Lloyd-Jones, that this may well not be any actual tunnel so much as some shift of consciousness giving the impression of one.

The particularly interesting aspect, however, is the profound change that seems to take place in the observing consciousness once this has emerged from the 'tunnel' and reaches the level in question, often dubbed by near-death experience researchers that of 'the Light'. For however strong the ties that the experient may previously have felt with his or her loved ones, now he or she may be surprised at their emotional detachment. Although they may feel no less love for their family than before, there is none of the shock/horror/grief that they would formerly have expected of themselves when confronted with separation from them by death.

Even more astonishing, however, is the way the observing consciousness now reacts to whatever scenes from the experient's earlier life may be 'replayed' before it. With some Power having 'tuned' this in so that all the physical and mental hurts that may have been inflicted upon others now appear as if highlighted by some searing magic marker, it is as if the experient suddenly views everything from the perspective of life values dramatically different from whatever he or she may have held before. Yet this change has almost invariably come about so swiftly and so imperceptibly that it is as if the experient has always had these values, yet has simply never before recognized them in himself or herself.

At the same time the experient may now almost palpably perceive the 'minds' of 'passed over' relatives and friends, communication occurring with these so naturally and spontaneously that he or she may fail even to notice that this is taking place without recourse to the spoken word. Among the communicating minds may be individuals who died before the experient was born, yet who, whatever their earlier failings, now seem to have the very same life values that the experient has now so mysteriously adopted. And whereas at level two it was touch, taste and smell that seemed to be absent, now it is time, all earthly time, past, present and future, seeming to be just one single now, and distance likewise having no meaning – thus explaining, it would seem, the absence of any feeling of separation from family members still living.

Furthermore, any confusions or uncertainties that the experient may previously have felt seem now to have been replaced by an absolute and automatic certainty and totality of knowledge, as if everything that is known can be instantly present in consciousness at the merest flick of an enquiring thought. The ancient Egyptian would have had little difficulty relating this level to his concept of the realm of the free-roaming and birdlike *ba*. It would also seem to be the same level that the medicine-men and shamans of many tribal peoples have spoken of in their descriptions of their ventures out of the body. It may also be this same level that St Paul referred to so cryptically when in his Second Letter to the Corinthians he remarked, apparently autobiographically:

> I know a man in Christ who fourteen years ago was caught up – whether still in the body or out of the body I do not know (God knows!) – right into the third heaven. I do know, however, that this same person – whether in the body or out of the body, I do not know . . . – was caught up into paradise and heard things which must not and cannot be put into human language (2 Corinthians 12: 2–4).

But inevitably the sixty-four-thousand-dollar question that we first asked much earlier in this book now resurfaces. Is all this just hallucination, as deservedly respected modern-day scientists such as Dr Susan Blackmore continue to contend? Or is it real? Even, as some near-death experients would express it, 'realer' than our normal 'reality'?

Now, as we noted in earlier chapters, we should avoid conceiving of the third level via any of the things that we can normally relate to: images, sounds, perfumes, etc. While any or all of these may be reported by experients, we have already found reasonable grounds for believing them to a greater or lesser degree to be illusions, simply aids to give us something to hold on to mentally. Far more important instead is that the third level essentially has one all-pervading characteristic: that it is a realm of *thought*, or, more accurately, *thought-patterns*. Thus as we may recall from

George Ritchie's description of the 'hellish' variant that he 'saw':

> These creatures seemed locked into habits of mind and emotion, into hatred, lust, destructive *thought-patterns*. Whatever anyone *thought*, however fleetingly or unwittingly, was instantly apparent to all around him, more completely than words could have expressed it, faster than sound waves could have carried it.'[1]

Likewise, as Howard Storm recalled of his dialogue with the Beings, following his asking them, 'Do you know what goes on in my mind?'

> They said, 'Yes.' And I said, 'What if I have a thought that I don't want you to know about?' And they said, '*We know everything that you think about* [italics mine] and have always known everything that you have thought about.'

And here we come to the nub of it. To us, entrenched as we are in a physical world bounded by time and space, our thoughts and feelings, even though we may regard them as more 'us' than anything else about us, invariably *seem* totally evanescent. After all, to all appearances they are completely invisible, inaudible and intangible to others. They have no taste and no smell. There is not a scientific instrument yet developed that can tap into them. We fondly *think* of them as private, known only to ourselves. And we also think that once they're gone, they're lost for ever.

Indeed such is their evanescence that as far back as the 1920s our science, under the influence of American 'behaviourists' such as John B. Watson and B. F. Skinner, effectively decided that thoughts were not even worth thinking about.

Since the behaviourist view is that only that which is measurable and observable is truly worthy of study, thoughts and everything to do with consciousness and our 'self'-awareness, had to be virtually banished from serious consideration. And scientific orthodoxy has shifted comparatively little from this viewpoint. According to the current *International Dictionary of Psychology*, 'It is impossible to specify what it [consciousness] is, what it does, or how it evolved. Nothing worth reading has been written about it'.[2] According to Professor Francis Crick, the co-discoverer of the structure of DNA, everything that we think and feel, including our 'self'-awareness, is no more than the behaviour of a vast assembly of nerve cells.[3] According to Guy Claxton, author of *Noises from the Darkroom: The Science and Mystery of the Mind*,[4] consciousness is just a useless epiphenomenon that appeared when evolving systems needed to find ways of redirecting attention. For these and for many others, 'we' are effectively little more than machines with a very finite brain which just happens to have developed sufficient complexity to be able to think about itself. There is absolutely nothing about us which we should not ultimately be able to match with a future generation of computers.

But could all this be akin to the thinking of those frogs at the bottom of the well? In Chapter 7 we mentioned the British Museum's papyrus that shows the dead ancient Egyptian Hunefer being brought to the god Osiris's judgment hall, where his heart was weighed against a feather. If we look again at this scene, we may interpret it in one of two ways. Thinking of it from the viewpoint of what we called 'level one', we may scorn the ancient Egyptians for supposing that any human heart could weigh lighter than a feather. Alternatively, if we think of it from the viewpoint of level three, we may admire them for the way they have visually conveyed that it is Hunefer's more metaphorical 'heart', that of all his thoughts and emotions, which is really being weighed, the feather, from that perspective, being a perfectly considered counterweight. The many 'heart' words that we still use in our language – 'heartened', 'soft-hearted', 'faint-hearted', etc. – together with the heart symbols that we use for Valentine cards and the like, all betray that we still instinctively associate our hearts with the true 'us', whatever science may say concerning our brains.

This leads us to the consideration of whether, instead of the 'heart' element of all our thoughts and emotions being as scientifically worthless as our modern science still supposes this to be, there could be a dimension in which this is every bit as solid and real and obvious as Hunefer's heart was depicted by the ancient Egyptians on those scales. Indeed, far more so. The serious consideration is of nothing less than a dimension in which our thoughts may be as instantly communicable as anything pertaining to our known visual, audible, tactile, olfactory and gustatory senses. And not just in respect of the present moment, but those of the entirety of our experience, and all others' experiences.

To go further, we are postulating that the world of all our thoughts, all our consciousnesses, all our minds, call these what you will, far from being so evanescent and just some mere epiphenomenon, actually represents some form of *third order of reality*, an order not only independent of the known dimensions of time and space, but actually reducing these latter to mere shadows. In this thought dimension, everyone that has ever lived, and arguably every creature likewise, *is still alive*, in a way as difficult for us to comprehend as it would be for people born blind to understand whatever we tried to tell them about sight. Intriguingly, none other than Jesus of Nazareth said very specifically, when referring to God's describing himself to Moses as the God of Abraham, Isaac and Jacob, that God is God 'not of the dead, but of the living; for to him all men are in fact alive' (Luke 20: 38). From a very different viewpoint, we are now saying much the same.

But can any such idea be equated with science? Certainly not with that of the frogs at the bottom of the well. For them our physical brains are all that there is to our thinking processes. Therefore when the brain dies, so does absolutely everything that we might identify as 'us' along with it. We have no 'mind' that could conceivably separate from the physical body, in whatever circumstances. Therefore all near-death experiences just have to be delusions of the dying brain. End of story. Or is it?

In fact, there are signs of at least the beginnings of change to such thinking. As this book was in preparation, Australian-born David Chalmers, thirty-year-old Professor of Philosophy at the University of California, Santa Cruz, published *The Conscious Mind: In Search of a Fundamental Theory*,[5] in which he has argued on straight philosophical grounds for a rein-statement of the old, so long-discredited 'dualist' notion of us being made up of both body and mind. Intriguingly, just as we suggested that *thought* might constitute the order of a third order of reality, so the nub of Chalmers' argument is that *conscious experience* may be 'one of the absolute funda-mentals of nature, rather like space and time'.[6] He calls it 'an extra, irreducible ingredient', and contends that it is actually unscientific to say that it does not, or cannot, exist.

Furthermore, there are some tantalizing glimpses of the possible workings of an invisible 'mind behind' in the world of nature, particularly in the case of marine organisms on the borderline between being a plant and an independent life form. Back in the 1950s an intriguing experiment[7] was conducted with two sponges, a red encrusting one called *Microconia prolifera* and a yellow one called *Cliona celata*. One of each of these was sieved into the same receptacle, and then all the cells mixed together, as if in a food blender. Astonishingly, when the resultant 'soup' was examined twenty-four hours later, all the red and yellow cells were found to have separated themselves from each other, and to have reassembled themselves once more as two separate sponges, with just a few lingering red cells in the yellow one. The inevitable question this experiment raises is: what and where was the invisible 'organization' that put these back together? Was it what we might call a 'mind'?

Although a sponge might be considered a cluster rather than a single organism, this is not the case with another marine creature, the humble sea cucumber, of which I was almost entirely ignorant until vacationing with my wife on Heron Island, a tiny tropical island that stands directly on the southernmost tip of Australia's Great Barrier Reef. In the course of our stay a young marine biologist kindly took us and others on a guided walk of the reef at low tide, during which she picked up various marine creatures from the sea floor, including one of the varieties of sea cucumber. She carefully explained how despite its name this was not a plant, but a completely independent creature, with a mouth, an alimentary canal, means of moving around, and some interesting sexual inclinations.

The really spooky part, she went on (and she told us that she had this on good authority from a colleague to whom it had actually happened), was that if she were to hold the sea cucumber out of the water for longer than half an hour, it would turn to slime and drip through her fingers, *only for it to reassemble as a sea cucumber once reunited with the water*.

Now, from enquiries subsequently made with the University of Queensland's School of Marine Science, it would appear that while this turning to slime is a well-recognized and established phenomenon, any observation of the reassembly is rather less so. However, more than a little making up for this deficiency is a video-recording of an as yet unknown marine creature, not unlike the sea cucumber in its shape, encountered over three days by the well-respected Australian underwater film-makers Ron and Valerie Taylor while diving off Observation Point, Papua New Guinea in January 1993.

Following my contacting the Taylors after they mentioned this creature on an Australian television programme, they kindly sent me a videotape of their full eight minutes' filming of it. From this it can clearly be seen that upon Valerie Taylor merely touching it, even though she did not attempt to remove it from the water, those parts with which her fingers came in contact dissolved 'like melted jelly', only to re-form again once the disturbance was over. As the footage further shows, when she tried to pick the creature up, again while still underwater, to all visible appearances it simply dematerialized, only, within a couple of minutes, to re-form again and, as she describes it, go 'undulating slowly along, as though nothing untoward had happened to it'.[8] Thus the inevitable question recurred: what and where was the invisible organization that put it back together again? Again, could we be looking at the operation of some kind of 'mind' at its most primitive level?

Although these are still only very tentative examples, in fact the 'thought dimension' that we have been trying to grasp, however inadequately, is not so very far removed from ideas first mooted some fifteen years ago by the then youthful British biologist Dr Rupert Sheldrake. In his book *A New Science of Life*[9] – described as 'fit for burning' in a trenchant editorial in the prestigious scientific journal *Nature*[10] – Sheldrake has argued that behind each life-form there lies an invisible, thought-like organizing principle, akin to an architect's mental concept of the house he plans, or to the score of a symphony in the mind of a musical composer. According to his reasoning, just as the human body may be killed, so the physical paper of an architect's plan, together with whatever energy and physical matter was used to translate it into a physical house, may become totally destroyed. But the thought-plan itself, off-puttingly dubbed by Sheldrake a 'morphogenetic field', will 'live' on completely unaffected by any such destruction. Lacking any energy or mass of its own, independent of both time and place and effectively existing everywhere at once, it may be re-translated at any time and in any place into new energy and materials without itself ever being observable or detectable in any possible way.

As further conceived by Sheldrake, each field or thought-plan interacts by what he similarly off-puttingly calls 'morphic resonance' – in essence, sympathetic vibrations or resonances along the lines of the ceaseless and fingerprint-like individual oscillations that are scientifically known to characterize all atoms, molecules, crystals, cells and other basic building blocks of life. And because such thought-plans lack any mass or energy of their own, their resonances or thoughts can transcend time and space and be 'just as effective over ten thousand miles as a yard, and over a century as an hour'.[11]

As may now be recognized, such a dimension of thought-forms, independent of time and space, resonating with those with which they are most in harmony, and existing everywhere at once, strikes some chords very similar to everything that we have deduced of the third level that is reached in near-death experiences. Furthermore – and mindful that we can often learn so much from thinking which is less 'developed' than our own – we find that it is intriguingly like the dimension of the afterlife as taught by many of the tribal peoples with whose 'mad' beliefs we began this book.

Among traditional Australian aborigines, the last surviving human beings to live entirely in a Late Stone Age phase of culture, whose *wirinun* or medicine men undergo a ritual near-death type experience as part of their initiation, this dimension is known as the *Dowie*. According to the late Cyril Havecker, who as we saw in Chapter 2 grew up in a predominantly aboriginal community in Murray Plains, South Australia, then becoming a blood-brother of the northern Waramunga tribe:

> the *Dowie* is the next life so far as we human beings are concerned. It is built of substance that is *frictionless*, but retains indefinitely *all of the emotions* imparted to it. In this sense, it is *thought built* and of a velocity greater than the speed of light. Inhabited by all kinds of entities and forms of life, the *Dowie* is not somewhere in space, *it is all about us* [italics mine] and it requires only the proper conditions to be contacted at any given time . . . [12]

'Built of substance that is *frictionless*': we may immediately recall how at the near-death experience's second level each experient describes moving ghost-like through solid walls without the slightest resistance. 'Retains indefinitely *all of the emotions imparted to it*': we may remember how during the near-death experient's third-level life review he or she describes finding preserved in entirety not only his or her own emotions, but those of all others. '*It is all about us*': was it not Howard Storm who said, 'They . . . are not there and we here. They are here,' just as Jesus said, 'The kingdom of God is among you' (Luke 17: 21)? '*Thought-built*': have we not, as recently as this very chapter, been arguing for thought as the universe's true number one building-block?

Importantly, this idea is not just something incidental to the traditional Australian aboriginal's understanding of the universe, it is central to it. Besides aboriginals having long been well known for their apparent telepathic powers, according to Havecker, they regard 'thought-power' as 'the most powerful force in the universe' . . . 'a force that may be used for good or evil, and . . . a potent weapon for black magic, as well as a healing-aid when administered for well-being'.[13] And indeed this pertains not only to Australian aboriginals. The power of concentrated thought has long been harnessed by the so-called 'witch-doctors' of many other tribal peoples, and by the so-called 'black' and 'white' witches who operate in our own Westernized society's occultic fringes.

Havecker also wrote of the *Dowie*, or afterlife dimension, in terminology strikingly similar to that of Sheldrake's concept of 'morphic resonance':

> The *Dowie* . . . requires only the proper conditions to be contacted at any given time.[14] Provided the *correct vibration or wavelength* [italics mine] . . . is obtained, contact between the two worlds [i.e. the present life and the dimension of the afterlife] can become regular practice.[15]

Indeed, the parallels between all that we have deduced from worldwide examples of near-death experiences, and the Australian aboriginal insights on their 'thought-dimension'-type afterlife as conveyed by Cyril Havecker are so many and so fascinating that only a completely separate book could do them justice. For instance, at least according to Havecker, aboriginals envisage their *Dowie* as existing in a dimension 'beyond the speed of light', therefore one in which, as we may glimpse even by present Einsteinian understanding, time and space would indeed become altogether different from the way we know them. Aboriginals also envisage this dimension as being one without gravity and as indelibly preserving the complete records of everyone's lives.

However, what must now command our attention are Cyril Havecker's earlier quoted words that this dimension requires 'only the proper conditions to be contacted at any given time'. Inevitably the importance of these is that if we can only find some way of replicating such 'proper conditions' in our Westernized society, we should be able to demonstrate that contact, hopefully by some means rather more satisfactory than anything so far produced either by spiritualist mediums, or by those associated with the various societies for psychical research. If we could only do this, then we might at last be able to make those frogs at the bottom of the well sit up and take notice. But can we?

Here, intriguingly, while I was researching the cases of apparently spontaneous 'drop-in' appearances of the recently dead to the living that we discussed back in Chapter 3, I happened to observe one repeatedly recurring curiosity. This was that where an experient 'saw' such an apparition while he or she was in waking consciousness, then the vehicle, or trigger, for the apparition was quite often *some mirror-like surface*.

In the case of Prince Victor Duleep Singh, for instance, it may be recalled from Chapter 3 that when he was 'visited' by his father the Maharajah on the latter's death, his father's face appeared to him as if from an oleograph picture that was hanging on the wall opposite him, the reflective surface being arguably either the glass covering the oleograph, or its own shiny surface. Similarly in the case of Krystyna Kolodziej, who as we may recall was visited in London by her father Kazimir when the latter had just died in Australia, it was again via 'a large mounted picture' that Kazimir's face appeared. As another instance, not previously mentioned, the travel writer Lawrence Blair, in his book *Ring of Fire*, has described how he and his brother Lorne had their plans for filming in Indonesia radically changed when their team-member Zac 'saw' behind him in the bathroom mirror the apparition of Sumba's elderly Raja of Pau, realizing from this that the Raja must have just died, which did indeed prove correct.

And while I was merely musing from such examples whether the repeatedly recurring mirrors or pictures might have facilitated whatever shift of consciousness by which the 'contact' was made – rather in the manner that hypnotists sometimes use a dangling bright object as an aid to hypnosis – I learned of clearly closely-related researches of that founding-father of modern-day interest in near-death experiences, Dr Raymond Moody. In 1987, ten years after the publication of his *Reflections on Life after Life*, Moody was apparently casually browsing in a bookshop when a volume entitled *Crystal Gazing* happened to fall off a shelf and land at his feet.

Whatever the chance or otherwise by which this happened, on Moody's looking through this book he came to learn that any form of mirror, or other shiny surface, has for a very long time indeed been regarded as an aid for shifting into what we may now term the thought dimension – typified, of course, by the gypsy's 'crystal ball'. With his interest duly whetted, Moody thereupon began to study the subject in depth, finding, for instance, quite apart from the examples cited above, that according to the distinguished French author Anatole France, the night that the French revolutionary leader Robespierre attempted suicide by shooting himself in the jaw, his [France's] own aunt 'saw' this event while she was looking in a mirror. Apparently she exclaimed, 'I see him [i.e. Robespierre]! I see him! How pale he is! Blood is flowing from his mouth! His teeth and jaws are shattered!'[16] Then she promptly fainted.

Researching further back, Moody learned that the Elizabethan seer Dr John Dee reputedly achieved many of his historically uncanny insights (he prophesied, for instance, that Queen Elizabeth I would have a long reign), via an obsidian mirror that apparently came from the Aztecs. He also discovered that the ancient Greeks had apparently used the shiny inside of a great bronze cauldron as an aid to visions of their dead when they visited the Nekromanteion, or 'Place of the Oracle of the Dead', the ruins of which still stand close to the banks of the River Acheron at what is now Ephyra in north-west Greece.

All this led Moody to try his own experiment at dimension-shifting by mirror-gazing, the particular person whom he aimed to make contact with being his deceased maternal grandmother, for whom he always felt great affection, as she had been a great influence upon him during his early childhood, when his father had been away with US troops fighting in the Second World War. After he had spent several hours re-evoking this grandmother's memory with the aid of old photographs of her and other memorabilia, he sat for 'at least an hour' in his own version of a Nekromanteion, a specially arranged dimly lit booth within which he gazed long and hard into the depths of a large offset mirror. To his disappointment, however, throughout all the time that he did this he felt 'not even a twinge' of his grandmother's presence, and eventually concluded that he was probably 'somehow immune to visionary reunions'.

His shock was accordingly all the greater when, a fortnight later, as he was sitting alone in a room, in his own words:

a woman simply walked in. As soon as I saw her, I had a certain sense that she was familiar, but the event happened so quickly that it took me a few moments to gather myself together and greet her politely. Within what must have been less than a minute, I realized that this person was my *paternal* grandmother, who had died some years before. I remember throwing up my hands towards my face and exclaiming 'Grandma!'

At this point I was looking directly into her eyes, awestruck at what I was seeing. In a very kind and loving way she acknowledged who she was and addressed me with the nickname that only she had used for me when I was a child. As soon as I realized who this woman was, a flood of memories rushed into my mind. Not all of these were good memories. In fact many were distinctly unpleasant. Although my reminiscences of my maternal grandmother are positive, those of my father's mother were a different matter . . . She once washed my mouth out with soap for having uttered a word of which she disapproved. Another time when I was a child, she told me in all seriousness that it was a sin to fly in aeroplanes. She was habitually cranky and negative.

Yet as I gazed into the eyes of this apparition, I quickly sensed that the woman who stood before me had been transformed in a very positive way. I felt warmth and love from her as she stood there and an empathy and compassion that surpassed my understanding. She was confidently humorous, with an air of quiet calm and joyfulness about her.

The reason I had not recognized her at first was that she appeared much younger than she was when she died, in fact even younger than she had been when I was born. I don't remember having seen any photographs of her at the age she seemed to be during this encounter, but this is irrelevant here since it was not totally through her physical presence that I recognized her. Rather, I knew this woman through her unmistakable presence and through the many memories we reviewed and discussed. In short, this woman was my deceased grandmother. I would have known her anywhere.[17]

Of this 'reviewing and discussing' of the 'many memories', Moody reveals that these included his grandmother's enlightening him on a very personal family situation of which he had previously been unaware, one which greatly helped his subsequent understanding. And he insists that while he 'heard' her voice, and very clearly – this having 'a crisp, electric quality to it that seemed clearer and louder than her voice before she died' – the communication was at one and the same time of a telepathic or 'mind-to-mind' character: 'Although most of my conversation was through the spoken word, from time to time I was immediately aware of what she was thinking, and I could tell that the same was true for her.'[18]

As he further insists, in no way did his grandmother:

appear 'ghostly' or transparent during our reunion. She seemed completely solid in every respect. She appeared no different from any other person except that she was surrounded by what appeared as a light or an indentation in space, as if she were somehow set off or recessed from the rest of her surroundings.[19]

Of similar interest is one other curiosity remarked by him, that his grandmother was very emphatic about him not attempting to touch her. In his words:

For some reason . . . she would not let me touch her. Two or three times I reached to give her a hug, and each time she put her hands up and motioned me back. She was so insistent about not being touched that I didn't pursue it.[20]

By way of possible explanation we may recall how for some near-death experients to touch anyone in the dimension of the dead represented a point of no return. This may possibly have been the reason why Jesus, in his very first post-Resurrection appearance, told Mary Magdalen, 'Do not touch me' (John 20: 17).

Whatever, Moody says that he found it impossible to estimate the time that his encounter with his grandmother took; in terms of his conversational exchanges with her it seemed to have taken at least a couple of hours, though in 'real' time he guessed that it was probably substantially less. His grandmother did not even disappear in front of him, as might have been expected of any 'ghost'. They simply said goodbye to each other, almost prosaically, in apparent full anticipation of their meeting again. He walked out of the room. Then when he returned, she had gone.

As Moody summed up this encounter, it was 'one of the most life-changing events' that he had ever experienced. He also insists that it was 'completely natural ... completely coherent with the ordinary waking reality that I have experienced all my life'. Despite all his earlier researches with those who had had near-death experiences, this personal encounter with his grandmother, which he describes as 'the most normal and satisfying' that he had ever had with her, more than anything previously in his experience left him: . . .'with an abiding certainty that what we call death is not the end of life ... If I were to discount this encounter as hallucinatory, I would be almost obliged to discount the rest of my life as hallucinatory too.'[21]

Having read Dr Moody's books, having heard him lecture at a London conference,[22] having seen so many of his insights checked out by others, and having checked these out myself with near-death experients of my own acquaintance, I have not the slightest doubt either of his critical judgment or of the truthfulness of this description of this successful 'contact' with his grandmother. Everything about it checks out with our earlier insights – the apparent solidity of his grandmother's appearance, the transformation that she had seemingly undergone, the thought transference, the all-knowingness she exhibited, the timeless quality of the experience, the slight sheath of light enveloping her (remember George Ritchie?), the prohibition on touching, and so much else.

However, this is very far from recommending that the means of confounding those frogs at the bottom of the well must now be for every reader to rush out, build their own Nekromanteion booth, and demonstrate for themselves that it is possible, while in a normal waking state, to get in touch with their dead loved ones. As needs to be very carefully noted of Moody's 'visitation', this quite specifically did not happen while he sat expectantly waiting for it in the darkened booth. Instead it was a fortnight later, when he was *not* expecting it.

Likewise, the visitation was not from the person whom he was trying to contact, his much-loved maternal grandmother. Instead it was from the distinctly unloved paternal one whom he had not even thought to try. Although Moody has glossed over both these points, they are arguably of more than a little significance. Furthermore, when he constructed a Nekromanteion-like Theatre of the Mind in Alabama specifically to encourage others to see whether they might have similar experiences to his own, his results, as published in his book *Reunions*, make distinctly uninspiring reading by comparison either to his own experience with his paternal grandmother, or to the corpus of near-death experience literature as gathered by himself and others. Indeed, although he received no shortage of volunteers, he has now apparently abandoned inviting such experiments.[23]

All this only serves to reinforce an impression that I have long held, and which nothing in my present researches for this book has led me to alter, that when it comes to making any attempts to contact the dead, the rules are essentially the same as what is archetypically told to actors after their auditions: 'Don't call us. We'll call you.'

Except . . . does this perhaps only apply to those attempts by us on 'this side' to 'get in touch' by what we may term first-level or 'worldly'-minded methods? By sitting before a mirror in some darkened Nekromanteion, for example, or paying money to a spiritualist medium, or staking out a purported haunted house with every form of recording equipment?

For by whose thinking are we actually *'out'* of touch? As we found those ancient and tribal peoples whose 'mad' beliefs we explored in Chapter 2 insisted, the world of those whom we illusorily call 'the dead' is not anywhere remote and out of touch. It is actually right here among us, and very capable of being 'felt' by those open to its reality. As we have learnt throughout this book, exactly the same is attested by near-death experients. Earlier in this chapter we recalled Howard Storm's words of his encounter with the Beings: 'They . . . are not there and we here. *They are here.'* Jesus of Nazareth said much the same with his words 'The kingdom of God does not admit of observation and there will be no one to say "Look here! Look there! For you must know, the kingdom of God is among you."'

This not only reminds us of the lesson we learned from Laurel and Edwin Lloyd-Jones's experiences described in the previous chapter – the importance of never leaving out God. It also explains that very curious characteristic which we noted every experient found when in level three of their experience. That is, they seemingly inexplicably found themselves suddenly judging themselves, as in their life reviews, by values that they had never previously considered before, but which now became so much 'them' that they stayed with them on their returning to life. In effect – and without their necessarily becoming in any way more conventionally religious – we may say that something we may call God had come into their daily lives in a way that they could 'feel' directly in touch with. But this contact took place not with a bearded old gentleman up in the sky but by means of a feeling of now belonging to that mind-blowing Thought that represents our connectedness to all creation through all time, and from which *only our clinging to material-mindedness* keeps us separate.

This is why very few if any near-death experients return to try to recontact those they met in the 'third level' via Moody's Nekromanteion-type séances in darkened rooms. Instead, without the slightest churchiness, and often even without directly recognizing that this is what they are doing, they return to live their lives in a way so closely resembling Jesus's teachings as enshrined in the Sermon on the Mount that, from our perspective at least, this can seem neither accident nor coincidence. For completely ordinary people to change their lives in this way bespeaks a true contact with that inconceivable dimension in which ultimately the thought-forms of all, through all time, meet as one. And it is *this way of living* that opens up our return to that dimension – from which we became separated only when some archetypal 'Adam' and 'Eve' first began running up fig-leaf suits by way of vainly covering themselves from that which is all-seeing and all-knowing.

Throughout recorded history mystics of many cultures have grappled, always inadequately, to describe this dimension. Among people from nearer our own time English school-master Dr F. C. Happold has very eloquently spoken of it following an experience that he had on the evening of 18 April 1936, the day that his first child was delivered still-born:

> As I lay in bed I was very anxious about my wife, and much disturbed in mind. And then a great peace came over me. I was conscious of a lovely, unexplainable pattern in the texture of things, a pattern of which everyone and every-thing was a part, and weaving the pattern was a Power; and that Power was what we faintly call Love. I realized that we are not lonely atoms in a cold, unfriendly, indifferent universe, but that each of us is linked up in a rhythm, of which we may be unconscious, and which we can never really know, but to which we can submit ourselves trustfully and unreservedly.[24]

Moira, an Australian who 'died' and had a near-death experience as a result of complications following an appen-dicitis operation, has given Dr Cherie Sutherland a similar description of an experience not unlike the Lloyd-Jones's concerning Edwin's hands. One day, following a lot of pain from her illness, she dragged herself into her garden, where there were two beautiful eucalyptus trees. She was lovingly admiring these when, in her words:

> as I looked at [one of] the tree[s], it was as if I had X-ray vision. I could see inside the tree. And I could see all these cells working away like mad. As I looked at them, I became a cell. And there I was. And I had a consciousness. I couldn't think or reason, but I had a feeling of joy that I was there doing something to help the universe go round, was helping bring up all this sap, or whatever it was, up into me to pass to the next one, to the top of the tree. And there

was a feeling of joyous participation in something that just went on and on.[25]

Although within a moment Moira was back in her body, as she began hanging out her washing:

the same thing happened again. I suddenly had this X-ray vision. I could see through all the trees, through everything. And I could see that absolutely everything in the universe was interconnected, and interdependent. There was nothing separate, not a thing. Then I saw that even the air between things was just teeming with organisms, and they were all interconnected and all for a purpose. They were all doing things. They were going into me, and coming out, going into the earth and coming out, going into the trees and coming out. I could see that absolutely everything was interconnected. And I thought, 'So that's how it works!' I completely lost consciousness of myself – I don't know how long it lasted – I could see through all the trees, all the buildings, and could see to infinity. Then the next thing I knew I was out in space somewhere, and I knew that the same power that was holding all the planets and everything in space was the same power that was in me. And it's a stupid thing to say, but I didn't see God – I felt I *was* God! I suddenly felt that I knew everything, that I was everything . . . Words won't explain it. I knew I knew everything. I knew there was an absolute reason for being, and I knew that the universe was all one – *almost as if the universe was me and I was the universe* . . . [italics mine][26]

As Moira summed it all up:

God is not a great big person sort of thing . . . Each of us is like a cell in the body of God, so we have all God's inherent qualities: love, peace, wisdom, et cetera. But we don't recognize it because we have this sense of separation. But once we can get over the sense of separation we'll know who we really are and then we'll be able to start expressing it.[27]

Indeed Edwin Lloyd-Jones expressed much the same sentiments from what he was 'given' in the course of one of his quiet reflections at Elm Grove Sanctuary:

I saw . . . this orange, and a knife. And I saw this knife cut the orange into bits and peel it. And each little segment of the orange was brought out, and each little tiny pip was taken out, and the whole thing was scattered, the whole orange was scattered, and then gradually re-formed again. And that's what I was told in this meditation, that is like God, it's a simplistic thing, we are like one of those tiny little pieces of that orange, and God won't be complete until we all come back together. I could relate to that.

And this is why neither God, nor any so-called 'dead' person who has ever lived in all God's creation, is to be found by any of the technologies of this world, any more than those same technologies can capture a thought in a test tube, or discover Beethoven by subjecting the CD discs of all his symphonies to every conceivable scientific test.

There is only one way of discovering these things, of making that so elusive 'contact'. This is by avoiding the mistake of that rich man of Jesus's parable who, by in life giving no thought for the poor beggar Lazarus who sat hungry and in rags outside his gate, so shut himself off from the God-who-knows-all-thoughts that when he died he lived on in the very same wretchedness that he had failed to alleviate in his neighbour the beggar. As we are told in Chapter 16 of St Luke's Gospel, when the rich man learned of his mistake, he urged that someone be sent back from the dead to give this message to his brothers who were still living. But he was told that they had already been given this message, just as he had. They had simply not listened to it.'Ah no,' he tried to plead. 'But if someone comes back from the dead, then they'll do the right thing then.'

So will they? This book has been about not a few twentieth-century people who have come back from the dead with this very message. A message that there really is an afterlife, and that its quality for each of us is critically dependent upon the values we adhere to in this one. A message that it is the treasures, of whatever kind, that we lay up for ourselves in this material world of time and space that hold us back from, and keep us out of touch with, that third level that is the realm both of God, and of all thoughts, and of everyone who has ever lived.

If we can only grasp this message, then we may indeed *know* that there is life after death. And be able to conceive the inconceivable . . .

Notes and References

Chapter One
'Back from the Dead?'

1. Peter and Elizabeth Fenwick, *The Truth in the Light*, London, Headline, 1995, p. 14.
2. Cherie Sutherland, *Within the Light*, New York and London, Bantam, 1993, p. 57.
3. Michael Sabom, *Recollections of Death: a Medical Investigation*, New York, Harper & Row, 1982, p. 136.
4. Dag Hammarskjöld, *Markings*, trans. W. H. Auden and Leif Sjöberg, London, Faber and Faber, 1966, p. 136.

Chapter Two
'The Oldest Belief'

1. Axel-Ivar Berglund, *Zulu Thought-Patterns and Symbolism*, C. Hirst and Co., 1976.
2. See Nicholas Reeves, *The Complete Tutankhamun*, London, Thames and Hudson, 1990, pp. 205–7.
3. Given on a cone of Urukagina, King of Lagash. See Alexander Heidel, *The Gilgamesh Epic and Old Testament Parallels*, Chicago, University of Chicago Press, 1949, p. 151.
4. According to the Chinese annals of the Wei Dynasty, when the Empress Regent Himeko (Jingō Kogu, according

to the Japanese lists), died in what is our AD 247, a large mound was piled above her grave and more than a thousand of her male and female servants were killed to accompany her into death.

5. Metropolitan Museum of Art, Geometric Greek vase no.40.130.15.

6. John W. Hedges, *Tomb of the Eagles: A Window on Stone Age Tribal Britain*, London, John Murray, 1985.

7. Susan Walker, *Memorials to the Roman Dead*, London, British Museum Publications, 1985, p. 10.

8. Lawrence Blair, *Ring of Fire*, London, Transworld, 1988.

9. A. M. Duncan-Kemp, *Where Strange Gods Call*, Brisbane, Smith and Paterson, 1968, p. 138.

10. Bart McDowell, 'The Aztecs', *National Geographic Magazine*, vol. 158, no. 6, December 1980, p. 751.

11. Berglund, op.cit., p. 78.

12. Adrian Boshier, 'The Religions of Africa', in Arnold Toynbee, Arthur Koestler et al., *Life after Death*, London, Weidenfeld and Nicolson, 1976, pp. 62–3.

13. M. S. Seale, 'Islamic Society', in ibid., p. 123.

14. Jung Chang, *Wild Swans*, London, HarperCollins, 1991, p. 111.

15. Sir J. G. Frazer, *The Belief in Immortality and the Worship of the Dead*, Gifford Lectures, London, Macmillan, 1913, vol. I, p. 361.

16. Cottie A. Burland, 'Primitive Societies' in Toynbee, et al., op.cit., p. 41.

17. John D. Ray, 'Ancient Egypt', in Michael Loewe and Carmen Blacker (eds), *Divination and Oracles*, London, Allen and Unwin, 1981, p. 179.

18. Lewis Bayles Paton, *Spiritism and the Cult of the Dead in Antiquity*, London, Hodder and Stoughton, 1921, p. 36.

19. Bart McDowell, 'The Aztecs', art. cit.

20. Edward Shortland, *Traditions and Superstitions of the*

New Zealanders, London, Longman, Brown, Green, 1856. p. 84.

21. Thompson, *The Devils and Evil Spirits of Babylonia*, 1, 53, quoted in Paton, op.cit, pp. 202–3.

22. Homer, *Iliad*, Book 23. In E. V. Rieu's classic Penguin Book translation, see pp. 413–14.

23. Arthur P. Wolf, *Gods, Ghosts and Ancestors*, p. 170.

24. Suetonius, 'Gaius Caligula', see translation by Robert Graves in *The Twelve Caesars*, Harmondsworth, Penguin, 1957, p. 178: 'His [Caligula's] body was moved secretly to the Lamian Gardens, half-cremated on a hastily-built pyre, and then buried beneath a shallow covering of sods. Later, when his sisters returned from exile they exhumed, cremated and entombed it. But all the city knew that the Gardens had been haunted until then by his ghost, and that something horrible appeared every night at the scene of the murder until at last the building burned down.'

25. W. Y. Evans-Wentz (ed.), foreword to *The Tibetan Book of the Dead*, Oxford, Oxford University Press, 1960, p. lxxv, footnote 2.

26. See 1 Samuel: 28.

27. Quoted in Paton, op.cit., p. 30.

28. Ibid., p. 33.

29. Cyril Havecker, *Understanding Aboriginal Culture*, Sydney, Cosmos, 1987, p. 30.

30. C. A. Valentine, 'The Lakalai of New Britain', in P. J. Lawrence and M. J. Meggitt (eds), *Gods, Ghosts and Men in Melanesia*, Melbourne, Oxford University Press, 1965, pp. 174–5.

31. Audrey Butt, in Stewart Wavell, Audrey Butt and Nina Epton, *Trances*, London, Allen and Unwin, 1966, pp. 43–61.

Chapter Three
'Sifting the Wheat from the Chaff'

1. Euripides, *Helen*, quoted in J. S. Morrison 'The Classical World', in Michael Loewe and Carmen Blacker (eds), *Divination and Oracles*, London, Allen and Unwin, 1981, p. 106.
2. Renée Haynes, *The Society for Psychical Research, 1882–1982: A History*, London, Macdonald, 1982, p. 145.
3. See my *Mind Out of Time*, London, Gollancz, 1981; also *The After Death Experience*, London, Sidgwick and Jackson, 1987, pp. 27–50.
4. Quoted from Myers in Sir William Barrett's *Death-bed Visions*, London, 1926, reprinted as an Aquarian Press paperback, 1986, pp. 87–8.
5. Gordon Thomas, *Issels, The Biography of a Doctor*, London, Hodder and Stoughton, 1975, pp. 161–2.
6. Quoted in George Gallop Jr (with William Proctor), *Adventures in Immortality*, London, Souvenir, 1983, p. 14.
7. Melvin Morse, *Closer to the Light: Learning from the Near-Death Experiences of Children*, New York, Bantam, 1992, p. 73.
8. Roy Jenkins, *European Diary, 1977–81*, London, Collins, 1989.
9. Melvin Morse, *Parting Visions: an Exploration of Pre-Dead Psychic and Spiritual Experiences*, London, Piatkus, 1995, p. 72.
10. Victor Duleep Singh, quoted in *Journal of the Society for Psychical Research*, vol. 6, 1894.
11. Letter from Krystyna Kolodziej to the author, and earlier quoted in my book *The After Death Experience*, London, Sidgwick and Jackson, 1987, pp. 98–9.
12. Harold Owen, *Journey from Obscurity*, vol. III, 1965.

13. I would have liked more information about this case, and contacted Bill Hamilton at the BBC to ask if it would be possible to be put in touch with Mrs Williams, only for him to put the phone down on me, as if stung by a wasp, when I explained my line of enquiry.

14. Barbara Wood, *E. F. Schumacher: His Life and Thought*, New York, Harper and Row, 1984, p. 367. Intriguingly, Schumacher does seem also to have given a symbolic signal at what was the time of his death. As recorded by his biographer daughter Barbara Wood: 'September 4th [the day of his death] had been a Sunday. At Holcombe a young mother's help called Tessa Midgely had gone into the kitchen sometime between ten and eleven while the rest of the family were at church to make herself a cup of coffee. As she put the kettle on she was startled by a crash on the kitchen floor. She turned to see a cup had inexplicably fallen out of the cupboard. It had broken into too many pieces to be repaired. She saw that it was Fritz's cup. Later that afternoon the police called with the news that Fritz had died.' Ibid., pp. 367–8.

15. This and subsequent quotations derive from Peter Underwood, *No Common Task*, pp. 117–20. Underwood does not, however, identify Robin Hayden, which I was only able to do with the kind assistance of Barbara and Duncan McKenzie. This case is dealt with at much greater length in my book *In Search of Ghosts*, London, Headline 1995, pp. 84–93.

16. Quoted in Andrew MacKenzie, *Hauntings and Apparitions*, London, Granada, 1983, p. 214.

17. From a letter written in 1769 to Anglican priest Revd Thomas Hartley: 'I have been called to a sacred office by the Lord Himself, who in the year 1743 most graciously manifested Himself in person before me, His servant, and

then opened my sight into the spiritual world and
granted me to speak with spirits and angels. . .'

18. Emanuel Swedenborg, Spiritual Diary, para. 2542, quoted
in David Lorimer, *Survival: Body, Mind and Death in the
Light of Psychic Experience*, London, Routledge and Kegan
Paul, 1984, p. 198.

19. R. L. Tafel, *Documents Concerning the Life and Character of
Emanuel Swedenborg*, London, Swedenborg Society,
1875–7, 3 vols, document 275P.

20. Quoted in William Gill, 'The Ghost Breaker', *Independent*
magazine, 29 January, 1994, p. 35.

21. See Eddie Burks and Gillian Cribbs, *Ghosthunter: Investigating the World of Ghosts and Spirits* London, Headline,
1995, Chapter 1.

22. Ian Wilson, *In Search of Ghosts*, London, Headline, 1995,
Chapter 17.

Chapter Four
'Something Everyone on Earth Has to Know About'

1. Raymond Moody's Foreword to George Ritchie, *Return
from Tomorrow*, Eastbourne, Kingsway Publications, 1992,
p. 9.

2. It should be pointed out that *Return from Tomorrow* has
gone into its 25th English Language printing, has sold
more than 200,000 copies, and been translated into nine
languages. Yet because it has been marketed predominantly in evangelical circles, it has not received anything
like the wide recognition enjoyed by Raymond Moody's
books.

3. George Ritchie wrote *Return from Tomorrow* in partnership
with the writer Elizabeth Sherrill. The first draft of this
chapter was based almost entirely on this book, and

when I sent it to Ritchie for checking he sent me a copy of his more recent *My Life After Dying*, entirely the work of his own pen, and which he felt to be the more accurate. Accordingly, where there are slight discrepancies between *Return from Tomorrow* and *My Life After Dying* I have followed the latter.

4. Ritchie, *My Life After Dying*, p. 13.
5. Ritchie, *Return from Tomorrow*, p. 40.
6. Ritchie, *My Life After Dying*, pp. 13–14.
7. Ibid., p. 14.
8. Ibid., p. 16.
9. Ritchie, *Return from Tomorrow*, p. 49.
10. Personal letter to the author, undated, received late September 1996.
11. Ritchie, *Return from Tomorrow*, p. 57.
12. Ibid., pp. 58–9.
13. Ibid., pp. 63–5.
14. Ibid., p. 79.
15. Ritchie, *My Life After Dying*, p. 35.
16. Raymond Moody, *Life after Life*, New York, Bantam, p. 14.
17. Ritchie, *Return from Tomorrow*, p. 16.
18. Ritchie describes his subsequent career as a psychiatrist in *My Life After Dying*.
18. Quoted in *My Life After Dying*, p. 9, from statements procured by Mrs Catherine Marshall, author of *To Live Again*.
20. Ibid., p. 9.
21. Ritchie, *Return from Tomorrow*, p. 122.

Chapter Five
'But Can You Really Leave Your Body'?

1. Kenneth Ring, *Life at Death: a Scientific Investigation of the*

Near-Death Experience, New York, Coward, McCann and Geoghegan, 1980, pp. 45–6.

2. 'Woman awake for surgery', report in the Manchester *Guardian*, 7 June 1985. For other examples, see J. M. Evans, 'Patients' Experiences of Awareness during General Anaesthesia', in M. Rosen and J. N. Lunn (eds), *Consciousness, Awareness and Pain in General Anaesthesia*, London, Butterworths, 1987, pp. 184–92.

3. Dr Thomas Stuttaford 'Some Sense of Hearing at Last', Medical Briefing column, *The Times*, 9 February 1989.

4. Jeremy Laurance, 'Buzzer Unlocks Mind Trapped in Useless Body', *The Times*, 5 July 1996.

5. Jeremy Laurance, 'Vegetative State Diagnosis Wrong in Many Patients', ibid.

6. H. R. Schoolcraft, *Travels on the Central Portion of the Mississippi Valley*, New York, Collins and Henry, 1825, pp. 404–20.

7. Bryant S. Hinckley, *The Faith of our Pioneering Fathers*, Salt Lake City, Deseret, 1959, p. 183.

8. Michael Sabom, *Recollections of Death: a Medical Investigation*, New York, Harper and Row, 1982, p. x.

9. Quoted in Margot Grey, *Return from Death, An Exploration of the Near-death Experience*, London, Arkana, 1985.

10. Cherie Sutherland, *Within the Light*, New York and London, Bantam, 1993, p. 86.

11. This confusion has significant parallels to ghost-laying Eddie Burks' and others' reported difficulties trying to persuade ghosts that they are dead, as we noted earlier of Eddie Burks' case of the old woman at Leicester, described in Chapter 3.

12. W. Y. Evans-Wentz (ed.), *The Tibetan Book of the Dead*, Oxford, Oxford University Press, 1960, p. 38.

13. Swedenborg, *Arcana Celestia*, op.cit., para 320.

14. Raymond Moody, *Reflections on Life after Life*, St Simon's Island, GA, Mockingbird, 1977, pp. 41–2.

15. From a tape-recorded account of her experience that Mrs McKenzie kindly supplied to the author. This is also quoted in Peter and Elizabeth Fenwick, *The Truth in the Light*, London, Headline, 1995, p. 100.

16. Moody, op.cit., p. 39.

17. Quoted in Fenwick, op.cit., pp. 34–5.

18. Moody, op.cit., p. 36.

19. Sabom, op.cit., p. 117.

20. There are rare examples in which the experient reports being able only to see but not hear everything going on around them, in particular a fifty-seven-year-old construction worker interviewed by Dr Michael Sabom who insisted, 'I couldn't hear anything. Some of these articles you read, the people say they can hear everything. I couldn't hear anything.' See Sabom, op.cit., p. 32.

21. Ibid.

22. Moody, op.cit., pp. 43–4.

23. Sabom, op.cit., p. 32.

24. Cherie Sutherland, *Transformed by the Light*, New York and London, Bantam, 1992, p. 6.

25. Ibid.

26. Sabom, op.cit., p. 73.

27. Barbara Walker, William Serdahely and Lori Bechtel, 'Three Near-Death Experiences with Premonitions of What Could Have Been', *Journal of Near-Death Studies*, Spring 1991, p. 191.

28. Sabom, op.cit., p. 34.

29. Kenneth Ring, *Heading towards Omega: in Search of the Meaning of the Near-Death Experience*, New York, Morrow, 1984, pp. 39, 40.

30. Cherie Sutherland, *Within the Light*, New York and London, Bantam, 1993, pp. 180–1.

31. Fenwick, op.cit., p. 26.

32. Ibid.

33. Ring, *Life at Death*, p. 45 [referring to his informant no. 33].
34. Sabom, op.cit., p. 116.
35. Moody, op.cit., p. 102.
36. It cannot be discounted that one or two books written by professed near-death experients may not be all they seem. Where I have suspicions of this (justified or otherwise), I have omitted giving the author's testimony any serious attention. But the generality of near-death experients seek no such publicity for themselves, and can have no motive for telling anything other than the truth.
37. M. Morse, D. Conner and D. Tyler 'Near-death Experiences in a Pediatric Population: A preliminary report', *American Journal of Diseases of Children*, 139 (1985), pp. 595–600.
38. Cherie Sutherland, *Children and the Light*.
39. Susan Blackmore, *Beyond the Body: An Investigation of Out-of-the-Body Experiences*, London, Heinemann, 1982.
40. See Fenwick, op. cit., pp. 36–7 for some cases of individuals who have perceived such cords when, like Susan Blackmore, they have had out-of-the-body experiences *not* involving their nearly dying. But among the generality of near-death experients, no such cords are reported.
41. Ibid., pp. 34–5.
42. Kimberly Clark, 'Clinical Interventions with Near Death Experiencers', in Bruce Greyson and Charles P. Flynn (eds), *The Near Death Experience, Problems, Prospects, Perspectives*, Springfield, Ill., Charles C. Thomas, 1984.
43. Ring, *Life at Death*, p. 92.
44. Ibid., p. 93.
45. Ring, *Heading towards Omega*, pp. 42–3.
46. Larry Dossey, *Recovering the Soul A Scientific and Spiritual Search*, New York, Bantam, 1989, p. 18.
47. In fact I have edited out here what Vicki said about

having had an earlier near-death experience as a result of acute peritonitis when she was twelve years old, during which she had also 'seen'. As, in her own words, the second experience was 'much the more vivid', the first one seemed best omitted from discussion.

48. From the tape-recording of a talk given by Vicki at a support group in Seattle, February 1994, as played during a talk given by Dr Kenneth Ring at the Stepping Stone Centre, Brisbane, Australia, 5 March 1996.

49. As quoted in Kenneth Ring and Sharon Cooper, *Midnight: A Study of Eyeless Vision in the Blind*, awaiting publication.

50. Quoted by Ring in his talk at the Stepping Stone Centre, Brisbane.

51. Ibid.

52. Ring and Cooper, *Mindsight*, op.cit.

53. Ibid.

Chapter Six
'And Can You Really Reach a Realm of the Dead?'

1. Father Louis Tucker, *Clerical Errors*, New York, Harper, 1943, pp. 221–5.

2. Cherie Sutherland, *Within the Light*, New York and London, Bantam, 1992, pp. 143–4.

3. Peter and Elizabeth Fenwick, *The Truth in the Light*, London, Headline, 1995, p. 50.

4. Ibid., pp. 173–4.

5. Sutherland, op.cit., p. 199. Here Laurel Lloyd-Jones is given the pseudonym 'Janet', but as Laurel will be referred to later in this book under her real name (having given me her permissioin to do so), I have used this here.

6. George Ritchie, *Return from Tomorrow*, Eastbourne, Kingsway Publications, 1992, p. 55.

7. Fenwick, op.cit., p. 76.
8. Sutherland, *Transformed by the Light: Life after Near-Death Experiences*, New York and London, Bantam, 1992, p. 11.
9. Kenneth Ring, *Life at Death: a Scientific Investigation of the Near-Death Experience*, New York, Coward, McCann and Geoghegan, 1980, p. 61.
10. Ibid., p. 63.
11. From the tape-recording of her talk as played during Dr Kenneth Ring's lecture at the Stepping Stone Centre, Brisbane, Australia, 5 March 1996.
12. Fenwick, op.cit., p. 25.
13. Maurice Rawlings, *Beyond Death's Door*, London, Sheldon, 1978, pp. 98–9.
14. Raymond Moody, *Reflections on Life after Life*, St Simon's Island, GA, Mockingbird, 1977, p. 16.
15. Fenwick, op.cit., p. 108.
16. Quoted in Johannes Brønsted, *The Vikings*, Hardmondsworth, Penguin, 1960, p. 282.
17. J. H. Hyslop, *Psychical Research and the Resurrection*, London, Fisher Unwin, 1908, p. 97.
18. Kenneth Ring, *Heading towards Omega: in Search of the Meaning of the Near-Death Experience*, New York, Morrow, 1984, pp. 39, 40.
19. Ring, *Life at Death*, pp. 63, 64.
20. Tucker, op.cit., pp. 221–5.
21. Michael Sabom, *Recollections of Death: a Medical Investigation*, New York, Harper and Row, 1982, p. 49.
22. For a fuller account of this experience, see my book *The After Death Experience*, London, Sidgwick and Jackson, 1987, p. 149.
23. Rawlings, *Beyond Death's Door*, p. 99.
24. Moody, *Reflections on Life after Death*, p. 56.
25. Sabom, *Recollections of Death*, p. 48.
26. Ibid., p. 47.

27. Sutherland, *Within the Light*, pp. 21–2.
28. Ibid., p. 192.
29. In the words of Allan Pring, 'the only senses I was aware of were sight and sound, but even these were very real', Fenwick, op.cit., p. 114.
30. W. Y. Evans-Wentz (ed.), *The Tibetan Book of the Dead*, Oxford, Oxford University Press, p. 32.
31. Quoted in Fenwick, op. cit., p. 94.
32. Sutherland *Within the Light* p. 193.
33. Ibid., p. 174.
34. Fenwick, op.cit., p. 108.
35. Ibid., p. 210.
36. Ibid., p. 62.
37. Betty J. Eadie, with Curtis Taylor, *Embraced by the Light*, London, Aquarian, 1994 (originally published by Gold Leaf Press, Placerville, California, 1992).
38. See Richard Abanes, *Embraced by the Light and the Bible*, Camp Hill, PA, Horizon Books, 1994, also a letter by Richard Abanes in the *Journal of Near-Death Studies*, Fall 1996, pp. 75–7.
39. Fenwick, op.cit., p. 114.
40. Ibid., p. 113.
41. Sabom, op.cit., p. 22.
42. Sutherland, *Within the Light*, p. 193.
43. From a tape-recording of her experience given to me by Mrs McKenzie and also quoted in Fenwick, op.cit., p. 100.
44. Ibid., p. 53.
45. Susan Blackmore, *Dying to Live: Near-Death Experiences*, London, Grafton, 1993, p. 259.
46. A. G. Khan, 'Come Back, My Child . . .' article in the part-work *The Unexplained*, issue no. 154, p. 3070.
47. According to my informant on this case, Peter Brooke-smith, this 'garden' corresponds 'very precisely' to the picture of paradise given in the Koran, yet that book was

not part of the life of the Khan household, the family being 'somewhat unorthodox in religion', the children neither being raised as Muslims nor attending a mosque.

48. Khan, art. cit., p. 3072.
49. Letter from Peter Brookesmith to the author, 24 February, 1990.
50. Sutherland, *Within the Light*, p. 194.

Chapter Seven
'A Question of Judgment'

1. Report by Ruth Gledhill, 'Synod backs rethink on traditional view of Hell', *The Times*, 15 July 1996.
2. From a tape-recording of a lecture in which Storm described his experience as given at the NDE Research Institute Fort Thomas, Kentucky in 1989.
3. From a tape-recording of a lecture by Howard Storm kindly supplied to me by Storm himself.
4. From the tape-recording of the lecture supplied directly to me by Storm.
5. From the tape-recording of Storm's lecture in Kentucky, as quoted in Arvin S. Gibson, *Glimpses of Eternity*, Utah, Horizon, 1992, pp. 280–1.
6. Raymond Moody, *Reflections on Life after Life*, St Simon's Island, GA, Mockingbird, 1977, p. 143.
7. Cherie Sutherland, *Within the Light*, New York and London, Bantam, 1993, pp. 106–7.
8. Maurice Rawlings, *Beyond Death's Door*, London, Sheldon, 1978, p. 19.
9. Sir Alfred Ayer, 'What I Saw When I Was Dead', *Sunday Telegraph*, 28 August 1988.
10. Peter and Elizabeth Fenwick, *The Truth in the Light*, London, Headline, 1995, p. 86.

11. Moody, op.cit., pp. 19–21.
12. See my book *In Search of Ghosts*, Headline, 1995, pp. 152–7, based on my personal interviewing of both Harry Martindale and Joan Mawson.
13. Quoted in R. Noyes and R. Kletti, 'Panoramic memory: A response to the threat of death', *Omega*, 8, p. 182.
14. Kenneth Ring, *Life at Death: a Scientific Investigatioin of the Near-Death Experience*, New York, Coward, McCann and Geoghegan, 1980, p. 117.
15. Moody, op.cit., p. 35.
16. Fenwick, op.cit., p. 114.
17. Quoted in Melvin Morse, *Parting Visions: an Exploration of Pre-Death Psychic and Spiritual Experiences*, London, Piatkus, 1995, pp. 104–5.
18. Sutherland, op.cit., p. 200.
19. Ring, op.cit., p. 196.
20. Fenwick, op.cit., p. 114.
21. George Ritchie, *Return from Tomorrow*, Eastbourne, Kingsway Publications, 1992, p. 54.

Chapter Eight
'On Time, Space and "Reality"'

1. Raymond Moody, *Reflections on Life after Life*, St Simon's Island, GA, Mockingbird, 1977, p. 101.
2. Peter and Elizabeth Fenwick, *The Truth in the Light*, London, Headline, 1995, p. 48.
3. Ibid., p. 114.
4. George Ritchie, *Return from Tomorrow*, Eastbourne, Kingsway Publications, 1992, pp. 49–50.
5. Cherie Sutherland, *Within the Light*, New York and London, Bantam, 1993, p. 138.
6. Kenneth Ring, *Life at Death: a Scientific Investigation of the*

Near-Death Experience, New York, Coward, McCann and Geoghegan, 1980, pp. 97–8.

7. Ritchie, op.cit., p. 50.
8. Sutherland, op.cit., pp. 180–1.
9. Ring, op.cit., p. 97.
10. Moody, op.cit., pp. 10–11.
11. Sutherland, op.cit., p. 170.
12. Kenneth Ring, *Heading towards Omega: in Search of the Meaning of the Near-Death Experience*, New York, Morrow, 1984, p. 74.
13. Sutherland, op.cit., p. 171.
14. Ronald Rose, *Living Magic: The Realities Underlying the Psychical Practices and Beliefs of Australian Aborigines*, London, Chatto and Windus, 1957, p. 130.
15. A. N. Exton-Smith and M. D. Cantaub, 'Terminal Illness in the Aged', *The Lancet*, vol. 2, 1961, p. 305.
16. J. H. Phillips, *Caring for the Dying Patient and his Family*, New York, Health Sciences Publishing Corporation, 1973, panel presentations on p. 45.
17. Melvin Morse with Paul Perry, *Parting Visions: an Exploration of Pre-Death Psychic and Spiritual Experiences*, London, Piatkus, 1995, p. 100.
18. From J. C. Barker, 'Premonitions of the Aberfan Disaster', *Journal of the Society for Psychical Research*, 44, 1967, pp. 169–81, quoted in Ivor Grattan-Guinness, *Psychical Research: A Guide to its History, Principles and Practices in celebration of 100 Years of the Society for Psychical Research*, Wellingborough, Aquarian, 1982.
19. Ring, *Life at Death*, p. 35.
20. Ibid., pp. 35–6.
21. Ibid., p. 36.
22. Morse, *Parting Visions*, pp. 38–9.
23. Phyllis Battelle, 'Triplets – and They Didn't Know It', *Reader's Digest*, UK edn, June 1981, pp. 51–5.

24. Ibid., p. 53.
25. Based on Peter Watson, *Twins*, London, Hutchinson, 1981, p. 47.
26. Stephen Hawking, *A Brief History of Time: from the Big Bang to Black Holes*, London, Bantam, 1988, p. 139.
27. Sir Alfred Ayer, 'What I Saw When I Was Dead . . .', *Sunday Telegraph*, 28 August 1988, p. 5.

Chapter Nine
'A Transforming Experience'

1. Peter and Elizabeth Fenwick, *The Truth in the Light*, London, Headline, 1995, p. 110.
2. Michael Sabom, *Recollections of Death: a Medical Investigation*, New York, Harper and Row, 1982, p. 45.
3. Cherie Sutherland, *Within the Light*, New York and London, Bantam, 1993, pp. 137–8.
4. Fenwick, op.cit., p. 80.
5. Sutherland, op.cit., p. 119.
6. Sabom, op.cit., p. 51.
7. The Australian near-death researcher Dr Cherie Sutherland has reported how on a trip to modern-day Japan she found particularly prevalent there the motif of a stream or river. One six-year-old Japanese girl who suffered a three-day coma saw herself on the banks of a river with a bridge upstream which she knew if she could reach it would take her to a place with beautiful flowers that she could see on the other side.
8. Fenwick, op.cit., p. 122.
9. Melvin Morse, *Closer to the Light: Learning from the Near-Death Experience of Children*, London, Bantam, 1992, p. 39.
10. Quoted in Fenwick, op.cit., p. 101.
11. Ibid., p. 48.

12. Ibid., pp. 116–17.
13. Ibid., p. 101.
14. Sutherland, op.cit., p. 21.
15. Ibid., p. 194.
16. Morse, op.cit., p. 44.
17. Raymond Moody, *Reflections on Life after Life*, St Simon's Island, GA, Mockingbird, 1977, p. 76.
18. Ibid., p. 105–6.
19. Sutherland, op.cit., p. 181.
20. Cherie Sutherland, *Transformed by the Light: Life after Near Death Experiences*, New York and London, Bantam, 1992, p. 214.
21. Fenwick, op.cit., p. 82.
22. Kenneth Ring, *Life at Death: a Scientific Investigation of the Near-Death Experience*, New York, Coward, McCann and Geoghegan, 1980, p. 156.
23. Ibid.
24. Sabom, op.cit., p. 132.
25. Sutherland, *Transformed by the Light*, p. 139.
26. Ibid., p. 137.
27. Sabom, op.cit., p. 126.
28. Sutherland, *Transformed by the Light*, p. 87.
29. Moody, op.cit., p. 95.
30. Fenwick, op.cit., p. 76.
31. Ring, op.cit., p. 144.
32. Sutherland, *Within the Light*, p. 184.
33. Quoted in Paul Pickering, 'Back From the Dead', *Observer* magazine, 12 December 1976, p. 31.
34. Ibid.
35. Sutherland, *Within the Light*, p. 142.
36. Ring. op.cit., p. 144.
37. Sutherland, *Transformed by the Light*, p. 136.
38. Barbara Harris and L. Bascom, *Full Circle: The Near-Death Experience and Beyond*, New York, Pocket Books, 1990, p. 150.

39. Using the Australian Values Study Survey of 1984, which quotes an average divorce rate of 11 per cent, Cherie Sutherland calculated the divorce rate among Australian near-death experients to be actually significantly worse than among the population as a whole. However, in view of the latest figures, which show a divorce rate of around 50 per cent, Australian near-death experients probably roughly reflect their national average. Certainly they are no better . . .

40. Mori Insinger, 'The Impact of a Near-Death Experience on Family Relationships', *Journal of Near-Death Studies*, 9, 3, Spring 1991, pp. 146–7.

41. Fenwick, op.cit., pp. 131–2.

42. Sutherland, *Within the Light*, p. 160.

43. Ring, op.cit., p. 164.

44. Ibid.

Chapter Ten
'On Not Leaving God Out'

1. Unless otherwise indicated, all quotes from Laurel and Edwin Lloyd-Jones in this chapter derive from my tape-recorded interviews with them on 1 and 2 July 1996.

2. Cherie Sutherland, *Within the Light*, New York and London, Bantam, 1993, pp. 201–2.

3. Ibid., pp. 202–3.

4. Ibid., p. 203.

5. Ibid.

6. Ibid., p. 207.

7. Ibid., pp. 207–8.

8. Ibid., p. 208. Sutherland, retaining the anonymity of her informants, has referred to an 'actress friend', which I have replaced with 'Rona'.

9. Anonymous account of a near-death experience: 'NDE Collision: The moment of choice', in IANDS News Bulletin Third Issue, Winter–Spring 1986–7.
10. Peter and Elizabeth Fenwick, *The Truth in the Light*, London, Headline, 1995.

Chapter Eleven
'Conceiving the Inconceivable'

1. George Ritchie, *Return from Tomorrow*, Eastbourne, Kingsway Publications, 1992, p. 64.
2. Stuart Sutherland, *The International Dictionary of Psychology*, quoted in Nigel Hawkes, 'What gives us our sense of self?', *The Times*, 5 August 1996.
3. Francis Crick, *The Astonishing Hypothesis*.
4. Guy Claxton, *Noises from the Darkroom: The Science and Mystery of the Mind* Willingborough, Aquarian Press, 1994.
5. David Chalmers, *The Conscious Mind*, Oxford, Oxford University Press, 1996.
6. From Igor Aleksander's review of Chalmers's book as published in *The Times*, 5 August, 1996.
7. J. G. Hoffman, *The Life and Death of Cells*, London, Hutchinson, 1958.
8. Valerie Taylor, fax to the author sent 3 July 1996.
9. Rupert Sheldrake, *A New Science of Life*, London, Blond and Briggs, 1981.
10. 'A Book for Burning?' Editorial in *Nature* 293, 1981, pp. 245–6.
11. Sheldrake, op.cit., pp. 95–6.
12. Cyril Havecker, *Understanding Aboriginal Culture*, Sydney, Cosmos, 1987, p. 19.
13. Ibid., p. 32.
14. Ibid., p. 19.

15. Ibid., p. 21.
16. Quoted in Raymond Moody, *Reunions*, London, Little, Brown and Co., 1993, p. 7.
17. Raymond Moody with Paul Perry, *Reunions: Visionary Encounters with Departed Loved Ones*, Warner Books, 1994, pp. 25–6.
18. Ibid., p. 27.
19. Ibid., p. 28.
20. Ibid.
21. Ibid., pp. 28–9.
22. Wrekin Trust conference: 'Life after Death'. Its relevance to the Living and the Dying', Regent's College, Regent's Park, London, 24–25 October 1987.
23. Rosemary Guiley, 'Odyssey for the Dead', in the Newsletter of the Ghost Club, London, April 1996.
24. F. C. Happold, *Religious Faith and Twentieth-Century Man*, Harmondsworth, Penguin, 1966, p. 15.
25. Cherie Sutherland *Within the Light*, New York and London, Bantam, 1993, pp. 135–6.
26. Ibid.
27. Ibid., p. 127.

Bibliography

Atwater, Phyllis, *I Died Three Times in 1977*, Dayton, Va., 1980

Ayer, Sir Alfred, 'What I Saw When I Was Dead', *Sunday Telegraph*, 28 August 1988

Barrett, Sir William, *Death-bed Visions*, London, 1926, reprinted as an Aquarian Press paperback, 1986

Blair, Lawrence, *Ring of Fire*, London, Transworld, 1988

Blackmore, Susan, *Beyond the Body: an Investigation of Out-of-the Body Experiences*, London, Heinemann, 1982
  Dying to Live: Near-Death Experiences, London, Grafton, 1993

Burks, Eddie and Gillian Cribbs, *Ghosthunter: Investigating the World of Ghosts and Spirits*, London, Headline, 1995

Chalmers, David, *The Conscious Mind*, Oxford, Oxford University Press, 1996

Chang, Jung, *Wild Swans*, London, HarperCollins, 1991

Conze, Edward (trans.) *Buddhist Scriptures*, Harmondsworth, Penguin, 1960

Davidson, Hilda R. Ellis and W. M. S. Russell (eds), *The Folklore of Ghosts*, Cambridge, Folklore Society, 1981

Duncan-Kemp, Alice Monkton, *Where Strange Gods Call*, Brisbane, Smith and Paterson, 1968

Eadie, Betty, J., with Curtis Taylor, *Embraced by the Light*, Gold Leaf Press, Placerville, California, 1992

Evans-Wentz, W. Y. (ed), *The Tibetan Book of the Dead*, Oxford, Oxford University Press, 1960

Faulkner, R. O. (ed.), *The Ancient Egyptian Book of the Dead*, London, British Museum, revised edn, 1985

Fenwick, Peter and Elizabeth, *The Truth in the Light*, London, Headline, 1995

Fiore, Edith, *The Unquiet Dead*, New York, Dolphin/Doubleday

Gallup, George Jr (with William Proctor), *Adventures in Immortality*, London, Souvenir, 1983

Gibson, Arvin S., *Glimpses of Eternity. Near Death Experiences Examined*, Bountiful, Utah, Horizon, 1992

Grattan-Guinness, Ivor (ed.), *Psychical Research: A Guide to its History, Principles and Practices in Celebration of 100 Years of the Society for Psychical Research*, Wellingborough, Aquarian Press, 1982

Grey, Margot, *Return from Death, An Exploration of the Near-Death Experience*, London, Arkana, 1985

Greyson, B. and Flynn, C. P. (eds), *The Near-Death Experience: Problems, Prospects, Perspectives*, Springfield, Illinois, Charles C. Thomas, 1984

Happold, F. C., *Religious Faith and Twentiety-century Man*, Harmondsworth, Penguin, 1966

Havecker, Cyril, *Understanding Aboriginal Culture*, Sydney, Cosmos, 1987

Hawking, Stephen W., *A Brief History of Time: from the Big Bang to Black Holes*, London, Bantam, 1988

Hedges, John W., *Tomb of the Eagles, A Window on Stone Age Tribal Britain*, London, John Murray, 1985

Hick, John, *Death and Eternal Life*, London, Macmillan, 1985 (revised from first edn published by Collins, 1976)

Hyslop, J. H., *Psychical Research and the Resurrection*, London, Fisher Unwin, 1908

Kessler, C., 'The Cultural Management of Death: Individual Fate and its Social Transcendence' in Crouch M., and Hüppauf, B., *Essays on Mortality*, Kensington Studies in

Humanities and Social Sciences, Faculty of Arts, University of New South Wales

Lawrence, P. J. and Meggit, M. J., *Gods, Ghosts and Men in Melanesia*, Melbourne, Oxford University Press, 1965

Lienhardt, R. G., *Divinity and Experience: The Religion of the Dinka*, Oxford, Clarendon Press, 1961

Loewe, Michael, and Carmen Blacker (eds), *Divination and Oracles*, London, Allen and Unwin, 1981

Lorimer, David, *Survival: Body, Mind and Death in the Light of Psychic Experience*, London, Routledge and Kegan Paul, 1984

Lundahl, Craig R. (ed.), *A Collection of Near-Death Research Readings*, Chicago, Nelson-Hall, 1982

MacKenzie, Andrew, *Apparitions and Ghosts. A Modern Study*, London, Arthur Barker, 1971

Moody, Raymond A., *Reflections on Life after Life*, St Simon's Island, GA, Mockingbird, 1977
with Paul Perry, *Reunions: Visionary Encounters with Departed Loved Ones*, Villard Books, 1993. Quotations here from Warner Books edition, 1994

Morse, Melvin, Conner, D and Tyler D., 'Near-Death Experiences in a Pediatric Population: a Preliminary Report', *American Journal of Diseases of Children*, 139 (1985), pp. 595–600

Morse, Melvin, with Paul Perry, *Closer to the Light: Learning from the Near-Death Experiences of Children*, London, Bantam, 1992
Parting Visions: an Exploration of Pre-Death Psychic and Spiritual Experiences, London, Piatkus, 1995

Osis, Karlis, 'Deathbed Observations by Physicians and Nurses', *Parapsychological Monographs* No. 3, New York, Parapsychology Foundation, Inc., 1961 [Fourth printing January 1982]

Owens, J. E., Cook, E. W. and Stevenson, I., 'Features of 'Near-

Death Experience' in Relation to Whether or Not Patients Were Near Death' *The Lancet*, 336 (1990) pp. 1175–7

Paton, Lewis Bayles, *Spiritism and the Cult of the Dead in Antiquity*, London, Hodder and Stoughton, 1921

Phillips, J. H., *Caring for the Dying Patient and his Family*, New York, Health Sciences Publishing Corporation, 1973

Pinch, Geraldine, *Magic in Ancient Egypt*, London, British Museum Press, 1994

Punzak, Dan, 'The Use of Near-Death Phenomena in Therapy', *Journal of Near-Death Studies*, 7, 3 (Spring 1989), pp. 173–82

Rawlings, Maurice, *Beyond Death's Door*, Nashville, Thomas Nelson, 1978, also London, Sheldon Press, 1978

Ring, Kenneth, *Life at Death: a Scientific Investigation of the Near-Death Experience*, New York, Coward, McCann and Geoghegan, 1980
Heading towards Omega: in Search of the Meaning of the Near-Death Experience, New York, Morrow, 1984

Ritchie, George, with Elizabeth Sherrill, *Return from Tomorrow*, Waco, Texas, Chosen Books, 1978 reprinted Eastbourne, Kingsway Publications, 1992
My Life after Dying, Norfolk, VA, Hampton Road, 1991

Rose, Ronald, *Living Magic: The Realities Underlying the Psychical Practices and Beliefs of Australian Aborigines*, London, Chatto and Windus, 1957

Sabom, Michael B., *Recollections of Death: a Medical Investigation*, New York, Harper and Row, 1982

Schoolcraft, H. R., *Travels on the Central Portion of the Mississippi Valley*, New York, Collins and Henry, 1825

Serdahely, William J., and Barbara A. Walker, 'The Near-Death Experience of a Nonverbal Person with Congenital Quadriplegia', *Journal of Near-Death Studies* 9 (2) Winter 1990, pp. 91–6

Sheldrake, Rupert, *A New Science of Life: The Hypothesis of Formative Causation*, London, Blond and Briggs, 1981

Shortland, Edward, *Traditions and Superstitions of the New Zealanders*, London, Longman, Brown, Green, 1856

Storm, Howard, Taped account of his near-death experience recorded in 1989 at the NDE Research Institute, 702 North Fort Thomas Avenue, Fort Thomas, Kentucky 41705
Second tape-recorded lecture, on different occasions, kindly supplied to the author

Sutherland, Cherie, *Transformed by the Light: Life after Near-Death Experiences*, New York and London, Bantam, 1992
Within the Light, New York and London, Bantam, 1993

Thomas, Gordon, *Issels, The Biography of a Doctor*, London, Hodder and Stoughton, 1975

Toksvig, Signe, *Emanuel Swedenborg, Scientist and Mystic*, London, Faber and Faber, 1949

Toynbee, Arnold, and Koestler, Arthur et al., *Life after Death*, Weidenfeld and Nicolson, London, 1976

Tucker, Louis, *Clerical Errors*, New York, Harper, 1943

Tylor, Edward B., *Primitive Culture*, 2 vols, London, John Murray, 1903

Ullman, Montague and Nan Zimmerman, *Working with Dreams*, New York, Delacorte, 1979

Walker, Susan, *Memorials to the Roman Dead*, London, British Museum Publications, 1985

Watson, Peter, *Twins: An Investigation into the Strange Coincidences in the Lives of Separated Twins*, London, Hutchinson, 1981

Wilson, Ian, *The After Death Experience*, London, Sidgwick and Jackson, 1987
Mind Out of Time, London, Gollancz, 1981
In Search of Ghosts, London, Headline, 1995

Wolfner, Ted, *Parallels – A Look at Twins*

Wood, Barbara, *E. F. Schumacher: His Life and Thought*, New York, Harper and Row, 1984

Wren-Lewis, John, 'The Darkness of God: A Personal Report on Consciousness Transformation Through an Encounter with Death', *Journal of Humanistic Psychology*, 28 (1988), pp. 105–22

Zaleski, C., *Otherworld Journeys: Accounts of Near-Death Experience in Medieval and Modern Times*, Oxford, Oxford University Press, 1987